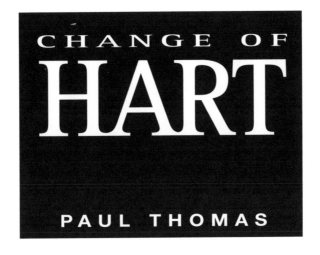

CHANGE OF
HART

PAUL THOMAS

Hodder Moa Beckett

DEDICATION

To Judy, Kay and Chris for their continued love, support and understanding. Hopefully the last two years have made the sacrifices worthwhile.

To the rugby players of today and tomorrow.

ACKNOWLEDGEMENTS

Thanks to James Gilbert Rugby Footballs (NZ) Ltd for their support; to Fotopacific, Photosport, Peter Bush and John Selkirk for the provision of photographs; to Lindsay Knight for his assistance in editing.

In the process of compiling *Change of Hart* I have sought the counsel of many of my friends and colleagues. They have given freely of their time and expertise for which I am very grateful.

In particular, my sincere thanks to Paul Thomas (with the support of his wife Jeni) for his professionalism, commitment and excellent literary skills.

ISBN 1-86958-571-2

© 1997 John Hart Consultancy Ltd

Published 1997 by Hodder Moa Beckett Publishers Limited
[a member of the Hodder Headline Group]
4 Whetu Place, Mairangi Bay, Auckland, New Zealand
Reprinted 1997 (twice)
Typeset by TTS Jazz

Designed and produced by Hodder Moa Beckett Limited

Printed by Wright & Carman (NZ) Ltd, Wellington

CONTENTS

INTRODUCTION

In 1993, Paul Thomas and I released *Straight from the Hart*, an account of my coaching career up until 1991 and a statement of the approach and philosophy which underpinned my coaching endeavours.

At that time, I was in the wilderness. Twice I'd sought to become the All Black coach; twice the Council of the New Zealand Rugby Football Union had decided I wasn't the man for the job. The book's final chapter, titled Change of Hart?, included this sentiment: "If the coaching career which I never actively planned but which grew like Topsy and gave my life a whole new dimension is in fact now over, the good memories will far outweigh the disappointments."

It seemed to be that way. The only coaching role in which I was interested was the All Blacks and many rugby people, including good friends and strong supporters of mine, were convinced that my time had passed. Perhaps I was, too.

But times change and with them people and institutions. The winds of change which buffeted rugby in 1995 induced an epidemic of changes of heart: the International Rugby Board embraced professionalism, the challenge of coaching in the new era inspired me to put my name forward again, and the NZRFU council saw me in a new light. I'd always argued that the technical side of coaching is just one aspect of the job and that, in fact, the better the players one is working with, the less important the role of technician becomes. In the professional era, the various aspects of coaching which can be grouped together under the heading of man-management have become even more fundamental to building a winning team. The message hadn't changed; everything else had.

On December 6, 1995, I turned 50 and became the All Black coach. Has any rugby man ever had a better birthday present? I shall be eternally grateful to those in rugby who put their trust and faith in me.

The All Blacks have achieved much in 1996 and 1997: 17 out of 18 tests won, an historic first-ever series win in South Africa, two Tri-Nations series won without dropping a game, the Bledisloe Cup retained. But victory on the field is only a step towards another goal. What motivates me is taking the game to a different plane and helping to make the All Blacks a team that all New Zealanders can support and take pride in. If the dramatic – and quantifiable – improvement in the All Blacks' standing with the public, the media, and the corporate sector are suitable yardsticks, we have made an enormous amount of progress towards that goal.

But an even bigger challenge awaits us. I believe New Zealand rugby should set itself the goal of transforming the All Blacks into a great international sporting brand. At present, the All Blacks are a great international rugby brand: notwithstanding the talk about rugby's global reach, the two are poles apart. Manchester United are a great international sporting brand; so too are the Brazilian soccer team; so too are the Chicago Bulls, although one suspects that they owe that status largely to Michael Jordan and may struggle to hold onto it once he passes from the scene.

Great international sporting brands are created by consistent success but it must be success with style. That combination is the key. The team become synonymous with excitement, with glamour, with class; they have the X factor in spades; they have a mystique. That's the reason they have supporters around the world, some of whom wouldn't otherwise take an interest in that sport, or indeed any sport. The main reason I criticise the excessive demands placed on the All Blacks is that, when too much is asked of them, it makes it much harder for them to win in style, to produce the sublime performances which make them the most exciting rugby team in the world.

Very few teams in any sport can aspire to becoming a great international brand: the All Blacks are one such team. First, of course, rugby must become a genuinely global game. We can't bring that about on our own but we can be in the forefront of the drive to globalise rugby and we can ensure that, if and when it happens, the All Blacks and New Zealand rugby are positioned to reap the benefits.

I know many people are uncomfortable when they hear the All Blacks talked about as a brand and rugby described as a product. They associate that language with what they see as a mindless rush to commercialise a game which is a fundamental part of New Zealand culture. They worry that in that rush something precious will be lost forever.

I share that concern. I don't, however, believe that rugby can quarantine itself from economic and commercial reality or from the rest of society. The challenge we face is to control and manage the process and use the revenue generated by the elite professional game to protect and nurture the traditional, amateur, mass-participation game without which the rest is meaningless. Professionalism and its attendant commercial pressures will only eat away at the soul of New Zealand rugby if the generation of revenue becomes an end in itself. If we have a vision of what we want our game to be which extends from the under-fives to the All Blacks, and if we can manage the commercial side of the game in accordance with that vision, the revenue generated can be the salvation of the grass-roots game which will otherwise struggle to withstand the grinding pressures of rising costs and competitive forms of leisure and entertainment.

It's against that background that the All Blacks have operated during the past two years. The stakes are very high. Because winning in itself is no longer enough, the management and players are on a mission to take the All Blacks to a new level: to win with style on the field and to be good role models off it. This book is an account of the mission thus far. It's a case-study in the practical application of the coaching philosophy set out in *Straight from the Hart* and a record of the achievements of a dedicated and immensely talented group of New Zealanders who set out to make history and have, so far, succeeded.

Straight from the Hart concluded with these words: "But the enduring memories will not be of record books or great eras but of the young men whose names will loom far larger than mine in the annals of the game and, in some cases, pass into rugby legend. Nothing will ever diminish the satisfaction of knowing that I walked a little distance with them on their road to greatness, pointing the way ahead and, once or twice, picking them up when they stumbled."

In the last two years I've walked a lot further down that road as part of a magnificent All Black management team. It is an enormous privilege to coach the All Blacks. They are the engine which drives our game: they fill the stadiums, they pull the television audiences, they inspire a small boy to chase a football around the backyard in the wintry twilight, they ensure that the great tradition continues by being the role models for the next generation of All Blacks.

This book is in their honour.

John Hart, Auckland, September 1997

1

STRIKE THREE

BROADCASTER Keith Quinn thinks he knows exactly when John Hart decided to have a third go at becoming the All Black coach: Wednesday, August 17, 1994 – the All Blacks against the Wallabies under lights at the Sydney Football Stadium.

"I commentated that game with John," recalls Quinn. "Afterwards he decided to walk back to his hotel in the city which was a fair walk. He wanted to think and I reckon that's when he decided to have a go."

It wasn't a decision to be taken lightly. To stand meant challenging an incumbent coach less than a year out from the World Cup. It also meant putting himself at the mercy of the New Zealand Rugby Football Union (NZRFU) council, the body which had already rejected him in 1987 and 1991.

That night's game would have given Hart plenty of food for thought: it was like a snapshot of the Laurie Mains era.

Three years of selectorial indecision were reflected in an All Black backline which contained only two survivors – Frank Bunce and John Timu – from the first test of the season in late June.

Three years of inconsistency were reflected in the All Blacks' schizophrenic display. After barely competing in the first half, they almost ran the Wallabies ragged in the second, only George

Gregan's last-gasp cover tackle on Jeff Wilson denying them victory.

Three years of media and public pressure on Mains were reflected in the rumour which swept through the press corps before the game that he'd resign if the All Blacks lost.

Three years of tense relations with the media were reflected in Mains' verbal assault on *New Zealand Herald* rugby writer Wynne Gray the next morning. Gray repaid the compliment by giving *Herald* readers an expletive-deleted account of the exchange.

Hart's unease with the Mains regime dated back to its earliest selection decisions in 1992, notably the calculated public humiliation of incumbent All Black captain and 58-test veteran Gary Whetton who wasn't considered worthy of a place among the four teams and reserves at the All Black trials. That was quickly followed by the casual dumping of Grant Fox and Graeme Bachop, the latter one of the few All Blacks to star at the 1991 World Cup. The new panel soon realised they simply couldn't do without Fox's armour-plated composure, tactical control, and precision goal-kicking. In Bachop's case, however, it took two years and three other halfbacks before the penny dropped.

After shaky series wins over an extravagantly-named World XV and a weak Irish team, progress was made on the tour of Australia and South Africa. There was some confident ball movement and, leaving aside the shockingly feeble display against Sydney, a hard-nosed, aggressive approach.

But in 1993 and 1994, the pattern re-emerged: erratic and inconsistent selections leading to erratic and inconsistent performances.

"To an outsider, there didn't really appear to be a plan," says Hart. "If you don't have a plan, selection becomes a bit blurred. I learned early on that if you don't select from a plan, if you don't know how you're going to play the game, you're going to make mistakes. If you have a plan and a consistent selection policy and get it right first time, then you get consistency of performance. If players aren't confident in the plan or in the position in which they've been picked, it's difficult for them to express themselves positively. That's what I saw in 1993/94 and, as someone who takes pride in selection, it frustrated me."

If 1992's selections were characterised by an apparent inability to recognise class, as evidenced by the dumping of Bachop and Mains' extreme reluctance to take Zinzan Brooke on tour, the trademark in 1993 and 1994 was an almost cavalier readiness to pick players out of position. On the tour of England and Scotland at the end of 1993, Marc Ellis was suddenly deemed to be an international first-five-eighth. When the Scots were overrun, the experiment was hailed by some as a stroke of genius. The reality check came in the form of a galling loss to England a week later.

Legendary former All Black and mischief-maker extraordinaire Andy Haden has an interesting perspective on the Ellis selection. Despite his official bogeyman status, Haden, at Mains' request, had attended All Black training sessions before the second test at Athletic Park against the 1993 British Lions with a specific brief to help the jumpers combat the giant English lock Martin Bayfield. Haden was surprised to find himself working primarily with Mark Cooksley rather than Ian Jones. He was taken aback when Mains told him that Cooksley would play instead of Jones. He was incensed when Cooksley appeared to be pulled off the field at halftime.

Was this a premature example of tactical substitution? Quinn thinks so: "The All Blacks' media liaison guy Ric Salizzo was adamant that we had to stay away from the halftime huddle. The cameraman wanted to have a fag but I told him to keep focused on the huddle. When we looked at the tape afterwards, we saw All Black team doctor John Mayhew hand a note to Sean Fitzpatrick. He read it and looked amazed; we saw him looking up at the stand. Then Mayhew went to Cooksley and gave him the message – you didn't need to be a lip-reader to figure out his reaction."

Mayhew provides the soundtrack: "Laurie would ring on the mobile just before halftime with three or four points for me to write down and pass on to Fitzy. One of them related to Cooksley – it was basically 'get him off.' Fitzy said, 'You tell him.' I said, 'No, you tell him.' I ended up having to do it."

Despite feeling that Cooksley had been "cut off at the knees," Haden agreed to take a lineout session before the third test in Auckland and, later, to work with the All Blacks in the UK.

"I was going to be there anyway," he says. "En route, I played for the Classic All Blacks in Bermuda. The All Blacks began the tour well and there was a suggestion in the UK press that they could be the best ever. A British journo in Bermuda asked me for a comment; I said it was a bit early to say but it'd be more likely if the team had been better selected.

"As arranged, I rang Mains when I got to Scotland – he didn't want to know. I didn't get near the team while they were in Scotland. They thumped the Scots who were about as good as the Bismarck Archipelago First XV. I went along to a training session in London before the England test. Earle Kirton breezed up and said, 'That should shut a few Aucklanders up' – he meant Marc Ellis' display at first-five. I said, 'You're telling me you think he's the answer.' Earle said Ellis would be remembered as one of the great first-fives to play for New Zealand. I told him I was going straight out to bet on England. I made £1350 which is still in my Barclay's Bank account. A few months later I saw Earle at the Trentham races. I was in the queue at the pay-out window and told him, 'This is the second win I've had lately – the first was thanks to you.'"

The selection sensation of 1994 was the choice of Jonah Lomu, aged just 19, to play on the wing against France. Hart had coached Lomu in a Coronation Districts team earlier in the season. "It was my first exposure to Lomu apart from seeing him playing touch at the Fletcher Challenge sevens. I'd heard about what he'd done at school and in his first year out of school. I was surprised at how raw he was – he was a converted loose forward and really hadn't played on the wing. He scored some good tries that day but was shown up on defence. I remember telling (All Black selector) Lin Colling that Jonah still had a lot to learn and didn't understand defence. I understand Ross Cooper, then coaching Counties, expressed the same concern.

"Throwing him into international rugby in a foreign position against opponents of that quality – guys with real speed who could turn a man – was a huge risk and I don't think you should take risks with young players at test level. I've always been a believer in promoting youth but you have to give the youth a chance to succeed. It was a serious mistake and a blow to Jonah as an individual. He then came under siege from rugby league and he must have gone through some difficult times in making up his mind. I think his manager Phil Kingsley-Jones played a positive role in keeping him in rugby."

At the end of the season, Hart chose Lomu as a flanker for the New Zealand Barbarians team to play their Australian counterparts in what was thought to be John Kirwan's farewell game. The decision was seen by some as a dig at the selectors.

"It wasn't; I still felt flanker was his best position. Eric Rush was also converted from flanker to wing but he had a lot of agility and the skill sets required. That was a successful move and one that I wouldn't have made myself. Jonah's size and inability to turn quickly, his lack of nous and experience in the position, made it very difficult for him. In due course, the experiment proved successful but learning the art of defence and of beating people takes time."

Perhaps the chopping and changing was partly a result of instability on the panel. Peter Thorburn lost his place at the end of 1993. Various theories circulated. The most intriguing was that Kirton, not Thorburn, had been the conspirators' target but they hadn't allowed for NZRFU geo-politics and Wellington's strategic position between Auckland and Dunedin, the rival centres of power. Thorburn was replaced by Lin Colling. While Colling had the technical credentials, Hart wondered if his personality was suited to the role.

During 1992/93, the All Blacks seemed to stagger from one public relations disaster to another, in the process tarnishing the All Black image at home and abroad. There was Richard Loe's swatting of Paul Carozza at Ballymore in 1992 and the dreadful facial injury inflicted on Phil De Glanville in England in 1993. England was also the setting for the Mike Brewer imbroglio: Brewer, accompanying the tour as a representative of Canterbury, one of the All Blacks' sponsors, materialised on the substitutes bench – and subsequently Twickenham – at the expense of Liam Barry and John Mitchell who'd performed more than adequately for the midweek team. It was a huge call which caused consternation at home and, reportedly, some bitterness among the touring party.

In Hart's view, these damaging controversies were symptomatic of a lack of pro-active, positive management. The media's readiness to play them to the hilt was hardly surprising given the suspicion bordering on outright hostility which pervaded the All Black management's dealings with the press.

Hart refrained from public criticism. "At the time, I was keeping a pretty low profile apart from doing the comments role on television. Even then, I took pains to ensure that I always restricted my comments to the game rather than the wider issues swirling about. The comments role gave me the perfect vehicle to get into the wider issues but I didn't do so because it would've been divisive."

Not everyone saw it that way. Mains complained to TV One about Hart's role, arguing that he was competing for the job and therefore shouldn't have a soapbox. Word even reached Hart that when Mains watched games on tape, he'd kill the sound so he wouldn't have to listen to Hart's voice.

Does that suggest a touch of paranoia? Doctor Mayhew, who

chooses his words more carefully than most, is in no doubt: "Laurie surprised me by asking me to hang in there in 1992 which made me the only survivor from the previous regime. Initially, he was a bit suspicious of me being an Aucklander and of my associations but we had a good working relationship although I disagreed with him on some issues.

"I found him equally as hardworking as Hart but absolutely paranoid. All coaches are a little bit paranoid but he continually worried about Hart and Haden running an active campaign against him. At the end of 1993, I felt I had to quit or make a commitment to go through to the World Cup but things weren't going the way I wanted and I thought it was better to get out. I left on good terms but I'd had enough of the paranoia – us against them."

History was repeating itself. The Hart-Wyllie rivalry which divided the country roughly along north-south lines in the late eighties and early nineties was being replayed with a vengeance. The All Blacks' losses to France in 1994 put Mains under fearful pressure. It was the time of the billboard campaign – 'The All Blacks need a coach, not a lorry.' Once again, there were accusations that the criticism was being covertly orchestrated by Hart and his supporters.

Hart: "I didn't agree with those billboards but they were nothing to do with me. Blaming me for all the criticism might've been comforting but it was unrealistic. What it showed is the passion and sensitivity surrounding the All Blacks. While it's always been there, it's grown in the past decade or so because of the emergence of talk-back radio which not only offers people an outlet for their views but also has a major bearing on their attitudes and opinions. Previously, you might've had the odd letter to the editor but people were generally pretty passive.

"The focus on me as a sort of coach-in-waiting was driven by three factors: the media who love personality conflict stories; Auckland's dominance which created a perception in some quarters that those who'd guided Auckland had got it right; and the lack of credible alternatives – Auckland's dominance made it difficult for coaches around the country to earn a reputation. Probably because he's an Englishman, there wasn't the same focus on Maurice Trapp who succeeded me as Auckland coach for five very successful years. There was also the unfair perception that he'd merely maintained the status quo."

When nominations were called for, Hart decided to throw his

hat into the ring. He did so partly because of his concern over what the All Blacks' performances in 1993/94 augured for the World Cup and partly because he believed a contested election would focus attention on and stimulate analysis of "where we were and where we were going."

He knew he had a lot of public support, not that that would count for much in the council's deliberations if history was any guide. In bottom-line electoral terms, he was aware that his concerns were shared by a number of councillors and he was getting "the same sort of signals from within the NZRFU that I'd had before."

That in itself would have been enough to persuade a less committed individual to forget the whole thing.

"I went in with my eyes open," says Hart. "I was quite philosophical about losing. I didn't have the sense that I'd be damaged if I lost but I wasn't putting down a marker for the future."

The process got under way. At first, the critical issue seemed to be timing. Mains' backers argued that it was too close to the World Cup to change horses, that they couldn't afford the upheaval, that their man deserved a chance to finish what he'd started, even that the players didn't want a change. Mains himself suggested that not too much should be read into the All Blacks' performances because he'd been keeping his powder dry for the World Cup, a claim which raised more than a few eyebrows.

Rob Fisher, then NZRFU Deputy Chairman, could see the issue preying on the minds of the undecided: "There were people around the council table who wouldn't have Hart at any price and others who'd voted for him every time he put his hand up. Then there were those in the middle who didn't think Mains was a great coach and were concerned about the All Blacks, whose record had been poor by historical standards, but who were apprehensive about making a change that close to the World Cup."

Hart addressed the issue in his presentation to the council's interviewing sub-committee – George Verry (Chief Executive of the NZRFU), Lee Smith (Director of Coaching), Peter Burke, John Sturgeon, Colin Meads, Richie Guy, Murray Inglis, and Mattie Blackburn. He pointed out that the successful 1987 World Cup campaign had been preceded by upheaval on the panel at the end of 1986 which led to a re-think of the game plan and selection philosophy.

However, as the interviewing process progressed, it became

clear that the hot-button issue was compatibility on the panel. Mains and Kirton indicated that they wouldn't work with Hart. Hart felt the same way about Kirton, seeing his influence in some of the experimentation and instability. But it created an immediate problem for him: with Colling out of the running, opting for Hart would mean a completely new panel.

Ross Cooper, who was prepared to work with either Mains or Hart, was looking like a certainty whichever way it went. That left Graham Mourie to complete a Hart panel.

"I felt he had enormous credibility," says Hart. "He was a visionary and a superb judge of a player. His candidacy was attacked on the basis that he lacked coaching experience but he wasn't standing for coach – once again, the confusion over the coaching and selection roles was influencing the decision."

It was going to be tight. According to Fisher, "John had taken enough soundings to know he was pretty close."

But Hart knew that he'd be in trouble if it got political. "Laurie's a highly intelligent person who networked well and used the system to his advantage. I was never in his class as a networker. People often said that I was political but Neil Gray, the All Black manager in 1992/93, reckoned I was a babe in arms compared to Laurie. Laurie had powerful allies on the council in John Dowling and Colin Meads who had considerable influence. Meads was driven by two factors: a belief in Mains and a fear that his position as All Black manager would be under threat if I became coach. It was actually suggested to me that I should ring him to say I'd be happy to have him as manager, to take the heat out of the situation. I didn't do so. It was pretty clear where he stood and, besides, it wasn't up to the coach to pick the manager."

There was a week between the candidate interviews and the council's vote which allowed time for politicking in earnest. The anti-Hart faction identified Mourie as his achilles heel and mounted a case against him, arguing that the former All Black captain wasn't qualified due to his lack of first-class coaching experience.

Thursday, September 15 – Decision Day. The sub-committee didn't put a recommendation before the council. It did, however, provide various scenarios to assist deliberations.

Mike Banks, current NZRFU board member and All Black manager, was in his first year on the council. He has vivid memories of the way the decision was reached: "The candidates' names were up on a whiteboard and it was demonstrated that A, B and C would work together and C and D would work together but candidate D was a problem – he could get a panel of two but not three. The argument was, there's no point picking Hart because he can't get a panel. It was a strategy which had been carefully thought through by those responsible for bringing back a recommendation."

Hart's supporters tried to counter. Banks asked whether the council was constitutionally bound to appoint the full panel there and then; if it wasn't, why couldn't they choose a convenor, then appoint the two selectors later, after consultation with the appointed convenor? Fisher supported him but the council opted to follow precedent on the grounds that Banks' proposal had been debated and rejected at a previous council meeting.

In a last-ditch attempt to cobble together a Hart panel, Neil Gray nominated Waikato's Ranfurly Shield-winning coach Kevin Greene from the floor. His name was added to the list of nominees.

It was all in vain.

Banks: "For anyone who was swinging or undecided, that presentation put to bed any thoughts of going for Hart. It was a very pragmatic approach."

Hart suspected that the concerns over compatibility were more tactical than genuine. He was amazed that the councillors could proceed to a vote without actually addressing the fundamental issue: which of the two candidates was better qualified to be the All Black coach. He was appalled that the election should have hinged on the systematic denigration of one of the great names in New Zealand rugby: "It was a sign of the times which said nothing positive about some of the people leading the game in New Zealand – they were still playing very hard politics over the All Blacks coach."

Within half an hour of the result being announced, the *Evening Post* hit the streets with a front-page banner headline: 'It's Mains.'

The election had generated a lot of emotion, even acrimony, but Hart believed it was all worthwhile: "I think my standing did have an impact. I don't believe there would've been a reappraisal of where the All Blacks were without a challenge. I believe that Brian Lochore was called in to manage the World Cup campaign as a direct result. Mains wasn't relaxed with the media and Brian was able to play a significant role in that area.

"The panel came under pressure to lift their game and the

Cartoonist Tom Scott's view of the 1994 election.

whole thing got a lot more disciplined. There was a new focus on selection and organisation and a much more balanced approach for which Ross Cooper can take some credit. Overall though, it's to Laurie Mains' credit that it came right and the team played very well at the World Cup."

Some councillors shared that view. "The election certainly focused the council's attention on the World Cup campaign which we were a bit late in getting under way," says Fisher. "There was a World Cup committee which probably wasn't as active as it should've been. Having said that, some saw Hart's standing as a destructive exercise."

Needless to say, few took a dimmer view than the incumbent coach. When the newly appointed Cooper joined the panel, he found Mains to be "an angry man. He was aware that Eddie Tonks (the then NZRFU Chairman) and some others didn't support him and saw Hart's standing against him as a major challenge."

That weekend, the *Sunday Star-Times* ran the results of their attempts to discover how each of the 19 councillors had voted. It wasn't particularly enlightening. Banks, Fisher and Gray said they'd gone for Hart; the others took cover behind the principle that council ballots should remain confidential. At the next council meeting, NZRFU President Peter Burke deplored the breach of that principle. Banks defended his action, arguing that the people he represented had a right to know how he'd voted.

Voting against Mains was a swift turnaround for Banks who'd joined the council earlier that year as a self-styled "100 per cent Mains supporter." What caused his about-face?

"There was a match between Fiji and New Zealand Universities in Palmerston North. I got a message to go and see Mains at the Motor Inn. I thought someone was pulling my leg – why would he want to see me? My secretary checked: there was a Mr Mains staying there so I went along. Mains and Colling were there; Kirton was meant to be there but was running late. Mains told me, 'You're new on council, there's a few things you need to know.' He started attacking Tonks and council member David Galvin and complaining about the All Black programme, particularly the midweek test under lights in Sydney. He told me, 'These are the people you should side with, these are the people you shouldn't.' That made alarm bells ring. It indicated to me that something was amiss. It was after that I saw there may be other options. Mains was a very political animal but not many people were aware of it."

Nineteen councillors – each, according to Banks, with his own agenda – had made their decision. Knocked back for the third time, Hart turned his attention to another momentous decision.

2
BATTLES OF
THE GIANTS

L ATE in 1994, John Hart decided to leave Fletcher Challenge Ltd, the company he'd joined straight from university in 1966.

It was a wrenching decision. He'd spent his entire career there, working his way up from an accounts clerk processing invoices to a senior executive overseeing the human resource function for the company with more than 30,000 employees worldwide. But the company was changing and he was closing in on 50. He wanted a new challenge and more time for himself and his family.

It was an amicable parting of the ways. Hart agreed to postpone his departure until March 1995 when he planned to set up a sports marketing consultancy.

The decision hadn't been announced when Sky Television came a-calling in November 1994. Frustrated by Television New Zealand's exclusive deal with the NZRFU, Sky executives had come up with a concept for a professional rugby competition involving eight teams from Australia and New Zealand – Auckland, North Harbour, Waikato, Wellington, Canterbury, Otago, New South Wales and Queensland. As well as earning $40,000 to $50,000, the players would get shares in the company which owned the competition. The shareholding arrangement would operate as a sort of superannuation scheme with the players receiving extra shares for each year they took part in the competition.

Sky needed someone who was plugged into the rugby scene to help them refine and sell the concept. Their timing was perfect: Hart was looking for something to get his teeth into. He agreed to come on board, firstly in an advisory capacity and, once he'd left FCL, as a consultant.

Although the Sky concept involved professionalism, it was never intended to be a rival competition to the established game.

"Our view was that the game was going to go professional and if we forced the International Rugby Board's hand, so be it," says Peter Scutts, a former Sky executive who became Executive Director of the Auckland Rugby Union in December 1995. "If we got the establishment on side, our concept would enable the All Blacks to earn money without jeopardising their ability to wear the black jersey. That was critical – if we couldn't guarantee that, we'd have to pay them much bigger money."

Senior players were approached and responded enthusiastically. As far as they were concerned, it was the only way they were likely to make any money out of the game. That was the easy part. When Hart, Scutts, and Sky's Chief Executive Nate Smith gave presentations to the national and provincial unions in New Zealand and Australia, they ran into a wall of suspicion, complacency, and self-interest.

"I was amazed at the administrators' lack of understanding of the changing environment and the arrogance, particularly in Australia, towards people who were trying to develop a concept for the benefit of the game," says Hart. "We were primarily interested in creating something which would help retain players, expand TV coverage, and attract sponsorship; they were only interested in what was in it for them."

He acknowledges, though, that the proposal had a fatal flaw. The Australians wanted South Africa involved. That was non-negotiable for Sky because of the time difference. They were looking for prime-time product.

Heavy artillery was brought to bear. "We didn't have a strategy to accommodate South Africa," says Hart. "Louis Luyt opposed it vigorously and you underestimate him at your peril."

After weeks of fruitless negotiations, Sky withdrew the offer on May 15. By then, it had been overtaken by events and Hart was in South Africa coaching the New Zealand Parliamentary team in the inaugural Parliamentary World Cup. The team comprised MPs, including ex-All Blacks Chris Laidlaw, Tony Steel, and Grahame Thorne, Beehive staff, MPs' sons, and the two ring-ins permitted under the rules – John Boe and Bill Osborne, who were still going strong in the Classic All Blacks. Cross-party relationships which continue to this day were forged and the crash-course in the value of teamwork was probably useful with an MMP election just around the corner.

New Zealand won the tournament but the real highlight was getting to meet Nelson Mandela. At late notice, the South African President met the teams in the gardens of Cape Town's Parliament House. He lingered well beyond the allocated 15 minutes – as someone said, when you've been locked up for 27 years, what's a few minutes here or there? – speaking to every person there. When his turn came, one of the Irish contingent told Mandela they had something in common. Happy to play the straight man, Mandela asked what that was. Back came the punchline: 'We've both got wives who are an absolute embarrassment.' Mandela hooted with laughter. One wonders how many political leaders would appreciate a joke that close to the bone. But then, as everyone who was there would testify, Nelson Mandela is no ordinary politician.

When Hart arrived in South Africa, he was surprised to find the media had firmly installed England and Australia as favourites to take the World Cup. The All Blacks hardly featured in the calculations. He'd been impressed with the All Blacks' build-up and was expecting them to do well. The management had spent a productive summer getting the players ferociously fit and restoring the public support and enthusiasm which had been frittered away during the previous two years.

Although Hart had few quibbles with the World Cup squad, he did wonder how there could be a place among the six loose forwards for Kevin Schuler, who'd swanned back from Japan into the All Blacks like some prodigal son, but not Michael Jones. Jones' unavailability on Sundays meant he'd miss the final pool game, the quarter-final, and the semi-final so his omission would have been understandable if they'd taken only five loose forwards. The selectors presumably felt that Jones couldn't go into the World Cup final without having played for three weeks and were concerned about the attrition rate among the loose forwards. As it was, Paul Henderson and Schuler played one full game each – against Japan.

"The panel had struggled in 1993/94, chopping and

changing," says Ross Cooper who joined the selection panel in September 1994. "They were undermined by poor selection but the work that was done at the camps and getting consistency of selection turned it around. I don't think what happened was a miracle – Lomu was a key element in it. I'm not sure about Mains' claim that he'd been hiding his tactics for the World Cup. I think we just started to get consistency and pick the team to play the game we wanted to play."

Hart was in the commentary box for the opening match of the tournament between the Springboks and the Wallabies at Newlands on May 25. The comparison with 1991 was irresistible: like the All Blacks then, the Wallabies were a team at the end of the line, distracted by money matters. Before long, everyone would be.

Hart returned to Auckland after that game. On May 31, he heard for the first time the acronym which would soon reverberate around the rugby world – WRC. He got a call from Australian coach Bob Dwyer who was in Port Elizabeth where the Wallabies were preparing to play Canada. Dwyer told him a professional rugby concept was being developed and he had confidence in the people who were driving it. Not wanting his whole team to get involved, Dwyer had allowed the World Rugby Corporation people to meet a few of his more level-headed players. They'd come away pretty enthusiastic. WRC had people working on its behalf in all the major rugby countries and now they were looking for someone in New Zealand.

Was Hart interested? If so, Dwyer would tell WRC to ring him; if not, the conversation never took place.

Hart said he'd be happy to talk. At that moment, rugby seemed under greater threat from rugby league than ever before. The split between the Australian Rugby League and Super League meant that rugby was now being stalked by two predators, one of them backed by the resources of a global communications empire. There was talk that Super League had a scout assigned to every team at the World Cup and would pay whatever it took to get Jonah Lomu.

WRC's prime mover Ross Turnbull, an ex-Wallaby prop, former Chairman of the New South Wales Rugby Union, and Australian delegate to the IRB, rang half an hour later. He outlined the structures of the proposed provincial and international competitions and indicated that everyone involved could expect to earn megabucks. A document outlining the concept in more detail and a contract would be sent forthwith. Hart said he'd want to get Andy Haden involved because of his experience in the area.

A courier package arrived the next day. Turnbull rang several times but Hart didn't take the calls. After he'd thought about it and discussed it with John Hood, a senior executive at FCL and one of his confidants, Hart contacted Turnbull to lay out his conditions: the game had to be controlled by the existing official national and provincial unions; he wanted to meet WRC's principals; he wanted to know the extent of the backers' involvement; he wanted to see a player's contract; and he wanted assurances that WRC would remain in force for at least three years. While he was at it, Hart also pointed out the need for a public relations strategy and what he saw as flaws in the proposed competition structure.

Turnbull's response was that WRC had started with a group of influential people becoming concerned over the threat from Super League. He was hopeful of getting the backing of the Australian Rugby Union; he hadn't approached any All Blacks yet. On the business side, Turnbull said he'd talked to US television interests and WRC would be shown on a pay TV network with 15 million subscribers. They were budgeting for a $40 million profit over three years, they'd allocated $5 million for a public relations campaign, and their budget had been verified by accountancy firm Ernst & Young. He couldn't confirm or deny Kerry Packer's involvement.

Hart agreed that he and Haden would attend a meeting in Sydney the following week. He met Hood and Haden to plan his strategy. Acutely aware of his responsibilities as a director of the Auckland Rugby Union, he briefed ARU Chairman Reuben O'Neill who took the view that at that stage it was useful to have someone like Hart talking to WRC. Hart undertook to resign from the ARU board if and when he signed a WRC contract.

Western Samoa's coach Bryan Williams rang from South Africa. Turnbull had told him of his discussions with Hart. Williams felt Western Samoa had no alternative but to go with WRC because they were sitting ducks for Super League. He mentioned that Turnbull had spoken to Springbok captain François Pienaar.

The Sydney meeting took place in the offices of business advisory firm Wentworth Associates, a company with close ties to the Packer organisation. Present were Turnbull, his partner Michael Hill, a former chairman of the Newcastle Knights rugby league club who'd signed up players for Packer's rebel cricket circus in the late 1970s, and South African-born lawyer Geoff Levy, a principal of Wentworth and a driving force behind WRC. Hart was asked to sign a confidentiality agreement; he declined, saying he was there on trust.

It was quite a successful meeting. Hart felt they'd thought the concept through from the players' perspective but their competition structure, which involved taking the game into non-rugby territory through franchises and divided the world into northern, central, and southern conferences, was naive and needed a lot of work. He made the point that there would be real problems in New Zealand if they didn't get the NZRFU and provincial unions on side. It was obvious what the deal with Packer was: if and when WRC had the players, he'd front with the money.

Stalling for time, Hart returned to South Africa for the business end of the World Cup. He met Dwyer who was understandably down in the dumps after Australia's flat showing. The WRC people asked Hart if he'd be prepared to test the water with the All Blacks. His position was: not directly while they were still in the tournament. The buzz was that the discussions the Australian, New Zealand, and South African rugby unions were having with Rupert Murdoch's News Corporation were well advanced so he wanted to see what emerged before going much further with WRC.

Hart rang Eric Rush to give him some background and see if he wanted to talk about it. After the All Blacks' semi-final against England in Cape Town, Rush and Schuler came up to the press box. They clearly had some idea of what was going on but, like Hart, thought that going outside the system would be futile. The chat lasted half an hour without getting into detail and they parted agreeing that there'd be no further contact until after the final.

On Friday June 23, the day before the World Cup final, the SANZAR deal was announced. In return for television rights for ten years, News Corporation would tip $US555 million into the coffers of the Australian, New Zealand and South African unions. That night Hart met the WRC people at the Johannesburg home of Harry Viljeon, a former coach of Transvaal and Natal who'd made his money in insurance and was WRC's point man in South Africa. Chez Viljeon was the most opulent dwelling Hart had ever set foot in.

Over dinner at a restaurant, Hart was surprised to find that the SANZAR announcement hadn't made any difference to their plans; if anything, they were more gung-ho than ever. He pointed out that the SANZAR deal seemed to address the issues which had brought WRC into existence in the first place and voiced his fear of a rugby league-style split occurring as two media barons slugged it out. None of the others seemed to share his concerns. Viljeon was very confident of signing the South African players. He had his recruitment network in place, even using a player – Joel Stransky – to sign up his Western Province teammates. Hart would soon hear from Western Province coach Alan Zondagh that Stransky's recruitment efforts were causing chaos and resentment.

For 24 hours the wheeling and dealing was suspended and all eyes turned to Ellis Park. Having arrived in South Africa comparatively unsung, the All Blacks had steadily gathered momentum. After their sublime first half performance against England, they were looking unstoppable.

South Africa, by contrast, had avoided a disastrous exit by a hair's-breadth in their semi-final against France at Durban when Abdelatif Benazzi body-surfed to within a centimetre or two of the tryline. They would benefit from another narrow miss in the final. The conditions at Kings Park were unbelievable. Hart was astounded to see a party of black women with brooms sent out to sweep the water-logged pitch. It seemed an awfully long way behind the times in more ways than one.

While the Springboks hadn't always impressed, their hard run-in may have been better preparation for the final. Their games with Australia, Canada, Western Samoa, and France had been quite physical whereas none of the All Blacks' opponents – the four home unions and Japan – had taken them on physically.

The final was played with great passion. The crowd and the Springboks were carried on a surge of optimism and pride in their new nation triggered by the sight of Mandela in Pienaar's jersey. South Africa gave a copybook exhibition of their traditional strengths: a strong scrum, relentless physical engagement especially in defence, and expert analysis of the opposition's game plan. After the years in the wilderness, it was a timely reminder to a forgetful rugby world that they are a truly formidable rugby nation.

"I always thought the All Blacks could win," says Hart. "We had the best game and had played it well up till then. I was a little concerned about the defence but the attack was good. I think the All Blacks went in believing that what was good enough to beat the other sides would be too good for South Africa. That didn't take into account that the Springboks would be a far tougher defensive nut than the rest. They did a brilliant tactical job on us: they worked out that they had to spread their defence and their defensive organisation was superb. Perhaps some of our younger players struggled to cope with pressure of an intensity they hadn't experienced before.

"We didn't get it quite right tactically. We seemed obsessed with getting the ball to Lomu and they handled him well. We didn't seem to have a back-up game plan in place: we didn't turn them enough, didn't put the ball behind them enough, didn't manipulate their defence and exploit the decision to play Mark Andrews at number 8. But it was very close: Mehrtens' dropped goal attempt was within inches of winning it for us and given the sickness afflicting so many All Blacks, it obviously wasn't to our advantage that the game went into extra time."

Keith Quinn regards the aftermath of that game as Hart's finest moment as a commentator: "We had 30 minutes to fill before the closing ceremony and he launched into a eulogy, doing a brilliant piece about the team and the management and saying that New Zealand should be very proud of them. He gave it everything and was very complimentary about Mains' contribution."

Hart: "Although in my heart of hearts I felt they'd got it wrong – as we did in 1991 – the management and players deserved credit for the All Blacks' performance at the tournament. We stumbled at the final hurdle but some of the rugby played was of a very high standard."

Johannesburg partied hard that night. The bitter conflicts of the past, the seemingly intractable problems of the present, and the awful uncertainties of the future were forgotten – for one night at least the Rainbow Nation was a reality. Rugby, the Afrikaners' game, had brought the nation together and seemed poised to play a significant part in the reconciliation process. In that context, the result didn't seem to matter quite as much. Twelve months later, there was precious little sign that South African rugby had grasped its historic opportunity.

Hart flew back to Auckland. On June 27, he wrote to Turnbull withdrawing from WRC. He wrote that:

• While he hadn't changed his views on the need for professionalism and changes in the game's administration and marketing, it was his strong preference that such changes be made in conjunction with the national and provincial unions.

• While he doubted that the national unions, via the IRB,

would embrace the WRC concept of a global game, they should be given the opportunity. If the IRB did take that step, then WRC wasn't necessary.

• While he had reservations about the SANZAR deal, particularly the ten-year time frame and News Corporation's involvement with the rival code, it had changed the climate and he was therefore surprised that it seemed to have given WRC added impetus.

• With SANZAR and WRC in competition, the game could split with the players becoming pawns.

Haden carried on as WRC's man in New Zealand. He met some All Blacks on their return and couldn't believe how fired up they were for WRC. They'd tried and failed to get a hard and fast financial commitment from NZRFU Chairman Richie Guy at a meeting in South Africa. Haden told the players that Hart was out of it.

On July 5, the All Blacks attended a parliamentary reception in Wellington. Afterwards, they off-loaded manager Colin Meads and went to a Haden-organised WRC presentation at a motel near the airport . Haden sat with Levy at the front of the room; Mains carefully positioned himself so that he didn't have to look at Haden.

But sporting takeovers, like misery and politics, make for strange bedfellows. It wasn't long before the big freeze started to thaw.

"Mains didn't want to talk to me until he realised that if he didn't, he might miss out," says Haden. "He started sending me faxes and ringing me to talk about team selections. He sent me a list of the top 100 players in the country ranked in relation to each other. I attended a meeting with him and two or three players at which he conducted affairs in relation to the type of salaries different players should be getting. Like some others, I became aware of the difficulties Mains was having negotiating with Josh Kronfeld who was procrastinating over whether or not he was making the right decision. Mains was acting as a selector for WRC if not a recruiter by proxy.

Although he had reservations about Turnbull, Hart had quickly come to respect Levy. They remained in contact. Hart's overriding view was that a split had to be avoided at all costs: if WRC had the players locked in, it was time for the two sides to make a deal which he was prepared to broker. By now, WRC was claiming it had signed 129 South Africans, 17 Scots, 20

Englishmen, 83 Frenchmen, 45 Welshmen, 60 Australians, 70 New Zealanders, and 16 Western Samoans.

He repeated his offer to act as a broker to Rob Fisher. He also approached Lion Nathan's Chief Operating Officer Kevin Roberts who had a foot in both camps. Roberts told him a compromise was in the works: Hart assumed that meant the NZRFU was using him as a go-between.

By now, the NZRFU counter-attack was under way. The players didn't want to deal with Guy so he'd been taken out of the negotiating process. The difficult assignment fell to Fisher, Brian Lochore, and Jock Hobbs. The two former All Black captains must have found it galling traipsing around the country trying to persuade players to remain loyal. For Lochore, it was probably hurtful as well given his close involvement with the All Blacks over the preceding nine months. But they responded to the call.

It wasn't easy. The All Blacks were being offered sums they wouldn't have dreamt of only a few months earlier but they didn't want to know. It was a bizarre situation: SANZAR had its News Corporation war chest but couldn't give money away while WRC, despite having no visible means of support, had players beating down its door.

The NZRFU's Plan B was to sign up the next generation – the 1995 vintage Baby Blacks. There were two problems with that. The first was Sam Chisholm, the New Zealand-born head of Murdoch's global television interests outside the USA – he made it crystal-clear that News Corporation wanted the World Cup squad. Secondly, unlike 1986, the 1995 Baby Blacks wouldn't have contained a few All Blacks and half a dozen players on the brink of significant – in a couple of cases great – international careers. Says Fisher, "If we'd lost, we'd have been fielding our tenth fifteen."

Hobbs, Fisher and Lochore chipped away at the edges, targeting senior players in the leading provinces – Otago, Counties, Waikato, Hawke's Bay, and Wellington. In Auckland's case, the focus was on the backs since the Auckland forwards were firmly in the WRC camp. Some players got paid too much but their market value had rocketed since Sky unveiled its scheme. Besides, time wasn't on the establishment's side and WRC had upped the ante since the World Cup.

"Turnbull was bloody-minded," says Haden. "He drove it hard because he felt the IRB had had enough time to sort it out. Of the 130 players the NZRFU agreed to pay, 30-odd have already disappeared – they were about 25 per cent wrong. Laurie's list was closer to the mark – I guess it's a pity he sent it to WRC instead of the NZRFU."

If there was a single, defining moment when the tide turned, it was when Pienaar failed to turn up for a three-way video TV hook-up with senior All Blacks and Wallabies, the leading lights in WRC and the Packer organisation. His no-show was a victory for Dr Luyt, albeit one whose bitter aftertaste would linger.

"The All Blacks were disappointed by Pienaar's dishonesty over WRC," says Fitzpatrick. "It was also common knowledge that Luyt had told him he'd get him one day for his role in WRC and the Transvaal players' strike."

Hart: "Luyt faced the problem we faced – if you lost your top players to an outfit unconnected to the game's administration, it could have a very serious effect. Whatever people say about him, Luyt's a very intelligent person who's passionate about rugby and will go to great lengths to protect it. He's also traditional, authoritarian, and an awfully powerful figure. Having to throw money at Pienaar to secure his loyalty would've hurt him."

David Moffett, then Chief Executive of SANZAR, agrees that the much-maligned (in New Zealand at least) Luyt played a key role: "One of the reasons we decided to make Luyt chairman of SANZAR is that he's a very good negotiator. He's not the easiest person in the world but a lot of successful people are like that. There are two sides to him: he can be a pain in the backside but he can be very gracious at times. His love of the game sometimes gets lost behind the manner of his delivery."

Finally, the establishment carried the day. There were winners and losers. The superstars were going to make big money whichever way it went but some All Blacks ended up signing with the NZRFU for less than they'd turned their noses up at when WRC seemed to hold the aces.

The case of Mark Carter, the Auckland and former All Black flanker, epitomised the money-go-round that rugby became in 1995.

Carter was a senior Auckland player who'd captained the team in Zinzan Brooke's absence. Seeing his way blocked by Kronfeld and not having received a hint of encouragement from the Mains regime, he'd signed on early with WRC. When WRC folded, he was offered $65,000 a year by the NZRFU. Carter's Auckland teammates who'd signed with the NZRFU when the bidding war was at its height were on salaries of between $100,000 and

$130,000. The Auckland Rugby Union topped the offer up but Carter decided to join the Auckland Warriors.

Auckland coach Graham Henry, a strong Carter supporter, got involved. With help from the private sector, he put together a package which wasn't far short of what the Warriors had offered. But Super League got wind of it: Carter got a blunt letter from Super League boss John Ribot telling him that they expected him to abide by his contract. Here was News Corporation, the same organisation which was providing the funds for the NZRFU component of Carter's rugby offer, raising the implicit threat of legal action if he didn't honour his agreement with their league enterprise. By that stage, News Corporation had had plenty of practice at juggling its dual roles of predator and white knight.

The battle for ownership and control of rugby was over. Hart felt the right outcome had been achieved but clung to the hope that some of WRC's better concepts, particularly that of a truly global game, would survive its demise. The signs are not all that good: the North-South divide now seems wider than ever with some in the south openly questioning the relevance of northern hemisphere rugby. Perhaps the British Lions' series win in South Africa has given them pause for thought.

WRC envisaged annual world provincial and international championships although the concept wasn't fleshed out. It would require a structured international season with these competitions taking place in the "windows" when the northern and southern seasons overlap – roughly March to June and September to November – and when weather conditions are favourable in both hemispheres. The outlines of such competitions are already apparent in the Super 12 and Tri-Nations in the south and the European Cup and Five Nations tournament in the north. It doesn't seem such a huge step to have the leading teams from the corresponding competitions play off to decide that year's world champion province and country.

Hart was also attracted by WRC's proposal to bolster the emerging rugby nations with players from the leading countries. If those players weren't required for international duty by their country of origin, they would then be available for their country of residence. To use a current example: if Graeme Bachop isn't wanted by New Zealand, he would become eligible for Japan.

"This is already happening de facto," says Hart. "Kiwis who can't make the All Blacks are turning up in other countries' teams – guys like Sean Lineen, Hemi Taylor, Kurt McQuilken, Dale McIntosh,

Ross Nesdale, and the 'Samoans'. Given that Japan has the resources to make a real dent in our talent pool, it also makes sense to devise a system which enables players who go to Japan to still play for the All Blacks."

While Hart continues to champion some WRC ideas, he isn't oblivious to the strains the whole business imposed: "They were difficult times. The players had mixed motivations – resentment at the way they felt they'd been exploited by the administrators, greed, and loyalty to the team. I'm sure the younger ones came under great pressure. The players didn't have it easy having to juggle conflicting advice but they reaped enormous financial gains.

"I never received a cent, never signed anything, insisted at every step of the way that WRC should work with the establishment. Even so, I was conscious that my position could be misinterpreted. A number of councillors in fact believed that I was WRC's New Zealand agent and I could see the issue being used as an excuse to oppose me if I sought a role in the game in future."

3
BIRTHDAY BOY

ART'S ties to WRC weighed on his mind when he started to toy with the idea of standing for All Black coach again. He addressed the issue head-on with Richie Guy, taking the NZRFU Chairman through his involvement step by step, showing him the correspondence, and explaining why he'd remained in contact with Geoff Levy after formally withdrawing from WRC. Hart didn't want to go through the wringer again any more than Guy wanted to see it happen. He undertook to take the council's pulse and warn Hart off if it was a lost cause.

However, it turned out that the councillors were more concerned about what the All Black coach had been up to. They'd been sent a document which apparently showed that Laurie Mains had done more than just 'sit on the fence,' as he'd put it.

This had a number of councillors, including some erstwhile Mains supporters, baying for his blood to the extent that his replacement by Ross Cooper for the tour of Italy and France was actively canvassed. Mike Banks, who'd managed the Cooper-coached Colts side which won the Southern Hemisphere Under-21 tournament in Argentina, was asked by senior councillors if he was prepared to take over as All Black manager if Mains got the axe.

"There was a strong view on the council that Mains had played both sides of the street," says Rob Fisher. "For a while, it looked like some action would be taken against him but, by the time the next council meeting came around, the rush of blood had subsided. Those of us who'd been through the pretty horrific period of negotiations with the players wanted to look forward not backward and the simple fact was that he'd been appointed for the calendar year."

Mains survived but Banks believes the affair put paid to any thoughts he may have had of seeking another term: "I suspect Mains' decision not to put his name forward wasn't entirely of his own volition; I suspect he was told not to stand again by people who'd been his supporters."

Hart, meanwhile, was having second thoughts. Given his track record, he would have been a blind, deaf, and dumb optimist if he hadn't occasionally despaired of ever being able to beat the system. Andy Haden sensed that Hart, worried that the game had moved forward without him, was having doubts that he could still coach at test level.

"I went through some self-doubt," says Hart, "but the support I received gave me confidence that I wasn't on my own, that there were a lot of people who wanted me to coach the All Blacks. And in terms of my own qualifications, I was hardening in the opinion that the job itself had changed: professionalism and its impact on the players and the playing of the game would require a different skill-set. It would be more about management in the wider sense than technical coaching ability."

Public support was all very well but in the end it would come down to those 19 councillors. For some of them, choosing the new coach would be their last hurrah as the council was to be replaced by a nine-member board in March 1996. As well as Guy, Hart consulted Fisher and Jock Hobbs. Between the three of them, they had a line into most of the council's shifting factions. A negative signal from two out of three would have put an end to it. Guy reported back that Hart's flirtation with WRC didn't seem to be an issue and none of them could see any reason why he shouldn't stand. Hart took that to mean they weren't picking up an anti-Hart mood among their colleagues.

Whether they'd vote for him was another matter. Hobbs was a supporter but wouldn't give a commitment until he knew who else was in the running. He added that if he did pledge his support, Hart could count on it. Fisher was in an awkward position since another former Auckland coach, his very good friend Maurice

Trapp, and the current Auckland coach Graham Henry were also likely to stand. (Fisher was to extract himself rather neatly from this dilemma by informing the three of them that he intended to support the interviewing sub-committee's recommendation. To his relief, they all accepted his non-decision.)

Hart also spoke to Colin Meads before the All Blacks left for Europe. In the wash-up from WRC, Meads' closeness to Mains had probably eroded his influence on the council but he remained a force to be reckoned with. Hart told him he was considering standing and was interested in his view. Meads replied that it would be a very important tour for Ross Cooper who was clearly the heir apparent. They agreed to talk again when the team returned.

Some of Hart's friends were adamant that he shouldn't stand, arguing that the factors and forces which had derailed his previous attempts were still pitted against him. Some advocated standing only if he was guaranteed the job, a suggestion which displayed touching naivety. The most poignant conversation was with his former Otahuhu and Auckland teammate Peter Murdoch, one of his closest friends. Convinced that Hart would get another kick in the teeth, Murdoch pleaded with him to give it away. The following day, Murdoch collapsed and died while jogging in the Auckland Domain.

Hart was worried about his family who'd been shattered by the previous disappointments. On the other hand, their lives wouldn't necessarily be a bed of roses if he was successful, given the All Black coach's profile and the pressures on him. They urged him to go for it.

As in 1994, Keith Quinn was on hand when the decision was made: "We were commentating a game at Pukekohe. He picked me up from the airport and told me, 'I'm going to have a crack,' his voice getting high the way it does when he's excited. I thought he was well and truly on the outer and his time had gone so I told him he was nuts. He reckoned he could get the numbers – I'd heard that before."

The nomination process had been changed to allow individuals to nominate in their own right. Hart knew from bitter experience that getting nominated by a lot of provincial unions meant next to nothing: the nomination wasn't binding on the province's nominee on the NZRFU council who could happily ignore it and vote for whomever he liked.

Even so, any candidate would naturally like to have the

clearcut backing of his own union. Here the Auckland Rugby Union faced the same dilemma as Fisher – having to choose between Hart, Henry, and Trapp. To complicate matters further, Hart was on the ARU board.

The pressure eased a little when Trapp, who was on the board of the Hawke's Bay Rugby Union, was nominated by that province. Trapp and Wayne Smith were soon being talked up as a dream ticket which surprised Hart a little: in 1992 and 1994, he'd promoted Smith as someone he'd like to have on board as an assistant coach. Smith later told Hart that he'd assumed he wouldn't stand.

Hart himself settled the issue for the ARU. Although he had every reason to believe that, if push came to shove, he would have been Auckland's nominee, he felt it would be improper to force the board to choose between the incumbent coach and a board member. Accordingly, he declined a nomination and seconded Henry's. Needless to say, he wasn't thrilled to discover that Henry, who was well aware of the circumstances, was claiming in an electioneering letter to NZRFU councillors and other unions that 'another strong element must be that I'm the preferred choice of the Auckland Rugby Union.' ARU Chairman Reuben O'Neill subsequently wrote to the councillors clarifying the situation.

Once again, the country was gripped by the impending election of the All Black coach. Unlike the previous year, there was no shortage of candidates: of the leading coaches only Smith and Vance Stewart (both of whom pulled out) and Mains weren't in the running. That left a field of six – Hart, Henry, Trapp, Cooper, Brad Meurant, and Gordon Hunter – with Andy Leslie, Earle Kirton and Frank Oliver seeking a selecting role only. It was difficult to predict how this embarrassment of riches would affect the process. Experienced observers of the council's machinations were inclined to think it would be more political than ever. Some feared an out-and-out lottery.

Hart's obvious weakness was his lack of recent coaching experience – his coaching CV since the 1991 World Cup contained just four one-off games. There were suggestions that four years off the scene was too much – that he'd be out of practice, out of touch. When Mains announced he was standing down, he insisted that his successor would have to have recent hands-on coaching experience and should therefore come from the All Black panel or the current crop of NPC coaches. You didn't have to consult the *Rugby Almanack* to work out who his target was.

The All Blacks' tour of Italy and France was a strange affair. It got off to a rocky start with Mains and the council bickering over how many players he could take. Mains, who wanted 30, lost the argument but one way or another ended up with 29. Kronfeld couldn't seem to get on the field while Cooper was in the invidious position of being promoted as Mains' successor, denied meaningful opportunities, and assessed by Meads, all at the same time. And then there was the mysterious players' poll.

Cooper didn't enjoy the tour one little bit: "I was going to learn the ropes but it was really a little false. Laurie let me do several things but losing the first test made it difficult and I never felt comfortable. I personally didn't feel I was his anointed successor – I think he just didn't want Hart to get it."

Quinn remembers there always being a different reason for Kronfeld's non-appearances and Mains not taking kindly to questions on the subject. He remembers the coach often being in a bad mood because he'd try to have secret training sessions and assorted Frenchmen would turn up. He remembers Meads cutting "a sad and lonely figure – we often saw him walking the streets by himself, maybe because some of the management team had other things on their minds."

When the team was in Paris preparing for the second test, Meads conducted a poll to find out who the players wanted to be the next All Black coach. A number of theories have been advanced as to what prompted Meads' snap poll and what he hoped to achieve. Sean Fitzpatrick believes Meads had gone away thinking Cooper would walk into the job but had developed doubts as the tour progressed; the poll was just a means of getting the players' perspective. A more cynical interpretation is that the poll was aimed at torpedoing Hart's run by demonstrating that he lacked support among the players.

Was that the case? "Some players had reservations," says Fitzpatrick. "In the Mains era there was always this undercurrent that he was trying to undermine us – it was probably a case of Mains and Kirton infecting us. I knew what he was capable of. I remember going to see him in 1991, possibly selfishly in that I knew he'd do something for me. His involvement in that World Cup campaign was seen as counter-productive but we might've been lucky to get to the semi-finals without him. I knew he had the skills to develop me further, to broaden me."

Hart found out about the poll when he and Meads had their chat on the team's return. The conversation was brief and strained. Meads brought the subject up, describing the result of the poll as interesting: Hart had got some support as had Cooper, Henry, and Hunter. Meads said he wouldn't reveal the actual results because he was going to submit them to the council.

Hart made no comment but he was surprised on two counts: at best, he would have expected to get one or two votes seeing he'd coached very few of the current All Black squad. Secondly, he would have thought Meads of all people, given his vast experience as a player, coach, and manager, would have realised that such a poll was misconceived simply because players tend to support whichever coach they think will pick them.

Hart kept it low-key, staying out of the media debate. Here again, experience had taught him that any comments he made to the media were likely to be selectively quoted back at him. Over the long haul, his support in the media had proved a two-edged sword: favourable coverage was likely to be taken as evidence of his orchestrating a campaign.

The council's interviewing sub-committee consisted of Mattie Blackburn (chairman), Lee Smith, Leo Walsh, Banks, and Lane Penn. Penn, who'd been a selector with Hart during the Alex Wyllie era, was added to the sub-committee to provide a coach's perspective. Hart and Brian Lochore had been used in a similar capacity by cricket and netball respectively. Lochore was in fact the council's first port-of-call; not surprisingly, given the year he'd had, he preferred to stay well out of it.

From Hart's point of view, the 1995 sub-committee was a huge improvement over the previous year's: there was no Meads and no John Sturgeon. Sturgeon, another throwback to the Wyllie era, had played a key role in Hart's defeat in the 1991 election. In fairness to Sturgeon, it was his decision to give up a place on the sub-committee and he did so knowing full well that his replacement would be the enthusiastically pro-Hart Banks.

The interview process was more professional this time around. The candidates were given clear guidelines on which subjects they should cover in their presentations. Hart devoted some time to what he saw as potentially damaging issues: his involvement with WRC, his lack of recent coaching experience, and his alleged inability to work with others.

In hindsight, Hart had probably done himself few favours in his 1991 presentation by suggesting that the panel should be done away with and the coach given the right to choose his own selectors and assistants, like an English soccer manager. That notion was never going to find favour with the council since it would entail a significant loosening of the reins. By suggesting it in the first place, Hart probably fed the perceptions that he was choosy to the point of arrogance about whom he would and wouldn't work with and that what he was really about was taking the show over – in league, of course, with the Auckland mafia.

This time he backed off, stating clearly that it wasn't the convenor's role to pick his fellow selectors and that he would happily work with any of the nominees and stressing the need for continuity from the outgoing panel. More tentatively than in the past, he drew a distinction between selecting and coaching, talking of the importance of the coach having "appropriate and compatible support staff with complementary skills." Experienced Hart-watchers would have recognised that as a code for bringing in coaching back-up from outside the panel.

Determined to leave nothing to chance, Banks persuaded him to back-pedal further: "He alluded to having coaching staff of his choice who may not necessarily be on the panel but I persuaded him to drop it because I believed it would've been detrimental – there'd be those who'd see it as a takeover and would've used it against him. I knew that pushing Cooper as his assistant would provide some peace of mind."

Hart left copies of his presentation with each member of the interviewing sub-committee and sought and received their permission to circulate his CV and presentation notes to the other councillors. He'd suffered by not doing so in 1994 when distorted versions of his presentation were peddled. He attached a brief note to the documents but had no direct contact with any councillor in the lead-up to the vote.

The other candidates were less inhibited. A puzzled councillor rang Hart the night before the vote wondering why he hadn't heard from him – every other candidate had been in his ear. Graham Henry criss-crossed the country making hour-long one-on-one presentations to most of the 19 councillors.

The sub-committee whittled the field down to four with Hart the clear front-runner. Banks "battled like hell" to get a unanimous recommendation but Blackburn wouldn't commit himself. Having reached a consensus, the sub-committee worked through how they were going to sell it to the full council, right down to framing counter-arguments to the objections they knew would be forthcoming.

It all seemed to be going along pretty smoothly. Too smoothly, in fact – it just wouldn't have been the same without a couple of nasty surprises.

The first came during a panel discussion on Sky Television chaired by Murray Deaker on the subject of who should be the next All Black coach. The panelists were former All Blacks Billy Bush, John Graham, and Graham Mourie, and Bob Templeton, a stalwart of Queensland and Australian rugby who'd been Bob Dwyer's assistant coach. Perhaps not surprisingly given that he wouldn't have known too much about some of the other candidates, Templeton went for Hart; so, predictably, did Mourie.

Hart was pleasantly surprised to get Bush's tick and looked headed for a clean sweep. After all, he and 'DJ' Graham went back a long way and hadn't the celebrated educationalist written a handsomely complimentary foreword to his 1993 book, *Straight From The Hart*, describing him as, among other things, "the finest thinker on the game since Vic Cavanagh"?

As they say in America, that was then and this is now. DJ plumped for Graham Henry. They also went back: Graham had been Henry's boss at Auckland Grammar School and his assistant coach with the Auckland team. Having given his verdict, Graham proceeded to justify it. He did so with such fervour that Deaker felt moved to point out that they were looking for the next All Black coach, not the next pope.

Once the initial shock had passed, Hart was philosophical: three out of four wasn't bad and, besides, that was DJ to a T: "He's always been a man of strong opinions which he expresses without fear or favour. He regarded Henry as an astute tactician who was more closely in touch with the game than I was. He also threw in a reference to the various controversies which have dogged me. It didn't bother me too much but it enraged my family."

Two days before the council was due to make its decision, Hart received a contract in the mail. The attachment explained that all candidates were required to indicate their readiness to sign the contract if they were appointed coach or selector. Hart was astounded: the contract was inadequate to say the least. It closely resembled the NZRFU's players contract and was short on detail and full of gaps. He got some legal advice which was that he shouldn't sign but should indicate a willingness to do so if and when appointed. He responded to the NZRFU to that effect.

December 6, 1995, was a big day for J.B. Hart: Judgement Day and his 50th birthday. He was having a surprise birthday morning tea with some former colleagues from Fletcher Challenge in his downtown Auckland office when he got a call from the NZRFU. The message was that he'd be getting a fax which he had to sign and return before the vote otherwise he was out of contention.

The fax arrived. It demanded his agreement to certain terms and conditions: a $200,000 salary, a one-year term, and an undertaking to avoid conflicts of interest. The money wasn't really an issue for him although whoever the new coach was, he'd be taking a pay cut before he'd even started work – Hart had been told by NZRFU Chief Executive George Verry that the salary would be $250,000. A one-year contract was disappointing but, at the end of the day, a professional coach stands or falls on performance and the only comfort a contract can provide is financial. What really worried Hart was the conflict of interest clause: rigorously enforced, it could blow his consultancy business out of the water.

He later learned that the NZRFU's hard line was instigated by Richie Guy who'd recently become something of an authority on contractual matters. Guy feared that if the NZRFU didn't set the terms in concrete in advance, they'd get screwed down the track.

Hart consulted his lawyer again but there was no way around it: he either bit the bullet or walked away when the prize he'd sought for ten years was within his grasp.

The council convened. Meads brought up the players' poll but got no takers – his fellow councillors didn't want to hear about it. To his credit, he didn't just stand up and announce the result as he could easily have done. Fisher, though, got the strong impression that Hart was not the players' choice.

The debate got under way. There was some revisiting of the past at Hart's expense. It was obvious to Fisher that nothing had changed as far as the Anyone-But-Hart brigade was concerned. The fact that Hart had done very little actual coaching in recent years was commented on. There was some interest in Henry: he'd sold himself well and had the attraction of not carrying any baggage.

But this time the momentum was with Hart. He was the interviewing sub-committee's clear choice and there was a feeling that, with the onset of professionalism, his time had come. The wheel had come full circle: his whole corporate-based approach with its accent on management rather than coaching *per se,* which had turned some councillors off in the past, had become a strong selling point.

Hart won on the first ballot, getting ten votes to Cooper's five and Henry's four. It was a decisive result given the size and strength of the field. There was an intriguing suggestion that Henry, the Auckland Rugby Union's nominee, had gained his support from the South Island. It appeared the southern bloc had calculated that Hunter was unlikely to get the top job but, as the only South Island candidate, was odds-on to make the panel. Perhaps, too, Henry, who hails from Christchurch, had persuaded them he was still a mainlander at heart.

The call came through twenty minutes before the announcement was made. Blackburn kicked off by asking, "Have you got a glass of champagne?" It beat the hell out of Eddie Tonks' standard opening line, "I've got bad news . . ."

It had finally happened. Having steeled himself to expect the worst, Hart couldn't switch off the self-control and let himself go: "The way I was looking at it, it wouldn't have been the end of the world if I'd missed out. There was an opportunity and I felt I had something to offer but there were a lot of other things happening in my life."

That night, a hundred guests gathered at Hart's place to help him celebrate his fiftieth. The party had been arranged before it was known that the council would decide that afternoon.

It was a pretty good party. Amid the revelry, it must have crossed people's minds that it would've been one of the all-time frosts if the birthday boy had gone down in flames again.

Some people felt the NZRFU would prefer absolutely anyone other than John Hart as All Black coach.

4

CHOOSE YOUR PARTNERS

THE next day, a conference call took place involving the three councillors who'd been on the interviewing sub-committee – Mike Banks, Mattie Blackburn, and Leo Walsh – and the new All Black coach. The subject: who would be his co-selectors.

John Hart was the first convenor to be granted the privilege of having a say in the matter – previously, the selectors had been chosen by council vote, along with the coach. Hart hadn't made any mutual support deals with other candidates beforehand but his analysis of what was needed on the panel had thrown up two names.

Firstly, he thought there should be some continuity from the outgoing panel. Earle Kirton was out of the question for a variety of reasons, the most pertinent being that he was on record as not being prepared to serve on a panel led by Hart. That left Ross Cooper.

"I'd seen a lot of Ross when he'd coached Thames Valley and Counties and liked him," says Hart. "He'd done a good job with the Colts and struck up a rapport with the players on the tour of France although he didn't get much of a crack of the whip – they may've seen him as a backroom boy."

He and Cooper had actually been in contact the previous day. Cooper recalls being on his way to Wellington for a media cocktail function "which in itself was amazing because we hadn't talked to the press. I got a call at the top of the Bombay Hills telling me I'd missed out – I thought, 'stuff it' and drove home. I rang Hart and congratulated him. I thought it was really neat for him and an astute decision."

Hart rang him back later that night. "I knew Ross would be the one hurting the most – he'd be sitting at home with the family thinking about missing out on a job he might've expected to get. I knew the feeling. I let him know he'd have my support as a member of the panel."

Secondly, Hart wanted a geographic balance for more than the obvious practical reasons. He was determined to break down the parochialism which had infected New Zealand rugby over the previous eight years. The All Blacks had been caught in the parochial crossfire and their previously monolithic public support had begun to erode. Much of the parochialism had centred around the coach: whether by accident or design, both Alex Wyllie and Laurie Mains were strongly identified with their provinces. So, too, was the man who'd waited in the wings.

While Hart has never revelled in the professional Aucklander tag, he was enough of a realist to know he was perceived that way in some quarters. As Peter Scutts, an Australian, puts it: "One thing I've learnt about New Zealanders, they love to pigeon-hole people. Hart's pigeon-holed as a typical Aucklander – that's a cross he has to bear."

A panel of North Islanders, or worse, North Islanders from north of Hamilton – which would have resulted under the NZRFU's previous system – would only reinforce the old negatives, entrench the north-south divide, and make it harder for the whole country to "buy into" the All Blacks.

The logic of geography pointed strongly to Gordon Hunter, the only South Islander among the candidates. They'd met once, in 1991 when Hart was an All Black selector and Hunter the coach of a Combined Services team which drew 19-all with North Harbour. Afterwards, Hart had complimented Hunter on a well-organised performance.

Hart had heard good reports of Hunter and thought he'd done a pretty good job with Otago. "He'd been Mains' assistant but he was his own man and I had no reason to think we couldn't work together."

Nor did the Dunedin detective: "People might've thought that being a confidant of Mains, there was no way I could be a strong Hart supporter or meet his criteria. When I was asked about it by the interviewing panel, I pointed out that if I was sent somewhere on a police inquiry, I'd work with whoever was on the case to get the right result. Besides, rugby has taken my horizons around the world – the Bombay Hills don't mean a lot to me."

While Hart appreciated being asked his opinion, he felt that the final decision should be made by the councillors who, as a result of the interview process, were in a better position to assess all the candidates. Their recommendation was Cooper and Hunter so everyone was happy.

The next item on the agenda was the assistant coach. During his interview, Hart had argued the case for having assistant coaches for both backs and forwards, a system Bob Dwyer had used with the Wallabies following the trend towards specialisation set by other sports, notably American football. At times under both Wyllie and Mains, Grant Fox had been the de facto back coach but in the new era players would be under too much pressure to shoulder that extra responsibility. He again made the point that two people can be of one mind on selection issues without necessarily gelling as coach and assistant.

The notion of coaches from outside the panel working with the All Blacks again failed to find favour: "They indicated quite strongly that it would be in my best interests to take Cooper as assistant coach," says Hart. "I was told that if I wasn't prepared to work with him, I should've said so at my interview and it would've counted against me. It wasn't a question of not being prepared to work with Ross but of never having worked with him. I talked about Peter Sloane because I had worked with him."

With that settled, Blackburn came back to Hart to get his views on the All Black manager. The candidates were Banks, Richard Crawshaw, and Colin Meads although the latter, rather like Kirton, had effectively eliminated himself from serious consideration. Hart hadn't worked with Banks or Crawshaw. Both were fresh faces, both had supported him, both appeared to have the organisational and planning skills needed in the professional environment. Hart said he'd be happy with either; Blackburn said Banks would be the recommendation.

In a TV interview after his appointment was announced, Banks said that he saw his role as helping to create an environment which bred enjoyment and success. That augured well – it was very much Hart's philosophy too.

The selectors met for the first time in Wellington on December 11, Cooper's birthday. He remembers Hart as being a little out of touch with NZRFU procedures but on the ball in other respects: when Cooper got home to Waihi, typed-up minutes of the meeting were on his fax machine.

Clearly, things were going to be different. "It was such a change," says Cooper. "Firstly, to be included in the discussion and planning and, secondly, the fact that everybody got the same stuff. There were no secrets. I'd got home from Argentina to find that Michael Jones had been picked ahead of Kronfeld; the team had left for Sydney and I had to go on radio to explain it not knowing a thing about it."

In his interview, Hart had floated the idea of taking a 36-man squad to South Africa on the basis that four tests against the Springboks in four weeks was a mission impossible unless the test side could be kept in cotton wool. That meant having another 21 players – the starting 15 and six reserves – for the midweek games.

The concept seemed to strike a chord with some members of the sub-committee. However, when Hart raised it at his first meeting of the NZRFU's rugby operations committee a week after his appointment, it got a mixed reception. Some committee members were receptive but a couple of councillors, including his old sparring partner John Sturgeon, opposed it on the grounds that a 36-man squad would be difficult to manage. It was even suggested that they'd have problems finding big enough buses. That sort of logistical detail was normally a matter for the team management rather than the council but some councillors were clearly more at home with logistics than strategy.

The media were speculating that the changing of the guard might extend to the captaincy. One theory was that Hart could neither forgive nor forget four grating years of the Sean and Laurie Show. Those who looked beyond personalities thought Fitzpatrick might be held accountable for the All Blacks' tactical inflexibility and poor decision-making in a couple of narrowly lost test matches.

When Fitzpatrick became captain in 1992, Hart had wondered if he was up to the job but had seen him grow in stature. He shared the concern about decision-making but saw it as a team – as opposed to a captaincy – issue. He suspected that Fitzpatrick's occasional palpable unease in the leadership role was caused by having to bear too much of the burden. Communication hadn't been the previous management's strong suit so Fitzpatrick had ended up as the main front man as well as the communications link between management and players.

Hart had heard from several sources that Fitzpatrick was not merely pro-Mains, he was anti-Hart. "That didn't ring true – although we'd never been close, we'd always had a positive relationship."

For his part, Fitzpatrick didn't feel he had much to fear from coach Hart: "There'd been talk of a rift between us, that I was Mains' man and so on. There never was a rift. I'd said in black and white that Hart was the best coach I'd ever had, that he pressed the right buttons for me, even though in the Auckland days you were aware of him manipulating people to get the best out of them. He'd tell me one thing and Abo (rival hooker Iain Abercrombie) another and although I didn't really like that side, I could see he was doing it to get the best outcome. Maybe in the 1992 to 1995 period we became more distant but I'd tell him that Mains was the coach so I had to support him and I'd take the same approach if he was the coach."

After meeting the other selectors, Hart went to see Fitzpatrick. They had a frank exchange. "I was quite open in telling him that certain players didn't like him and what they didn't like about him," says Fitzpatrick. "Mostly it was based on hearsay and unfamiliarity and the fact that he hadn't really coached in the nineties. It was interesting to watch him turn all that around. I remember after a training session in Durban, seeing Zinzan and Harty lying in the middle of the field, talking and joking. I said to Robin Brooke, 'You wouldn't have seen that six months ago.'"

Hart found Fitzpatrick slightly ill at ease, as if half-expecting unwelcome news. The first issue to be resolved was: did he want to play? "Sean said he would've retired if there hadn't been a change of coach and management. This wasn't intended as a criticism of Mains so much as a statement that the burden had become too great. But it was clear he was hugely motivated by the South African series – he'd taken the loss in the World Cup final deeply and personally and would relish the opportunity to lead the All Blacks back to South Africa. I told him it came down to his desire and form: if he was still the best hooker, I'd pick him. And as I didn't see anyone who'd bring more quality to the leadership, if he was in the team, he'd be captain.

"I also told him I had real concerns about the lack of overall leadership within the All Blacks – the players had become too programmed and weren't taking individual responsibility. We had to grow the leadership capacity within the team to take the pressure off him in terms of decision-making – I wanted shared decision-making under the captain's direction. In sport or business, the leader shouldn't carry all the responsibility; the more he can share, the more effective the team will be and the more the leader can demonstrate leadership quality. It was imperative that we used players like Zinzan and Robin Brooke, Ian Jones, Michael Jones, Frank Bunce and Olo Brown as key decision makers which would ultimately assist him."

Hart's concerns over leadership extended to the succession. The only alternatives weren't much younger than Fitzpatrick; no potential successors from the next generation had been identified, let alone groomed. He emphasised that the South African tour would be an opportunity to try to develop potential leaders and the captain would have an important part to play in that.

As it turned out, Fitzpatrick's Super 12 form was outstanding and the panel decided very early on that he was their man. He and Hart worked on their relationship. The fact that Fitzpatrick wasn't captain of the Auckland Blues, with all the day-to-day responsibilities that entailed, freed him up to spend time with Hart during the Super 12.

"I talked to him about the trial teams, what we were trying to achieve, what our areas of concern were," says Hart. "We spent so much time together. I found him very perceptive when it came to assessing players although he was mindful of his role and never attempted to push a point of view."

The selection of the 1996 All Blacks was the culmination of a long, painstaking process. In the first phase, the three selectors talked for hours on end about every aspect of selection except individual players. They identified the personal qualities they saw as important and the requirements of individual positions. They established principles, they agreed on what they wouldn't put up with on and off the field. They analysed the opposition. They dwelt on the subject of leadership, focusing on the theme of supporting the captain by developing leadership skills throughout the team to improve decision-making and the ability to react under pressure.

Hart found these sessions stimulating. None of them had come in with fixed views and they sparked well off one another. From time to time, when the discussion turned to philosophy and strategy, Banks would join in. They were well aware that they could stand or fall on what they achieved before a ball had been kicked in anger in 1996. "We had to get it right first time," says Hart. "If we didn't, it would impact on the team and undermine the public's confidence in us."

They analysed the previous panel's performance. Mains had handed over a test XV in pretty good shape but there were alarming shortcomings at the next level, compounded by the exodus to Japan and rugby league of five fringe All Blacks. The analysis led Hart to the conclusion that he should talk to Mains to tap into his knowledge of players' strengths and weaknesses.

Hart believed in handovers. He'd done it with Bryan Craies when he became Auckland coach and again with Maurice Trapp when he stood down. He felt the lack of a handover in 1992 had contributed to the misguided decisions to replace some proven performers with players who simply weren't up to it.

That was fine in theory but his relationship with Mains was non-existent and their rivalry had taken on bitter overtones. Would Mains co-operate? Hart had his doubts but Cooper kept at him to make the approach: "We were sitting in the Koru Lounge at Wellington about to get on a plane and I was pushing John to ring Mains. He rang and Mains said, 'I'm having dinner, ring back in twenty minutes.' He took that as a fob-off and was tempted to forget it but I pushed him to try again."

They met at Carisbrook just before Christmas. The meeting lasted several hours; Mains was guarded at first but gradually loosened up. They went through the players he'd picked and some he hadn't with Mains giving his assessment of their strengths and weaknesses. They covered up-and-coming talent, the Wallabies and the Springboks, even matters like adjusting to altitude in South Africa.

Hart, who'd gone in with limited expectations, came away thinking that he and his predecessor weren't all that far apart on most issues: "He was fair in his assessment of someone like Lee Stensness although I didn't think he'd handled him that well. It was a valuable exercise, both in terms of gaining information and showing our intention to build bridges."

Cooper, the instigator, took a bleaker view: "The meeting itself was awkward and uncomfortable – I felt like the meat in the sandwich. It was good PR going to Dunedin but to be quite honest, while it was a useful exchange of information, I don't think it achieved a lot in terms of breaking down the barriers between Hart and Mains."

A key element in formulating the game plan which would drive selection was thinking through the implications of the new rules.

The most significant rule changes were those allowing support of the jumper at the lineout and requiring loose forwards to remain bound to the scrum. The effect of the latter was to be partially negated by the double-stacking system devised by the Auckland Blues brains trust.

Hart explains how the panel saw the changes impacting on various positions:

Number 8/blindside flanker: "The reduced defensive screen at scrum-time meant that, more than ever, the number 8 needed ball skills, distribution, and power as well as speed off the mark which hadn't necessarily been a requirement before. Under the old rules, the number 8 could stand off on the blindside; now the guy picking up and driving from the back of the scrum had more opportunity to get outside the tackler.

"It all added up to a lot more pressure on scrum defence: the blindside flanker in particular had to have vision, quick reflexes, and the ability to react quickly and accurately, plus real aggression in the tackle to halt the momentum of the attack. Players like Glenn Taylor and Blair Larsen were now far better suited to lock than blindside flanker. Previously, you might've wanted height in a blindside flanker but body position and intimidating defence had become the key requirements."

Hooker/locks/props: "The lineout changes created a cleaner, more easily policed environment which made height and bulk less important and in some ways even a negative since the bigger you are, the harder it is to support you. Ball-winning was now primarily a matter of co-ordination between the thrower, the jumper and the supports. Genuine leaping ability was less important, accurate throwing-in even more important. With the amount of interference that went on under the old rules, there was always an element of 50-50 ball. Under the new rules, a poor throw is the most likely way to snare opposition ball because, if the timing is right, it's almost impossible to contest successfully. Props needed the strength to support and give the jumper extra height and stability on the take and the co-ordination to synchronise with the thrower and jumper. A prop whose timing is out can upset the whole lineout."

Halfback: "To capitalise on quick, clean lineout possession, you needed to get the ball quickly to the midfield so length of pass became important. A halfback with good speed off the mark could exploit the fact that the loosies had to stay bound. On the other hand, that same restriction required the halfback to do more defensive work around the fringes."

Centre: "With the ball being moved more to capitalise on the extra space available, big defence out wide became critical. Centre rather than second-five would be the key defensive position in the backline making big, hard centres like Frank Bunce and Alama Ieremia invaluable."

Wings/fullback: "Wings with experience at fullback and the ability to retrieve and clear efficiently in defence became a real asset because the new lineout rules meant the premium kick was the one which put the ball hard up against the touchline in the opponent's danger zone, forcing them to put it out close to their line. Good handling and kicking skills were needed to clear the ball quickly, preferably back into the opponent's territory forcing them to make a decision. Genuine pace in the back three would be more important than ever with the extra space opening up.

"In general terms, there'd be less kicking to touch which placed far more emphasis on ball retention. That in turn made upper body strength even more vital: attackers had to be able to take the ball aggressively into the tackle without losing control while defenders needed the ability to turn the ball carrier. Increased ball movement also meant more rucks and mauls and wrestling for possession.

"Some commentators were suggesting that kicking possession away had become almost a criminal offence. We didn't entirely agree: if the kick is poor, yes, but with defences getting very flat and one-off, especially off rucks and mauls, the ability to manipulate defences with kicks behind the opposition backline was a valuable variation. Out wide, players in possession had to avoid being bundled into touch if possible so the kick parallel to the touchline which maintained the momentum of the attack while still offering a chance to recover the ball was an important skill and one which Jeff Wilson was to master."

Graeme Bachop's superb performances at the World Cup and in the subsequent Bledisloe Cup games had only served to increase Hart's long-held admiration for him. Following his appointment, the new coach was keen to explore the possibility that Bachop might not be lost to All Black rugby despite his move to Japan. IRB regulations were no barrier: if his Japanese club would release him, New Zealand could select him. The omens were good since he'd already been granted a release for the World Cup and the tests against Australia. Hart met Bachop over Christmas to sound him out. For Bachop, the big attraction of

Japan was a three-year contract with a substantial income and the opportunity to improve his career prospects. However, his roller-coaster ride at the hands of the All Black selectors after 1991 had made the decision a lot easier.

Bachop's Japanese employer had shown some interest in investing in the International Rugby Hall of Fame, a venture on which Hart squandered time, money, and pride in varying quantities. He took the opportunity to raise Bachop's case and found them amenable: providing his absences fitted in with their season and adequate compensation was paid, they could see benefits in having a current All Black in their team. All he needed now was the thumbs-up from the NZRFU. Hart put his case to the new board and was turned down flat. Notwithstanding the precedent set by Kevin Schuler's inclusion in the World Cup squad, the board wanted the All Blacks chosen from New Zealand-based players.

It was a major setback and, in Hart's view, a decision which might come back to haunt New Zealand rugby. With the money on offer in Japan and the UK, he worries that New Zealand could be systematically stripped of its back-up talent, some of which could end up in other national teams and therefore gone for good given the IRB's ruling that players cannot represent more than one country.

This time, Rob Fisher wasn't on his side: "I was firmly of the view that Bachop shouldn't be considered. I had nothing against him but I thought it was sending the wrong signal to young players – that they could go overseas and still get an All Black call-up." He concedes however that, "it remains to be seen how long that stance can prevail."

Win a few, lose a few. Hart got his way on the 36-man squad for South Africa and a pre-season All Black camp. In early February, the panel got together to choose the players for the camp. Apart from 1995 form, the key consideration was their assessment of an individual's capacity to meet both the skill demands of their position under the new rules and the on- and off-field standards which would apply. After much discussion, none of which centred on the likely test side, Hart drew up a list of 45 players with his co-selectors.

Hunter was in the slightly difficult position of being both All Black selector and coach of the Otago Highlanders. It wasn't an ideal arrangement but he'd already been appointed to the Highlanders job when the panel was elected and was reluctant to give it up: "I'd spent a lot of time putting the combinations together. I knew we were lightweight but I'd come up with an exciting plan and didn't really want to hand over to someone else. The others agreed to me carrying on with the Highlanders even though it was clearly going to increase their workload."

There was a dearth of quality tighthead props after Olo Brown but that wasn't the only position where the lack of suitable back-up was worrying: halfback was another, hence the strenuous efforts to keep Bachop in the frame, and the situation at lock, number 8, and centre wasn't too flash either. The jury was still out on what was Jeff Wilson's best position: if it was wing, then fullback also came into that category.

The panel met the Super 12 coaches to get their input. They were effectively the panel's suppliers so Hart wanted them on side. Eroni Clarke, who'd been a borderline case anyway, was added to the list at Graham Henry's request. Super 12 commissioner Peter Thorburn and the coaches then signed off on it.

Less successful was the attempt to co-ordinate fitness programmes. "We ran up against different agendas," says Hart. "I found Thorburn very supportive in getting some co-ordination going but there was a fair amount of tension at that meeting. Some of it was between Thorburn and the coaches which might've been a spill-over from the Super 12 selection process in which he'd played a big part."

The list featured up-and-comers like Christian Cullen, Roger Randle, Adrian Cashmore, Chresten Davis, Scott McLeod, and Charles Riechelmann. Glenn Taylor re-emerged from the obscurity into which he'd disappeared after his nightmarish experience against Sydney in 1992. The announcement met with a generally positive reaction. There would have been something seriously wrong if it hadn't: squads of 46 give selectors enough leeway to please most people.

Richard Loe's omission was probably the closest thing to a controversy. It wouldn't have surprised anyone who knew Hart's views on the importance of discipline but in fact it was as much to do with Loe's lack of mobility.

Over the years, Hart and Loe had had something of a love-hate relationship, quite unconnected to Loe's family ties to Alex Wyllie. Before the squad was announced, Hart sent Loe a note saying that the door wasn't closed but adding that he'd seen a newspaper report that the All Blacks were no longer the veteran prop's priority. Loe wrote back from South Africa, where he was on a pre-season tour with the Canterbury Crusaders, to set the record straight: he certainly hadn't indicated his unavailability for the All Blacks; on the contrary, he was "fit and available."

The significance of those words wasn't lost on Hart. The 1995 World Cup squad plus Michael Jones were on lavish NZRFU contracts which guaranteed their handsome salaries whether or not they were selected. All they had to do was remain "fit and available."

5

BACKROOM BOYS (AND GIRL)

WHEN John Hart became All Black coach, he knew exactly who he wanted as his medical support team. Getting them was another matter.

The men in question were Doctor John Mayhew and physiotherapist David Abercrombie who'd worked together with the All Blacks under Alex Wyllie (and Hart in Japan in 1987). Hart had sounded them out beforehand and both were keen in principle. Next thing, Mayhew rolled up to Hart's fiftieth birthday party with a humdinger of a contract from the Auckland Warriors in his pocket.

The Warriors' timing was spot-on. Although Mayhew is a rugby union man to the core, his years of involvement with the All Blacks and North Harbour had taken a heavy toll on his medical practice. Furthermore, Mayhew's wife Sue and his young family were, as he puts it, "rugby-ed out" – they'd had enough of his being away from home on rugby duty.

"I didn't think Harty would be appointed in 1995," says Mayhew. "When I was approached by the Warriors, I thought my rugby time was over and it'd be another adventure in my sports medicine career. I turned their initial offer down but the day before Hart got the job, they came back with a revised offer which had everything I'd asked for."

Hart wanted Mayhew badly and not just because he was the best sports medicine doctor in the country: he also had the skills and personality to make a valuable contribution in a quasi-management role. He was officer material, the sort of cool, capable hand you need on a tough campaign. Hart kept asking and Mayhew kept saying "no." Mayhew thought he was making himself pretty clear but Hart knew that, deep-down, he didn't really mean it.

Hart: "I don't believe in persuading people to do things they don't want to do because they'll inevitably fail but Doc's strong preference was to work with the All Blacks and maintain his medical career. It was a matter of getting the structure right, providing support for his family life and medical practice, and exercising some gentle persuasion on his wife."

For "getting the structure right" read "screwing more money out of the NZRFU." In the old days, that would have been difficult if not impossible but the winds of change were swirling through the Huddart Parker Building in downtown Wellington.

"Traditionally the NZRFU would've taken the view that plenty of people are itching to get involved with the All Blacks so why should they pay people to do it?" says Hart. "I argued that in the professional era we had to have the best. To their credit, the NZRFU came up with a reasonable package – not as much as the Warriors were offering but enough to neutralise the financial issue. It was a major fillip – Doc was such a key figure that him not being there would've had a big impact on my effectiveness."

Money was also an issue for Abercrombie – like Mayhew, he'd had to kiss plenty goodbye during his previous stint with the All Blacks. When Hart put Abercrombie's case to the NZRFU, however, the winds of change suddenly dropped to a gentle zephyr.

"Some of those on the NZRFU's medical advisory committee – which had control over the appointment – felt that when Abo had done the job under Wyllie, he'd got bigger than the role warranted because he'd been ahead of his time in seeking to have his costs reimbursed," says Hart. "That reflects his self-confidence which is well-placed; he's world-class in his injury assessment and rehabilitation ability. Because of the NZRFU reaction, I didn't push as hard and the result was a package which wasn't as attractive as it should've been."

Abercrombie could live with it and the promise of a review in 1997: "My motivation was to be involved with the first year of professional rugby. There was also the motivation of a series in South Africa. I could remember as a kid the old man getting us up to watch those games and thinking that would be something. It was also a chance to get a change of environment and stimulate my work ethic. I was right on that count; it was seven days a week, up to 14 hours a day."

Hart had been expected to reintroduce the Auckland-based fitness guru Jim Blair to the All Black set-up. He'd met the Scotsman in 1983 at a low point in his coaching career; a season which had promised much for Auckland had crumbled away to nothing and he'd even contemplated stepping down. The introduction to Blair and his revolutionary ideas on grid training and individualised conditioning was one of the most significant events in Hart's development as a coach.

On the other hand, the All Blacks' impressive speed and aerobic fitness in 1995 spoke volumes for the incumbent fitness adviser Marty Toomey who had the backing of the other selectors. There was also the fact that Toomey was from Dunedin and Blair from Auckland; Hart's drive to position himself and the All Blacks above parochialism would stall at the starting line if he was seen to be purging all Mains' men and replacing them with Aucklanders. Blair was understanding, telling Hart he'd do the same in his shoes.

Toomey, who'd never met Hart, had suspected he'd fall victim to the new broom syndrome. He was caught off guard when the call came: "My wife said it was John Hart on the phone and I went, 'oh yeah.' I thought it was someone taking the mickey because I didn't know his voice."

Recent All Black touring teams have been accompanied by representatives of the team's various sponsors. Hart's research showed that this arrangement hadn't worked particularly well for anyone, including the sponsors themselves. The 1993 tour of England and Scotland featured the vexatious Mike Brewer affair and Steinlager representative Tim Barry, brother of All Black Liam, found himself in some invidious positions in France in 1995 when his role became blurred.

Hart was determined that there'd be no more than one sponsors' representative and no repeat of these distracting contretemps. He approached Lion Nathan's Kevin Roberts seeking the release of the former Auckland, Counties, and North Harbour player Richard Fry to accompany the All Blacks throughout the season as the sole sponsors' representative. Like

Mayhew, Fry's personal and professional attributes meant he could contribute in areas beyond his strict job description. Roberts obliged.

Through his television work, Hart had observed the All Blacks' prickly relationship with the media at first hand. In their dealings with journalists, the players tended to follow the management's lead which was to be offhand at best and hostile at worst. The inevitable upshot was a certain amount of negative coverage which coloured the public's perceptions of the All Blacks and was a factor behind the public's sometimes luke-warm support for the team.

The first step towards turning it around was establishing just how bad the situation was. Hart decided to conduct his own media survey. He enlisted the aid of Paul Lewis, a former *New Zealand Herald* rugby writer who'd joined the Baldwin Boyle Group public relations company. Together, they drew up a survey consisting of twenty or so questions which was sent to some ninety media people, a cross-section of reporters, presenters, and opinion-makers, some of whom regularly dealt with the All Blacks and others who didn't. They were spread across the country and the three branches of the news media – newspapers, radio, and television.

Hart wanted a quick response so that he could present the results to the 46 prospective All Blacks at the seminar on professionalism scheduled for February 25. He got it – responses flooded in from 80 per cent of those surveyed. There was no need to feed their answers into a computer to make sense of it all. The near-unanimous view was that the All Blacks were arrogant, unapproachable, inaccessible, and indifferent to the media and their requirements – and that was the good news.

The respondents were asked to rate the performance of the 1995 All Blacks and management in a number of media-related areas on a scale of one to ten. Their highest rating was six; on most counts, they rated in the three to five range. As well as completing the survey, a number of respondents had attached notes – screeds of them in some cases. It was hair-raising stuff. Those in the All Black camp who'd complained about negative media coverage didn't know how lucky they were.

The bottom line was that while there was still a reservoir of latent goodwill towards the All Blacks, it was drying up fast.

The next step was a face-to-face session between Banks and the panel and 20 leading rugby journalists from around the country. Once again, no punches were pulled. Murray Deaker supplied some anecdotal evidence which he felt summed up the sorry state of affairs: "I got to South Africa halfway through the World Cup and met Richard Becht in the hotel lobby. He's one of the most influential people in the New Zealand sports media, the guy who decides what sport goes on the One Network News. He said to me, 'Murray, there are two types of All Blacks: ***** and big *****.'"

Others were slightly more specific, detailing the endless frustrations involved in covering the All Blacks who didn't seem to accept that they had any obligations to the media and therefore felt the media should be grateful for whatever co-operation they got. Hart believed this attitude was dangerously misguided; the media are the conduit to the public on whose support the game depends and whose ticket purchases, TV subscriptions, and support for sponsors' products ultimately pay the salaries of professional rugby players.

Another message which came through loud and clear was the need for a media liaison officer in the All Black management team. From Hart's observation, particularly at the World Cup, the role hadn't worked – Ric Salizzo, who'd done the job since 1992, had come to be referred to as "the media prevention officer." Hart had therefore told the NZRFU board that he wouldn't require an MLO – he and Banks would look after the media. The journalists were able to convince him that the problem stemmed from the All Black management's negative attitude towards the media which resulted in Salizzo having an essentially obstructive brief. It seemed the system had been at fault, not the individual; the much-maligned Salizzo was only following orders. The journalists were equally adamant that Banks and Hart couldn't handle day-to-day media liaison effectively.

Sensibly, Hart had taken the precaution of inviting NZRFU Chief Executive David Moffett to the session. Having adopted the stance that the MLO role was part of the problem rather than part of the solution, Hart was grateful for Moffett's support when he performed his U-turn before the board.

At media lunches in the four main centres before Super 12 games, the panel and Banks presented the survey's results and outlined how they intended to operate. One journalist made the comment that it sounded great but talk was cheap. They put their credibility on the line by making a commitment to an open, inclusive relationship and promising improved access to the players, a user-friendly MLO, and Sunday press conferences after tests. Salizzo had usually sat with the reserves during matches, a practice which helped earn him the nickname 'Number 31' (as in the 31st All Black). It was agreed that his successor would sit with the press to get their feedback on which players should attend the post-game press conferences.

The Sunday morning press conference was mainly in response to the daily newspaper rugby writers' complaint that, by the time the Sunday papers had finished with a test match, there wasn't much left for Monday. Hart was planning to introduce Sunday morning team de-briefings and some of that analysis could be shared with the media. By Sunday morning, too, the injury situation would be clearer than immediately after the game.

The hunt was on for an MLO. Although Salizzo wasn't an option, he was helpful in explaining his role and suggesting how it could be done differently. The search led to TVNZ sports reporter Jane Dent who was about to quit television. Her swansong would be the Atlanta Olympic Games which meant she'd miss the tests in Christchurch and Brisbane and the first game in South Africa. The compromise was for the Baldwin Boyle Group to provide cover – in the form of consultant Michelle Lewis – while Dent was in Atlanta. Hart had misgivings about this arrangement but went along with it because he was convinced that Dent was the right person for the job.

Dent wasn't unduly daunted at the prospect of being the sole woman in such a testosterone-rich environment: "Sport in television was a fairly male-dominated area in the early eighties and we mostly covered blokes' sports so, for me, the intimidating part was back then. I'd had 12 or 13 years' experience of the All Blacks and knew a few of them – I must've interviewed Zinzan Brooke about twenty times on whether or not he was going to league. Hopefully, I hadn't antagonised too many of them."

Some things still took a bit of getting used to. "I had a meeting with Fitzpatrick and Fry to discuss the players' concerns about having a woman in the set-up – their biggest one seemed to be having a woman on the bus. I didn't know what that meant and I'm still a bit bemused by it – it was never made clear exactly what worried them. Maybe it's superstition. It's very territorial on the bus – even Mayhew and Abercrombie have to sit together. In the end it got to me too – on the Barbarians tour I was quite put out to find Dylan Mika in my seat. He said he always sat there on the Auckland Blues bus."

Hart had also been inclined to do without a masseur; this time the players persuaded him otherwise. Toomey had done some massage work in his student days and while Hart wasn't prepared to take him on tour purely as a fitness advisor, he'd do so if he could combine the roles – help with the pre-training warm-ups and grids and do rubbing work when needed. This arrangement worked well when it was trialled during the home leg and Toomey duly became a full member of the increasingly versatile management team. Hart was getting the NZRFU's money's worth.

Even at this early stage Banks had a good feeling about the team Hart had assembled: "John's ability to get the right mix and integrate the components is one of his real strengths. It's all about getting the right balance of personalities and workloads and from very early on I got the sense it would work well."

He and Hart had decided that a reconnaissance trip to South Africa was vital. They put a proposal to the council which was only prepared to cough up for the manager. Hart and Banks decided they would split the cost of the second ticket although, subsequently, the NZRFU agreed to pay for both.

Before they left, the full management team discussed touring South Africa with Fitzpatrick, Andrew Mehrtens, and Ian Jones, the All Blacks' representatives on the NZRFU's players committee. They also went through the whole season, getting the players' input on how things had been done in the past, what they liked and didn't like, and which were their preferred hotels.

The pair made a three-and-a-half day swing through Cape Town, Durban, Pretoria, Port Elizabeth, and Johannesburg. They met Johan van Bloemstein, the liaison officer appointed by the South African Rugby Union (SARFU). He'd been the All Black baggage manager at the World Cup. He was enthusiastic but, as it turned out, didn't have the connections in SARFU to get things done and found it difficult coping with the organisational demands of what were effectively two teams.

The baggage manager was Edwin Nkula, whose appointment was part of the development programme designed to involve blacks and coloureds in rugby. Nkula told them he was looking forward to the free tickets and free meals which was commendably frank of him but not quite the attitude they were looking for. He was to prove as good as his word, becoming known as Edwin Who? because he was rarely sighted anywhere but in restaurants.

They changed unsatisfactory arrangements: SARFU wanted the team to travel in the mornings which was when they preferred to train. Eastern Province wanted a night game; they insisted on an afternoon game so the team could travel to Durban that night and train there the next morning.

The party had been booked into a Cape Town hotel for almost two weeks at the start of the tour. Hart and Banks wanted to get the team out of the city to somewhere where they could relax and slowly build up for the challenge ahead and the enlarged squad could come together. They asked the Southern Sun/Holiday Inn chain, which was providing all their accommodation through its sponsorship of South African rugby, if they had any resort-style properties off the beaten track. The company suggested the Beacon Isle Hotel at Plettenburg Bay, between Cape Town and Port Elizabeth. It looked ideal in the brochures and, since it wouldn't be peak season, Southern Sun would charge the same rate as at the other hotels. Hart wanted to delay their return to Cape Town until a few days before the test so while Banks checked out Plettenburg Bay, he scouted the Stellenbosch area for another hotel. Banks returned waxing lyrical. Hart was equally enthusiastic about his discovery, the Lord Charles Hotel; unfortunately, it wasn't a Southern Sun property. After a major debate and with great reluctance, Southern Sun agreed to them staying there.

They met the manager of every hotel they would stay at, presenting them with detailed wish-lists which went right down to where the various members of the management team should be located. There was much discussion about food: the hotel chain was painfully aware that the All Blacks were returning to the Sandton Crowne Plaza in Johannesburg, the scene of the crime or the misfortune, depending on your point of view.

They checked the training grounds. Discovering that some of the scrum machines weren't up to scratch, they decided to bring two scrum and two ruck machines with them. That further complicated the logistics since it would require two trucks shuttling around South Africa, one following the team bus and the other on a positioning haul to the next stop.

The provincial unions, particularly Western Province and Natal, were helpful and hospitable; they were looking forward to hosting the All Blacks. However, the pair came away with the feeling that SARFU would do as much as it had to and no more. They never met SARFU Chief Executive Rian Oberholzer nor, in any real sense of the word, President Louis Luyt. As guests of the Northern Transvaal union, they watched the Blue Bulls Super 12 game against Transvaal at Loftus Versfeld Stadium. Luyt was there wearing his Transvaal hat but scarcely deigned to acknowledge them. It was a sign of things to come.

One person they did meet was Andre Markgraaff, the new

Springbok coach. The encounter took place in Kimberley where the All Blacks were to play Griqualand West. Markgraaff, who was also Chairman of the Griqualand West union, took them back to a friend's house for a barbecue and later drove them to the airport. The two coaches discussed professionalism and discipline. They were of like mind on the need to manage professionalism carefully and Hart undertook to send Markgraaff details of the professionalism seminar he'd staged in February. Judging by Markgraaff's remarks on the subject of discipline, James Small and James Dalton would need to get their acts together. Hart got the impression that François Pienaar wouldn't necessarily be the Springbok captain because he wouldn't necessarily make the team. Clearly, Pienaar's role in WRC hadn't been forgotten, much less forgiven.

Hart enjoyed the discussion which left him in no doubt that he was up against a formidable adversary. The relaxed and friendly tone of that first meeting was never to be recaptured. As the season progressed and the pressure on Markgraaff intensified, Hart would find it increasingly difficult to communicate with him.

In passing, Markgraaff had revealed that he'd had the South African-based Alex Wyllie down to Kimberley and was thinking of using him during the series, particularly to work on the Springboks' rucking. That would have been more of a bombshell if Hart and Banks hadn't run into the former All Black coach at their hotel in Pretoria the previous Saturday. Hart had asked Wyllie if he'd be prepared to help the All Black cause during the tour. Wyllie didn't answer but the unspoken message was, 'don't hold your breath.'

6

TRUST ME –
I'M A PROFESSIONAL

THE thorniest issue confronting the new coach was professionalism. John Hart believed that, handled badly, professionalism had the potential to undermine a hundred year tradition of All Black excellence and success.

The warning lights were already flashing. There was Glen Osborne on television acting like he'd won Lotto, talking about buying this and buying that. There were Lee Stensness and Charles Riechelmann, asked what professionalism would mean to them, saying it was just a matter of being paid to play. Simple as that.

The end of amateurism resembled the collapse of communism. Both systems had lasted for decades and, almost to the very end, seemed immune to both their internal contradictions and external pressures. In both cases, many of those who ran the old systems shed their ideological skin overnight and remained in place to implement changes which swept away everything they'd previously held dear. In both cases, the abrupt transition was managed better in some countries than in others. In both cases, the new order which was supposed to be the answer to everything was soon beset by problems of its own.

John Selkirk

Another Decision Day, another rejection. Hart studies the form on the morning of the NZRFU's vote to stick with Laurie Mains.

John Hart collection

End of an era. Hart bids farewell to Fletcher Challenge and, from left, Sir James Fletcher; Fletcher Challenge executive and lifelong friend David Sixton, and FCL Chief Executive Hugh Fletcher.

The call from the NZRFU began, 'Have you got a glass of champagne?' On his 50th birthday, Hart becomes the All Black coach.

The voice of rugby – Keith Quinn at work.

Andy Haden – rugby great, WRC point man, mischief-maker extraordinaire.

Inconsistent selections put pressure on Laurie Mains (left) but no-one could quibble with his faith in Frank Bunce (right) and promotion of Andrew Mehrtens.

'Have you heard the one about . . .' John Hart meets Nelson Mandela, Cape Town, 1995.

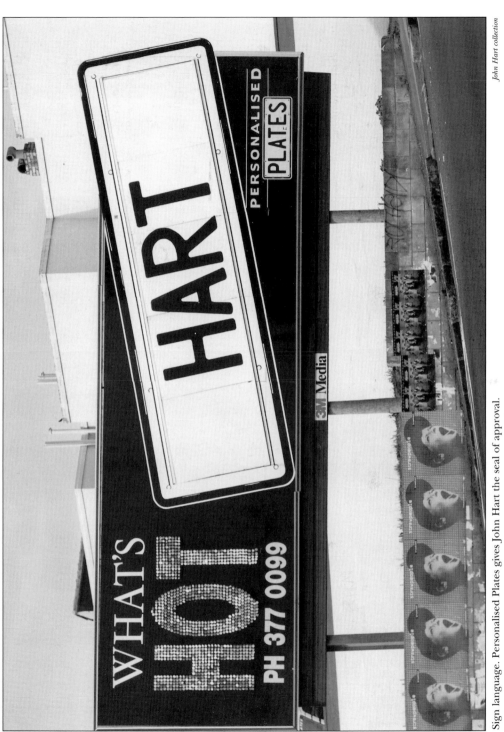

Sign language. Personalised Plates gives John Hart the seal of approval.

John Hart collection

Part of the New Zealand Parliamentary team who swept all before them in the 'other' World Cup. Back row, from left: Trevor Mallard MP, Doctor John Mayhew, the coach, Murray McCully MP; in front are the ring-ins: Bill Osborne (left) and John Boe.

Although New Zealand had managed the transition better than most, there was still a danger that it could go terribly wrong. The mad scramble for the players' services when WRC's takeover bid was at its height had radically altered the balance of power within the game; for a time, at least, the players held the whip-hand. The change in players' expectations was permanent and, in many cases, accompanied by a shift in focus away from the game's wider interests to narrow self-interest. New Zealand's pre-eminence was a reflection of rugby's place in the nation's culture but how long would it take the public to become alienated from a mercenary elite? How long before the base began to crumble? How long could New Zealand remain a dominant force without mass participation at the grass-roots?

Having brooded on these issues over the summer holiday and feeling it was time for the leading players to meet the new All Black management team, Hart organised a seminar on the theme of Professional Rugby: Opportunities and Responsibilities. It took place at the Waipuna International Hotel in Auckland on Sunday, February 25.

Forty-six players, prospective All Blacks in 1996, were invited. One cried off sick, another turned up late. Michael Jones took part even though it was a Sunday. The Super 12 coaches, Commissioner Peter Thorburn, and key NZRFU councillors and executives were invited to attend as observers as were a number of ex-All Blacks.

In addition to the management team and Paul Lewis of Baldwin Boyle, the presenters were David Jones, a specialist in company law who'd assisted some players in their negotiations with the NZRFU in 1995 (and still does today); Jan Torrance, an accountant who'd provided financial advice for a number of New Zealand's top professional athletes; Tim Castle, Senior Vice-President of the NZOCG, the Olympic and Commonwealth Games organisation and a specialist in sports law; Doug McKay, Managing Director of Lion Nathan International; Riki Ellison, who'd won three Superbowl titles with the San Francisco 49ers; and the ubiquitous Paul Holmes whose abilities and influence Hart held in high respect.

As well as their presentations, there was a series of player-led workshops covering contracts, relationships with the NZRFU, the media, the social and financial implications of professionalism, agents and managers, and the need to maintain public support.

Putting the programme together, Hart had been encouraged by the number of people, many of them high-powered, who were eager to help. The All Blacks were still a special breed even though they were now some of the highest paid people in the community.

When Hart sought suggestions for an experienced professional sportsman or woman to provide a player's perspective, the Auckland Warriors were the names on most people's lips. Eighteen months on, the notion of a roomful of All Blacks respectfully taking advice from a Warrior could only be a product of the Mad Butcher's fevered imagination.

Hart wanted a wider perspective and Ellison was perfect: a Maori who'd gone to the USA as a young man and enjoyed a highly successful gridiron career while obtaining a degree in international relations and positioning himself for a rewarding life after football. Ellison's presentation was a revelation; he stopped after half a minute, sat down, and threw away his notes, saying he needed to get his thoughts together. An All Black then asked him a question which set off a worthwhile discussion. When it was over, Ellison's hesitancy disappeared and he was once again the confident individual Hart had met beforehand. He'd simply been overawed by his audience.

When Hart described the incident to George Seifert, the 49ers' former head coach, he found it hard to believe that getting up in front of a bunch of fellow jocks had unnerved Ellison. These weren't just any old jocks, though – they were All Blacks. It was a timely reminder to the players that New Zealanders, even those who are highly successful in their own right, tend to place the men in black on a pedestal.

The players were given the results of the media survey. They were told how professionalism had changed the public relations landscape, why the media were critical towards Hart's goal of presenting the All Blacks as appropriate role models on and off the field, and what the new management intended to do differently. Holmes advised them on dealing with the media in terms of interview techniques and preparation.

Holmes gave an impressive performance: his self-effacing, even humble, demeanour might have had his regular viewers checking the programme guide but, to Hart, it was symptomatic of the media personality's increasing acceptance of rugby's fundamental place in New Zealand culture.

The management team were quite nervous, some more than

others. Many of the players were getting their first taste of Hart and it was realistic to assume that there were a few sceptics and a few cynics in the audience. It cut both ways. John Mayhew, who was close to the players, recalls that some of them regarded Hart with out-and-out apprehension: "There was a fear that they'd get the Gary Whetton treatment, meted out by the former administration."

Hart provided some comfort by making the point that they wouldn't be there unless they were firmly in the panel's thinking. On the other hand, Super 12 form would be the main basis for selection so players who weren't there weren't out of the frame. He trod a careful line with Sean Fitzpatrick, not designating him as captain but giving him a leadership role so that the players could see he had the new panel's support.

He explained the thinking behind taking 36 players to South Africa and the fact that six of them would be on development contracts although still full All Blacks. He discussed the style of game the panel wanted to play and the impact of the new rules on the game as a whole and on the various positions. He summarised the season, providing details of announcement and assembly dates and hotels for each game.

"I felt that if we were going to demand professionalism from the players, we had to demonstrate it ourselves. We gave that information to the media on the same principle. They came to lunch and had access to the players."

Keith Quinn immediately noticed something different: players smiling at journalists.

Hart had two key messages: one was about continuity, the other about change. The black jersey and the All Black heritage remained paramount but, off the field, things had changed beyond recognition: "In the amateur game, the players could say no, they could manage their time. As professionals, things were different and we had to ensure that they understood the responsibilities which went with that without making them feel like hired help. It was a matter of doing things not because they were paid to but because it was part and parcel of their position."

He warned them that the public's expectations would be even greater now that they were earning massive amounts of money by New Zealand standards. Not only would the public demand commensurate levels of performance, they would be even less forgiving of what they perceived as arrogance and taking the All

Blacks' exalted status for granted. He warned them that player greed was driving some unions towards bankruptcy. Players kept pushing for more money without giving a passing thought to where it was coming from or whether there'd be enough left over to meet the cost of running the amateur game.

He quoted chilling statistics from American football: length of average professional career – three-and-a-half years; percentage of players flat broke at the end of their careers – 50 per cent; failure rate of their marriages – four out of five; average life expectancy – 54 years.

"Some might say it's stretching things to compare the two," says Hart, "but everyone who worships at the altar of football runs the same risks. These were warning signals which we had to take heed of."

The combination of inexperience and the sudden influx of large amounts of money had made rugby fertile ground for agents and managers of varying quality. Some players were easy marks and were already being preyed upon.

"Managers manage time, they sift through what's good and what's not," says Hart. "It's the high-profile players who need a manager, the guys who have a lot of commercial opportunities coming at them. The rest are like everyone else: they need a mixture of good advice – legal, financial, tax, medical – and they should go out and buy it like everyone else. Agents take ten or twenty per cent of everything that comes in but most of them aren't adding value and twenty per cent's a huge amount to take if a project's nothing to do with them."

The seminar was also an opportunity for the players to get together with their mentors. Mentoring was a concept which Hart had borrowed from business in the belief that players, even experienced All Blacks, could still learn about their positions from former players who'd mastered those positions. Secondly, it gave the players a sounding board outside the management team while the panel could use the mentors to keep an eye on aspects of a player's game.

The 46 squad members were allocated an appropriate mentor from this distinguished line-up: Robbie Deans, Craig Green, Bruce Robertson, Warwick Taylor, Terry Wright, Grant Fox, Dave Loveridge, Wayne Shelford, Graham Mourie, Alan Whetton, Andy Haden, John Drake, Peter Sloane, and Steve McDowell.

Eight former All Black captains – Wilson Whineray, Brian Lochore, Ian Kirkpatrick, Andy Dalton, Stu Wilson, Gary

Whetton, Jock Hobbs, and David Kirk – also attended the post-seminar dinner to reinforce the panel's message that traditional All Black values could not be lost sight of in the rush to professionalism. Kirkpatrick, who has great presence, proposed a toast to the black jersey. His speech was perfectly pitched, a powerful evocation of the All Black heritage and an acknowledgement that times had changed.

Hart regarded the event as a qualified success: "In retrospect, maybe it was a bit tough to make the boys sit in a classroom all day. The players did well in the workshops and I should've given them more time – the younger guys were a little restrained in front of the older ones, not wanting to make fools of themselves. Generally, I felt that there was a better understanding of the issues but still a huge distance to go.

"Our biggest advantage was that the All Blacks have always been pretty professional so it wasn't all brand-new. Auckland was another example of a professional team which already had a lot of the disciplines in place. We had a good base to build on, especially compared with some other countries. Fitzpatrick would prove to be an outstanding professional rugby player; he understood the need to be aware of the interests of the public, the media, and the sponsors, and to look after the younger players. If they're not comfortable, you don't have a team, which is what happened in 1991."

How did the players rate it? "Maybe the professional, almost corporate approach was heavy going for some of the younger guys but I thought it was excellent in terms of bringing us up to speed on the issues of pro rugby," says Fitzpatrick. "We took a lot away from that and applied it to the Auckland Blues set-up, making sure guys had accountants and the right sort of managers. It showed the guys that the management had taken the next step up and it was up to us to do the same.'

Mayhew considered that the seminar had also succeeded in its secondary aim of kick-starting the relationship between the new management and the players: "They quickly got the players' confidence. Banks was a superb organiser and it was clear the three selectors got on well together which wasn't the case under the previous regime."

Sponsorship had been on the agenda. The issues weren't complicated and the players' obligations to team sponsors weren't unduly demanding although they would need to be reminded of them from time to time. One such occasion was after a player jeopardised a hugely advantageous arrangement – All Blacks are supplied with a new Ford every six months – by returning a car in an appalling state.

Where Hart did foresee trouble was in the grey area where team sponsorships overlap with individual deals and endorsements. Trouble duly arrived, escalating into a crisis which very nearly terminated his All Black coaching career before it had even started.

The Nike boots affair had its seeds in the end-game of rugby's takeover battle. When Jeff Wilson and Josh Kronfeld broke ranks with the All Blacks to sign with the NZRFU, they understood that their deal freed them to wear Nike boots when playing for the All Blacks, despite Mizuno's status as supplier of boots by appointment. In February, players alerted the management that they had a problem on their hands. Anxious to have the matter dealt with and out of the way before the international season started, the management passed the message on to the NZRFU. Nike had a number of other players on their books but most of those deals recognised that the Mizuno team sponsorship had precedence when the individuals concerned were playing for the All Blacks. The exception was Ian Jones, who saw himself as being in the same position as Kronfeld and Wilson.

When Mizuno found out that three All Blacks were planning to wear Nikes, they threatened to sue the NZRFU. What gave the whole affair the potential to seriously destabilise the All Blacks was the fact that Mizuno was represented by Jock Hobbs: the same Jock Hobbs who'd negotiated the disputed contracts in the course of luring the two Otago golden boys out of the clutches of WRC – and of their teammates. As it was, some All Blacks were surprised that Hobbs, as a comparatively recent All Black himself, would line up against the players.

It all came to a head when the players gathered in Napier for the trial which was held a week before the first test of the year, against Western Samoa. The rival sportswear companies had dug in, Nike promising its trio it would back them all the legal and financial way, Mizuno telling the NZRFU that if all 15 All Blacks weren't in the right boots, they'd see them in court.

No-one budged. The three players were locked in tight with Nike – the relationship went beyond the problem endorsements. For its part, Nike was staking a claim: the company had recognised that the All Blacks had international cachet and was signalling that it wanted a piece of the action. The stand-off continued into the following week. The NZRFU responded to Mizuno's threat of legal action by informing the All Black management that any players who refused to wear Mizuno boots could not play against Western Samoa. Now the fuse was well and truly lit.

Hart was angry that the NZRFU and the two companies had failed to act on his warning. Instead of settling it through arbitration, they'd sat on their hands for four months allowing the thing to come to the boil at the worst possible time. "I'm not anti-Mizuno – they're boots of the very highest standard – and I support the concept that all team members should wear team sponsors' gear. But there was a clear difference of opinion as well as the argument that boots, unlike the playing strip, are tools of trade. It had to be arbitrated.

"I wasn't prepared to drop them – it would've been unfair on the other players to change the team at the last moment. That would've put me in breach of my relationship with the NZRFU so I would've had to resign. Mike Banks supported my stance so he would've had to go too."

It went right to the wire. On game day Ian Jones had three pairs of boots in his kit – Nikes, Mizunos, and Nikes with the swoosh blacked out. A deal was reached that the three players would wear Mizunos and the dispute would be put on ice, to be revisited at a later date. That's where it remains.

The Nike boots affair wasn't the only time WRC cast its shadow over the All Blacks. In a long and somewhat rambling interview, Zinzan Brooke tossed in a comment to the effect that if Wilson found himself sniffing boot leather at the bottom of a ruck, the other All Blacks wouldn't bust a gut to look after him. It was said jokingly but, as we learn at an early age, many a true word is spoken in jest.

Brooke's remarks caused uproar. Hart took it up with Fitzpatrick who confirmed that the pair's defection – as it was seen – had caused hard feelings. "The others felt let down," recalls Hart. "They didn't want to force anyone to do what he didn't want to do but couldn't understand why Wilson and Kronfeld hadn't communicated. I could – it would've been very tough for young guys to break ranks. I admired Wilson and Kronfeld – they'd taken a principled stand in defence of the black jersey, no different from John Kirwan's over the Cavaliers tour. Perhaps the comparison was with David Kirk who pulled out at the last minute and was then cast as a hero."

The All Black management tried to downplay it but it was an issue which had to be faced. They talked to the senior players and discovered for themselves that feelings ran deep.

"I asked them how were they going to handle it," says Hart. "They talked about it among themselves. We talked about it once as a team, then put it behind us – it was dead and buried. When Wilson scored in Wellington, one of the first guys to embrace him was Zinzan Brooke. We put it on the players to sort it out and that's what they did."

Like true professionals.

7

TRIAL RUN

THE decision to field regional teams covering the whole country in the Super 12 championship was a boon for the All Black selectors. It meant that the top 125 players were on show every week throughout the early part of the season in a competition which was the next-best thing to test rugby. That was the theory anyway.

While the NZRFU Super 12 Commission did a lot of good work in establishing a base for regional rugby, the process proved more difficult than anticipated. To the dismay of the coaches, the strong-willed commissioner, Peter Thorburn, had a lot of say in selection. With Buck Shelford as his right-hand man, Thorburn had been the driving force behind the rise of North Harbour and he took a particular interest in the Waikato Chiefs. His perceived influence may have contributed to the disharmony which was evident within this marriage of inconvenience from the moment the knot was tied.

Overall, the selections left something to be desired. Not enough thought was given to positional requirements in the light of the new rules. The Chiefs ended up with far too many of the leading locks – Ian Jones, Mark Cooksley, Steve Gordon, Blair Larsen, and Glenn Taylor – because the last two were still regarded as blindside flankers. As a result, some of them didn't get enough rugby, other teams were seriously under-powered at lock, and the panel didn't get to see much of Larsen or anything of Taylor in the position for which they were All Black contenders.

Gordon Hunter, then in his dual role of All Black selector and Otago Highlanders coach, recalls Thorburn's determination to impose his view that the Super 12 was no place for greenhorns: "As far as he was concerned, you had to be a proven force to go in. I could understand that but there were certain players like Andrew Blowers, who'd been identified by Graham Henry, who were young but special and others on contracts who weren't good enough for Super 12. It was difficult because the NZRFU had made a large financial commitment and I guess it made it easier if the people they were paying were picked."

Selection issues aside, the competition suited the panel's purposes. It was a big step up from NPC; the selectors were able to see how players coped under pressure in terms of vision, defence, and the pace of the game.

Some of what they saw provided little comfort. The five New Zealand teams lost all their games in Australia and all but two in South Africa. That sort of away-game strike-rate wasn't a good omen for a four-test tour of the republic. The new rules were increasing attacking opportunities but some of the inflated scorelines owed more to feeble defence – an awful lot of soft tries were being conceded.

When Natal put 63 points on Waikato, it was a sign that all was not well in the Chiefs' camp. The all-star outside backs weren't making much impact although that had to be seen in a team context. "The Chiefs had more ball-winning capacity than they could possibly use but they had an inadequate scrum and average inside backs," says John Hart. "Selectors have to take these things into consideration – when teams are going well, individuals can be carried along. It would've been easy to see Eroni Clarke as being ahead of the other contenders at centre – Clarke was playing well all right but he was in a very good team with a tremendous pack and slick inside backs providing good service."

On his way back from the reconnaissance trip to South Africa, Hart spent a depressing evening at Ballymore watching the full-strength Auckland Blues being methodically taken apart by Queensland: "Auckland had faltered against ACT but this was disaster. Queensland were outstanding, Auckland out of sorts – some players did their reputations little good. Mike Banks and I were sitting in front of a group of Queensland players' wives and partners – they were very vocal in their appreciation which made it even harder to take.

"Auckland being the only New Zealand team to make the semi-finals raised questions about our depth and where we stood in the international arena. The fact that South Africa had two teams in the semis and a third – Transvaal – had beaten Auckland gave us an idea of their depth. Natal had started slowly but when they put it together, as they did against New South Wales, they looked superb. Queensland came to grief at Carisbrook first up but were very consistent from then on, reaching real heights against Auckland, while ACT were the surprise packet showing that Australia had more depth than many believed."

The crowded playing programme meant that the All Black trial had to take place a week after the Super 12 final. The panel had a lot riding on Auckland's final pool game against Natal in Durban: if Auckland lost, they'd have to stay on in South Africa for their semi-final; if they won that and Queensland lost their semi-final, Auckland would then have to stay in South Africa for the final. The Blues – who contributed a third of the players involved in the trial – would be stuck in South Africa for three solid weeks, arriving home thoroughly jet-lagged as the other trialists were assembling in Napier. As it turned out, Auckland beat Natal to earn a home semi-final and the worst-case scenario wound back to having to travel to Brisbane for the final. It's a telling commentary on the relentless schedule – the Blues' All Blacks had 13 Super 12 matches followed by a trial, then ten tests in 13 weeks – and the Super 12 coaches' reluctance to employ the squad system that the panel came to regard injuries which kept potential All Blacks sidelined for a game or two as blessings in disguise.

As the competition moved into its final phase, it became clear that the indifferent form of Frank Bunce, Walter Little, and Glen Osborne couldn't be completely explained away by the Chiefs' shortcomings. Bunce looked particularly lifeless. In late April, the coach decided it was time for a Hart-to-heart. That wasn't as easy as it sounds; while the competition was in progress, he had no control over the players and couldn't be seen to interfere. On the other hand, if a key player had lost his appetite for the big-time – and it was starting to look that way with Bunce – the panel needed to know, pronto.

Hart: "Frank and I go back to 1986 when he came into the Auckland squad but our paths hadn't crossed for many years and he might've thought I wasn't an admirer of his. He hadn't helped himself by not warning us that he couldn't make the seminar and leaving me to cover for him – we wondered if he was sending us a message. He'd been a tremendous servant for the All Blacks and gone further than I thought he would but I was worried about his form and speed. I wasn't prepared to play him if he wasn't on top of his game; when players near the end of their runs, there's always the concern that, once their form slides, it's harder than ever to pull it back up to international level."

Without trying to gloss over his indifferent form, Bunce explained that niggling leg injuries had prevented him from doing the training he needed to get up to All Black sharpness. But the desire was still there: he was excited by the challenge of the Tri-Nations and South Africa; he still wanted to be an All Black.

Hart told Bunce that he fitted the game plan and had the capacity to provide leadership within the team. There were six weeks to the trial; now that he was over his injuries, he had to get into a concentrated fitness routine and show some form. If he did, they'd put him in the trial with the intention of putting him in the All Blacks. But if his speed didn't pick up dramatically . . . "I told him I didn't want to drop him so if he wasn't in the frame come decision-time, we'd manage it together. If he'd felt his time was up, the discussion should've cheered him."

For a man who'd been fast-tracked into the All Blacks as a 20-year-old and played 36 tests, Walter Little had probably never enjoyed the luxury of feeling that his place was secure. Getting dropped for Bernie McCahill in 1991 would've scarred him, especially by the time his provincial coach Peter Thorburn had finished having his indignant say on the matter. Little and Bunce had struck up their productive midfield liaison in 1992 but then, partly due to injury, he'd found himself on the outer again for much of 1993/94 with Lee Stensness, Matthew Cooper, and Alama Ieremia all getting a run in the number 12 jersey. He'd re-established himself as the test second-five-eighth in 1995 but now the big question-mark was hovering over him again.

Like his midfield partner, Little wasn't making a strong case for himself. Compounding his problems with form and fitness, his confidence had been shot to pieces when he tested positive to a banned substance – propoxypene, a mild painkiller which he'd taken for toothache – after the Chiefs' game against Natal and got hit with a two-game suspension. Hart was beginning to doubt that he'd make it.

Osborne was exhibiting the same worrying symptoms as his illustrious Chiefs teammates at a time when the panel was coming to the view that, under the new rules, he was better suited to wing than fullback. To make matters worse, he wasn't handling professionalism well.

"Here was a young guy from Wanganui who suddenly found himself having money thrown at him from all quarters," says Hart. "He was an example of someone who lost his way and needed good advice."

Then there were the injury worries. Top of the list were Josh Kronfeld and Andrew Mehrtens who'd have minimal on-field time before the first test. Michael Jones' struggle with a chronic achilles problem wasn't helped by the Auckland Blues management putting him under pressure to play when he would've been better off resting.

Illness and injury respectively restricted Simon Culhane and Tabai Matson to just five Super 12 appearances between them. Matson's situation was particularly aggravating as he was a contender to replace Bunce if the veteran didn't come up to scratch.

On the positive side, there was a new star in the firmament – Christian Cullen. Hart had come across Cullen when he'd played for the Junior Barbarians against the New Zealand Secondary Schools in 1995; he'd dropped a couple of up-and-unders but looked the goods otherwise. He was the toast of Hong Kong at the 1996 Sevens tournament, his record swag of 18 tries including a mind-boggling effort against Fiji. Not content with a mere length-of-the-field runaway try, he ducked, wriggled, and ghosted past most of the opposition – some of them, it seemed, more than once – behind his own goal-line before setting sail. The panel was enthused by his ability to exploit the new rules with ball in hand, less so by his tackling and positional play.

The new sensation returned from Hong Kong in a blaze of publicity. The panel watched him play for the Hurricanes against Natal at Athletic Park on April 6. He didn't let his fans down but Hart thought he looked very tired by fulltime. A week later they watched the Canterbury Crusaders thump the Hurricanes in New Plymouth and pulled back on the idea of Cullen being the All Black fullback. He made a dismal showing in defence, conceding several tries. Three days of aerobically demanding non-stop rugby in Hong Kong had left him running on empty. Cullen was still very much in contention but more for a place in the reserves; Jeff

Wilson was the front-runner for fullback, at that stage still his preferred position, with Eric Rush firming on the wing.

With the test programme getting under way a week later, the panel decided that the trial would be first and foremost a shakedown for the test squad. The logical extension of that was that the reserves should train with the President's XV – as the shadow test side was called – rather than play against them, moving the trial even further away from the traditional approach of pitting the top 30 players against each other in a dog-eat-dog contest.

The rationale for selection, therefore, was that the President's XV and reserves would be the nucleus of the test squad for the first part of the international season while their opposition – the New Zealand Barbarians XV – would consist of the players the panel expected to fill the remaining 15 places in the 36-man touring party.

The teams were announced at a formal press conference in Auckland. Hart has long believed that selectors who can't or won't explain their decisions make a rod for their own backs. Just about everyone has an opinion on who should be in the All Blacks – the media are paid to have them – so if selectors don't explain their decisions, the vacuum will be filled by conjecture. The media and the armchair selectors will come up with their own reasons why so-and-so was picked and such-and-such wasn't which won't necessarily show the panel in a competent or even honourable light. Hart therefore spent 15 minutes outlining the overall philosophy behind the selection process and explaining the purpose of the trial and the thinking behind the decisions likely to provoke discussion.

Olo Brown was being rested as he'd played all of Auckland's Super 12 games and, secondly, because he was indisputably the first-choice tighthead prop. If Brown was injured, the panel's inclination would be to move Craig Dowd across so the trial was an opportunity to give him some experience on the tighthead side. If Dowd handled it successfully, that would clear the way for Mark Allen, very much a specialist loosehead, to be the reserve prop. One of the three props in the squad must be able to play on both sides of the front row; ideally, it's the reserve otherwise one injury forces a double change. No doubt that's why the previous panel was so reluctant to dispense with Richard Loe's services.

Michael Jones was also rested to enable the medical team to do some intensive work on his injury. He was replaced by Charles

Riechelmann who'd had a storming Super 12 alternating between lock and blindside flanker. The trial would provide a further examination of his suitability, especially in terms of speed, for the side of the scrum. In the event, the shoulder injury he suffered against Natal took him out of consideration altogether.

The choice of Scott McLeod in the shadow All Blacks was a straight-forward matter of form but the panel made no secret of the fact that McLeod versus Little would be one of the few old-fashioned head-to-heads. Cullen had finished the Super 12 in style, scoring another freakish try against New South Wales. Coupled with the panel's growing conviction that Wilson should stay on the wing, it was enough to persuade them to give the wonder kid his chance. Bunce had recovered his zest while Mehrtens and Kronfeld were on the comeback trail. Kronfeld had managed three Super 12 starts but Mehrtens had missed the entire competition and had to test out his knee in invitation games; his goal-kicking was all over the place but the knee felt fine.

Rhys Duggan, who'd made an impact with the Hurricanes, was given an opportunity at halfback in the Barbarians. The panel had seen plenty of Ofisa Tonu'u in the Super 12 and wanted to try Jon Preston at first-five-eighth to see if he was up to covering both inside back positions on the bench. Whoever covered for Mehrtens had to be a goal-kicker so Carlos Spencer's inconsistency in that department weighed against him. Adrian Cashmore and Osborne would swap positions at halftime giving the latter one last chance to impress at fullback and some valuable experience on the wing.

As night follows day, injuries forced changes: Taine Randell replaced Riechelmann; Matson did a hamstring at training and was replaced by Eroni Clarke; Richard Turner was replaced by Errol Brain. Brain wasn't quite All Black material but he was a great competitor who'd bring some leadership and stability to the Barbarians side.

Con Barrell, who headed the worryingly short list of back-up tighthead props, was forced to withdraw by the asthmatic condition which had inhibited his development. Given Barrell's obvious potential, it surprised Hart that North Harbour hadn't recruited him to shore up their inadequate front row.

Frank Walker, Wellington's NPC coach and a Hurricanes selector, was one of the few to find fault, criticising the choice of James Kerr ahead of Tana Umaga in the Barbarians. Kerr had been in the unenviable position of being the Blues' third wing behind Jonah Lomu and Joeli Vidiri but had impressed in his four outings. He had size and speed but was very raw and his concentration tended to drift, especially in defence. His inclusion in the trial was mainly to give him some of the experience he'd missed out on during the Super 12.

The management team was also on trial. They'd done a huge amount of work behind the scenes but now they were on display. Good intentions and favourable impressions were all very well but the players and the press would make judgements on what happened in Napier. Hart knew from his conversations with Sean Fitzpatrick that some players wondered if he still had the juice after four years away from coaching. He couldn't really blame them – so did he.

It was a moment of truth for Jane Dent. She had to make a presentation to the players en masse knowing that her effectiveness in the job virtually depended on making the right first impression. She'd thought she wouldn't be intimidated; she was wrong.

"I was very, very nervous," she recalls, "more so than ever going on TV and that's saying something. One camera is nothing compared to a sea of rugby faces. Basically, I wanted to get across that I wasn't their mother even if I looked old enough to be – I wasn't going to do their ironing or sew on their buttons. I also wanted them to know that I wouldn't be shocked or judgemental about bad language or anything else. I expected them to be disciplined but I'd worked in newsrooms which can be pretty blue."

After the players had undergone fitness tests, the panel had a session with both teams to spell out what they were looking for in the trial and to look ahead to the South African tour. Conscious that many of those opposing the shadow All Blacks would be touring with them in two months' time, the management went to some lengths to avoid a them and us situation.

On the Thursday before the trial, the three selectors sat down with each player in the Barbarians squad to tell them where they stood, what was expected of them, and in which areas they had to improve. The most revealing session was with Osborne; frustrated with his form and constant injuries and generally out-of-sorts, he was far from being in the right frame of mind for test rugby.

Originally Ross Cooper had been going to assist Hart with the shadow All Blacks, with Hunter coaching the Barbarians, but that didn't square with the plan to use the trial as a dress rehearsal for the management as much as the players. Peter Sloane and Robbie Deans took the Barbarians instead. Sloane, a no-nonsense character with a firm grasp of the intricacies of forward play, had assisted Hart with the New Zealand XV in 1991 while Deans was a refreshing personality and creative thinker. Neither had any representative coaching experience; politics and disorganisation had deterred Sloane in Northland and he'd missed out to Brad Meurant on the Waikato Chiefs job in 1996. Deans had been active in Canterbury country rugby and in 1997 would follow the trail trod by Alex Wyllie from Glenmark to the Canterbury NPC team. The pair were re-united in the Canterbury Crusaders management team in 1997, Deans as manager and Sloane as Wayne Smith's assistant.

"They did a good job," says Hart. "If you field a shadow All Black side in the trial, it's vital that those coaching the other team understand what the panel is trying to achieve and work towards that goal rather than pursuing their own agendas. Naturally they were disappointed with the outcome but it's always difficult for the second stringers to compete against the shadow All Blacks, especially when they're largely the previous year's side."

For Hart, the challenge was to ease himself back into coaching with the help of Hunter and Cooper while leaving the players in no doubt who was "running the cutter," as Brian Lochore said of a similar arrangement at the 1987 World Cup. A reference at the after-match function to "All Black coach Laurie Mains" showed that not everyone got the message.

Under the McLean Park lights the Barbarians were extinguished 72-18. While the one-sided nature of the game made it hard for the second-stringers to impress, it allowed the panel to watch them under pressure. Players who weren't prepared to hang in and work for eighty minutes would be no use in South Africa and the pressure definitely got to a couple of Barbarians.

The trial hardly allayed the selectors' concerns over depth but it did show that they were on the right track in terms of the test side. Picking it wasn't a difficult exercise.

Cullen had shown huge potential at training and confirmed it with his three-try performance. Not even Earle Kirton's comment on television that Osborne was the best option at fullback could dissuade the selectors from backing their judgement. Little had suffered a recurrence of his hamstring injury but McLeod had shown he was ready although his selection meant there'd be two new caps in the backline.

Mehrtens and Kronfeld proved they were sufficiently match-fit to warrant selection and Marshall's development, which would gather pace as the season progressed, was evident. The old hands Bunce, Zinzan Brooke, and Fitzpatrick were very definitely still in business. Among the Barbarians, Blowers' promise and Larsen's competitiveness caught the eye.

Finalising the reserves was almost as straightforward. Preston had shown he could do a solid job at first-five which took care of the inside backs. Ieremia, who'd demonstrated explosive speed off the mark in fitness testing, being the fastest man over ten and forty metres from a standing start, had played impressively when he'd come on for Bunce. He'd cover the midfield and Rush the back three with Wilson going to fullback if Cullen left the field.

Up front, Norm Hewitt remained Fitzpatrick's understudy although Anton Oliver was clearly a player of immense potential; for a 20-year-old, he came through the trials of strength well and had the asset of rare leg speed. With precision even more important under the new rules, his throwing to the lineout needed concentrated work. By handling the tighthead role with aplomb, Dowd had done his nearest rival on the loosehead a favour and Allen came in as the reserve prop.

The decision on the final forward reserve who'd cover the back five of the scrum was trickier. Since none of the three loosies in the test XV had experience at lock or was tall enough to cover for a frontline jumper and since Michael Jones would cover number 8 and, at a pinch, openside flanker, the reserve had to be equally at home at lock or blindside flanker. That required someone who could lock the scrum and win lineout ball or, alternatively, do the tough defending and support work of a blindside flanker. With his spring, mobility, and punishing defence, Riechelmann had looked tailor-made for the role but his injury opened the way for Larsen or Taylor. Both had chopped and changed between lock and blindside flanker; neither really possessed the speed, handling ability, and vision needed in the latter position under the new rules. In the end, Larsen's test match experience and big match temperament carried the day.

The test team was announced the morning after the trial. Hart had earlier broken the news to Little and Osborne, test incumbents now out in the cold. Of the others missing from the team who'd played in the final test of 1995, Rush was a reserve while injury and illness had ruled out Liam Barry and Culhane.

Osborne took it hard; Little's injury made him more resigned to his fate. Hart reassured Little that he still figured in the panel's thinking and would be restored to the squad as the midfield back reserve as soon as he proved his fitness. He'd made an excellent impression during the week with his commitment to the Barbarians team and leadership at training and had tried hard to stem the tide while he was on the field in the trial.

"Maybe missing the first two tests didn't do Walter any harm," says Hart. "It gave him time to reflect on where he was. He played extremely well on his return despite battling a chronic knee injury. There's no question of giving up with Walter Little – he doesn't look for short cuts and has an incredible pain threshold."

8

LIONS TO THE CHRISTIAN

I N the lead-up to the Western Samoan test, the All Black management worked hard on building a relationship with the team and putting in place operational guidelines for the long winter campaign. At training, the coaches set about instilling an ethos of self-discipline, composure, boldness and imagination in attack, and consuming aggression in defence.

A routine was established. At breakfast, the management team would go over the day's programme ensuring that everyone understood their responsibilities. The local liaison officer would confirm arrangements. The coaches and the fitness advisor would discuss and finalise the structure of the training session. The captain would take part if he hadn't already been consulted. The heavy work would be done earlier in the week with training tapering off with a light half-hour run or just a "walk in the park" at the venue the day before the game.

John Hart was nervous at the early training runs, unsure how the players would react to him and his style: "When I became Auckland coach, I was moving in from several years of club coaching – I knew most of the players, they knew me, I knew the environment. This was a bit of a venture into the unknown. Apart from when I'd been a candidate, I hadn't really given coaching much thought since 1991 so I hadn't made a conscious effort to keep up-to-date with the latest thinking and techniques and people like John Graham had questioned my grasp of the technical side of the game. I actually went to a couple of Auckland Blues training runs to see how they did it."

And while Hart had been off the scene, the players had had four years of Laurie Mains, a technically proficient coach who ran good training sessions. He wouldn't be an easy act to follow. The rest of the management team weren't fretting for Hart. They could see that his off-field organisation was already making an impact.

"Hart stamped his mark by letting the players know there was a structure that was going to be followed in terms of the training plan and the game plan and the plan for the whole week," says David Abercrombie. "Everyone knew exactly what was going on from day one."

Ross Cooper: "The players were getting information, they were being talked to. You could see them grow, you could see the culture change from all that back seat of the bus rubbish. Whatever handover issues there were, the planning we did defused them and Fitzpatrick helped in that.

"Hart was open and honest. We'd be talking about tackle suits and ruck machines and he made no secret of the fact that he'd never seen them. I thought it was a great strength that he could admit there were gaps in his knowledge. He utilised Gordon and me. He stood back a little bit, watched and learned. It was fascinating."

Besides, as Mike Banks points out, what were the players going to do? The king is dead, long live the king – Hart was in charge now and that was that. "The players are adaptable. It's like employees getting a new boss – they have to adapt. That's the reality of the work-place."

Like a lot of the players, Marty Toomey was seeing Hart up close and personal for the first time. He didn't detect any stage-fright: "You can hide anything behind gregariousness but I don't think the players picked up any lack of confidence. There may have been some doubts on their part but they didn't last."

The big development in team preparation since Hart had last coached at this level was opposed training with all its protective paraphernalia. Seeing the players knock hell out of one another was a bit of a shock to his system.

"Jim Blair devised grids to put players under pressure but without physical contact," says Cooper. "They evolved into contact with tackle suits and hit shields and so on and training became really physical in the 1993/94 period. Things almost got out of hand at the World Cup camps with the amount of pain the players were put through. I think John was a bit surprised by the ferocity of it."

Hart soon came to terms with it: "Physical, opposed sessions are important in getting correct body positions, working on ball control in the tackle, and organising defence. Looking back on the season, some of the best performances followed training sessions where we'd bring in local players to provide opposition in ruck, maul, and tackle situations. These sessions certainly have their place but you need to get a balance because they can be very draining as we were to find in South Africa."

Hart introduced some innovations of his own, notably by giving senior players with technical expertise responsibility for their specialist areas. His view was that, firstly, they knew as much if not more about them than the coaches – "am I going to tell Ian Jones how to jump?" Secondly, by taking responsibility for a particular function at training, the players would improve their execution and decision-making in games. A further aim was to develop leadership support for Sean Fitzpatrick so that he'd no longer have to shoulder the burden alone.

Hart: "The danger with this approach is that individual players can take over and you go from having an authoritarian coach to authoritarian players, as perhaps happened with Auckland when Gary Whetton and Grant Fox ran things. The difference here was two-fold: we were encouraging players to take responsibility for the execution of their specialist responsibilities, not the overall tactical approach, so it was a matter of spreading responsibility rather than handing over the reins. Secondly, it wasn't a case of elevating one or two very experienced players with strong personalities who could dominate their teammates. We had a core of players – the Brookes, the Joneses, Brown, Little, and Bunce – all of whom could make a contribution."

The allocation of portfolios was Andrew Mehrtens: backline moves; Zinzan Brooke: scrum moves; Robin Brooke: kick-offs; Michael Jones: scrum defence; Frank Bunce: backline defence; Olo Brown: scrummaging; Ian Jones: lineouts. If there was confusion or disagreement, Hart stepped in to adjudicate and resolve it.

The rest of the management team sensed a new atmosphere as the players responded to Hart's style. "Hart identified the key players, gave them ownership of particular phases of the game, then brought them around to where he wanted them to be," says Banks. "That empowerment didn't happen under Mains – if anyone questioned him, he thought they had an ulterior motive and took them to task. In this environment, they could talk freely without being punished."

Abercrombie spoke to a lot of players during the ten days in Napier: "I got the feeling that Mains did what he thought was best for the players but his personality inhibited them. Hart's sessions were more fun – they could experiment but if they screwed up, he'd let them know. He put a lot of the onus to perform back on them – 'we've put the structure in place, now it's up to you to do your thing.'"

The training sessions were structured to ensure that the three-coach system didn't cause confusion. Toomey would take the warm-up and grids with Hart using one of his greatest natural attributes – his penetrating voice – to focus the players on correct body positions, effective communication, and accurate handling. The backs and forwards would then go their separate ways with Cooper usually taking the forwards, Hunter the backs, and Hart moving between the two units overseeing activity.

The forwards would generally practise taking and receiving kick-offs, scrummaging, lineouts, rucks, and mauls. The backs would work on defence, counter-attack, and set-piece moves. Cooper and Hunter would then take a back seat as Hart brought the backs and forwards together for a team work-out incorporating the unit drills practised earlier.

"I enjoyed this system," says Hart, "because it enabled me to watch what was happening rather than calling it all the time. Then I'd bring the pack and the backline together and hopefully get them to jell. Ross adapted quickly – the assistant's role fitted him comfortably. Gordon found it more difficult – he was used to running things with Otago and the Highlanders and being an assistant takes some getting used to."

The role of assistant All Black coach has an unhappy history. After missing out on the convenor/coach position in 1988, Hart declined to serve on the panel, a decision which damned him for all time in some people's eyes, because he felt that being Alex Wyllie's assistant would be an exercise in futility. He was right: Wyllie wasn't into power-sharing. On the eve of his first test as coach, he told the *Auckland Sun*, "I understood [Hart's] thinking – to be standing around while another person is running the show can be frustrating."

The poisoned chalice was handed to Lane Penn who, in his words, "didn't get a look in" – he took just two training runs in almost four years. Disturbed by the All Blacks' slide in 1991, the NZRFU council shunted Penn aside and instituted the doomed co-coach system for the World Cup, a decision which "took out three men with one shot," as Brian Lochore memorably put it. Perhaps Earle Kirton had the right idea, settling for the role of jester in the court of Stern King Laurie. W.C. Fields' attitude to death was that, all things considered, he'd rather be in Philadelphia; that's pretty much how Cooper felt about being assistant coach in France in 1995.

If the system worked better this time around, it was because Hart let Cooper and Hunter be what they wanted to be – coaches. Says Hunter: "It was neat to be involved because what I really wanted to do was help coach the All Blacks."

Looking back, Hart gives himself a mixed report card: "I'm not sure those sessions were as fluent as they should've been – I was trying to establish my position at the same time as introducing a culture of more input and decision-making by the players and getting the balance wasn't easy. But I needn't have worried about the coaching side – Ross and Gordon were right up-to-date and the players themselves were experts. Working with the All Blacks is a humbling experience – they have an enormous knowledge of the game, they know what works and what doesn't. You can't fool them and you shouldn't try. What would've caused problems was if I'd come in and tried to change everything.

"Fitzpatrick said to me that my style was different from Mains' – less hands-on. I took it as a compliment because I'd gone in first and foremost to manage the overall process and get the team to do things themselves rather than do what they were told."

Playing the trial under lights at McLean Park was a good preparation and gave the All Blacks a head-start over the Western Samoans which Hart was happy to capitalise on: "You must maximise the advantage of playing at home. You don't often get a level playing field preparation-wise when you're on tour, as we were to discover."

The All Blacks were under no illusions about the challenge which awaited them. The Western Samoan game is based on physical confrontation and they had a lot to prove. The Samoans were still bitter over their exclusion from the Super 12: they believed it effectively marginalised them since, without regular international competition, their player base would swiftly erode.

They felt abandoned and their resentment was probably tweaked a notch or two by the knowledge that they would have been big winners under WRC.

On the other hand, 12 of Western Samoa's starting side were New Zealand-based players, a number of whom had experienced Super 12 rugby for New Zealand teams. Restricting Super 12 selection to players eligible for the All Blacks – which, arguably, would be in New Zealand's best interests – would, in the long run, undermine Western Samoa's ability to field a competitive side, so to claim that they'd been abandoned was an exaggeration. Western Samoan rugby has also benefited from an injection of financial, administrative, and management support from Sir Michael Fay. That's not to deny the difficulties they face getting a team together with players being enticed to Japan and the UK but, for the time being at least, they remain in the game and available for Western Samoa.

The agreement between News Corporation and SANZAR contained a provision for cameras in the dressing rooms during the count-down to kick-off. Hart was once bitten, twice shy: in Japan in 1987, TVNZ had filmed in the All Black dressing room for all of one minute before the tour's opening game. The sequence featured Hart striding up and down barking urgently at his men and concluded with Wyllie – on that tour the assistant coach – appearing to shut the dressing room door on the camera. Jock Hobbs, acting as comments man in a Wellington studio, saw it as a self-promotional stunt and compared the Auckland show-pony with bluff, down-to-earth Grizz who didn't want a bar of it. He wasn't the only one.

In fact, Wyllie had simply acted on a pre-arranged signal and the whole exercise was a TVNZ initiative, agreed to by the tour manager Malcolm Dick after the players had given their okay, which had nothing to do with Hart. But the damage was done and the episode counted against Hart when the NZRFU council voted to elect the All Black coach after the tour.

This time he was taking no chances: "We spoke to Sky Television about what they were trying to achieve: they wanted to capture the tension and nervous energy of a test match build-up but that had to be balanced against what was feasible and fair. We didn't want the team's preparation affected by the camera. In the event, the camera in question was a small piece of equipment and its positioning wouldn't bother the team. We agreed that they could show the team arriving in the dressing room, warming up, and doing ball skill exercises with no audio. They'd also ensure that the players' privacy was respected – we didn't want a repeat of the Andrew Ettingshausen shower shot."

Hart regards the dressing room as primarily the captain's domain and likes to drift in and out. As kick-off approached, he went out onto the field. On the sideline was a TV monitor displaying scenes from the All Black dressing room where the players were getting changed. The images weren't going to air but a privileged group of spectators in the grandstand were getting an eyeful – ET's exposé was a very minor affair by comparison. Hart had the monitor switched off and, from then on, the management took responsiblity for turning the dressing room camera on and off.

The match was New Zealand's first test under lights and the first outside the four main centres. It was an extremely cold night with a lot of dew on the surface. Night rugby has its pluses but the weather is the big minus; cold hands and a slippery ball aren't conducive to a free-flowing spectacle.

The referee was the South African Tappe Henning whom Hart had met during the reconnaissance trip. Both managements had had a session with him the previous day to discuss interpretations, especially at the lineout. Henning's early rulings were at odds with the New Zealanders' understanding of what had been agreed on; it wasn't the last time they perceived a discrepancy between what a referee said beforehand and what he did on the field. At least Henning was open to discussion and Fitzpatrick was able to sort it out.

As a rule, Hart doesn't get nervous before games but he was keyed up for this one: "The outcome wasn't so much in question but it was important that we put up a solid performance as a springboard for what lay ahead. I was also aware that the eyes of the public were on me as much as the team."

The Samoans confronted the haka with their own challenge. There was electricity in the air. Mehrtens announced that he was back by banging over an early dropped goal. Christian Cullen was welcomed to test rugby with a couple of Samoan specials, the sort of shuddering collisions which galvanise reserves and stretcher-bearers.

"From the panel's perspective, the way Cullen bounced up from those two immense hits was enormously reassuring, much more so than the tries he scored," says Hart. "It showed he had mental and physical resilience to go with his speed and skill."

The Samoans threw everything at the All Blacks. They closed

to 10-13 with a 24th minute charge-down try but that was as good as it got for them. Mehrtens kicked brilliantly for Jeff Wilson to catch and score and Cullen's second try took the All Blacks out to 27-10 at halftime. However, the Samoans never gave up and it wasn't until the final ten minutes that the pressure eased.

"They were innovative but suffered from having a halfback, Joe Filemu, at first-five," says Hart. "While the new rules provide a lot of opportunity to run and pass, you can't underestimate the importance of kicking. As lineouts become more predictable, the ability to kick long and accurately, to drive the opposition back and perhaps force them to take the ball into touch, has become critical and Western Samoa struggled in that regard."

The new coach was pleased with his first test in sole charge of the All Blacks. The 51-10 scoreline, the solidity up front, Marshall's strength, and Mehrten's control, albeit with a mixed goal-kicking performance, amounted to a good base to build on. Cullen, the new star, was blazing more brightly with each outing while Scott McLeod was solid on defence and showed some deft touches to create space for his outsides.

Most of all, he was delighted with the team's composure and discipline in the face of the Samoan onslaught which once or twice exceeded the fairly broad licence to commit mayhem granted international rugby players. Brian Lima made a good fist of containing Jonah Lomu until he appeared to decide that mere containment wasn't enough. To say that Lima was fortunate that his stamp on Lomu's head was spotted by the South African touch judge is to highlight the absurdity of closing the file on incidents seen and dealt with by the match officials. If they'd missed the incident and Lima had been cited to appear before a judiciary able to study video replays at its leisure, he would have found himself at a loose end on a couple of Saturday afternoons.

Hart: "I see no justification for excluding from the judicial process incidents which are acted upon by match officials, especially if it's a touch judge's report – it's difficult for a referee to order a player off if he didn't actually see the offence himself. In fact, that's the only argument I can see in favour of flying touch judges around the world: how would a foreign referee respond to a local touch judge telling him he should order a visiting player off?

"It cuts both ways. Frank Bunce got the first yellow card of the 1997 Super 12; it was a petty incident and he was more sinned against than sinning and it seems strange that it couldn't be challenged. There's no point in insisting that referees are always right when everyone with access to a television knows otherwise. What's important is getting it right and being fair."

The post-match press conference was a tame affair, as they often are. Hart soon learned that the sharper and more competitive reporters would keep their powder dry and seek him out afterwards to pursue their angles away from their rivals' flapping ears.

That evening, Hart went out with his parents and family. The mood was one of quiet relief that the first hurdle had been negotiated. Then it was back to the hotel to watch the match video and prepare for the next morning's team debriefing. The great value of these sessions was that they compelled the players to review their individual and collective performances and contribute to the analysis.

That wasn't all they had going for them. "With a debrief at 8.30am," says Cooper, "the boys couldn't get on the turps."

9
SCOTCH FILLET

SCOTLAND went into the first test at Carisbrook with a mixed record: wins over Wanganui, Southland, and a South Island Divisional XV; losses to Northland and Waikato. Touring teams from the northern hemisphere tend to use the early games to try out different combinations as they work through the selection process so the results didn't necessarily reflect the strength of their test XV.

The selectors saw all the Scots' lead-up games live or on television. They looked to have a good scrum, a rugged, mobile pack built around the captain Rob Wainwright, and – with the exception of their skilful playmaker, Gregor Townsend – solid rather than brilliant backs. The series promised to be competitive and enjoyable: traditionally, the Scots have shared New Zealanders' robust attitude to the game and their preference for the ruck in phase play. Under the guidance of manager Jim Telfer and coach Richie Dixon, both firm admirers of the New Zealand game, they could be relied upon to take a positive approach.

The panel's focus on Scotland didn't extend beyond an analysis of their strengths and weaknesses. There were no modifications to the strategy, no tailor-made tactics. They were confident that the game plan they were developing for Australia and South Africa would prove potent against the Scots.

"Some may see that as folly," says John Hart, "but we hadn't taken our eye off the Scots. It was similar to the exercise the 1987 panel went through for the World Cup: we prepared a plan which we felt, executed correctly, would be effective against the teams we identified as our likely opponents in the final but which would also get us through the preliminary rounds."

There was one change to the All Black squad: Walter Little had proved his fitness in North Harbour club rugby and, as promised, took the midfield back spot in the reserves, replacing Alama Ieremia.

For Scotsmen, Dunedin is a home away from home. When sleet, snow, and howling winds blasted through the city early in the week, the test must have shaped as the nearest thing they could have to a home game without actually playing at Murrayfield. The All Blacks trained indoors on Tuesday but the icy conditions persisted. The weather was so foul on Wednesday morning that the liaison officer and at least one member of the coaching staff wanted to delay training until the afternoon. Sean Fitzpatrick and Zinzan Brooke vetoed that proposition; they didn't care what the weather was like, they wanted to train.

So train they did. It was snowing at Tahuna Park and Hart had never been so cold in his life. It was an important lesson for him; he'd been prepared to take the soft option which isn't the All Black way. Training went well; Hart sensed that the urgency had gone up a notch from Napier as the team set themselves for a traditional opponent who'd take them on across a broader front than the Western Samoans.

Scotland opened the scoring with a penalty. In the tenth minute, there was one of those events which make a commentator's day: Ian Jones scored a try in his 50th test. In 1990 he'd made his test debut on the same ground, against the same opponents, marking the same player – Damien Cronin. He scored a try that day too.

The Scottish fullback Rowen Shepherd kicked a second penalty which gave his side back the lead and triggered an All Black blitzkrieg. Jonah Lomu's blindside stampede to the line was followed by breathtaking tries by Christian Cullen and Zinzan Brooke, taking the All Blacks out to 24-6. Then sloppiness crept in. The Scots pulled it back to 24-16 after half an hour and 31-19 at halftime. The second half was more of the same: the All Blacks ran in another five tries – Cullen scything past bewildered defenders en route to three of them – and conceded two. While the navy-blue line was at times thin to the point of anorexia, Cullen went through the full repertoire in the course of a sublime performance.

The Scots must have wondered what they'd done to deserve these All Black ambushes. They were on the receiving end of Jeff Wilson's three-try debut in 1993, they were Lomu-ed in the World Cup quarter-final, and now they'd been scorched by another supernova. They played with a lot of spirit, probably doing enough to win the forward battle on points, but when it came to strike-power, they were massively out-gunned. It was cannons against laser-guided missiles; the All Blacks' attack was swift, surgical, and devastating.

Not that you'd have got that impression when the television cameras picked out the panel in the grandstand at the end of the game. Coaches learn to mask their feelings – it comes from many afternoons spent in the company of those twin imposters, triumph and disaster – but these guys weren't just deadpan, they were downright grim.

"The bleak looks reflected deep dissatisfaction with the defensive display," says Hart. "It's pointless scoring tries and then conceding them – you just have to start all over again – and we'd conceded some soft tries. We had a pointed message to deliver at the next morning's debrief."

The downbeat mood after a nine-try, 31-point test win staggered the celebrated Scottish commentator Bill McLaren. Perhaps he had a point: to seek perfection is to condemn yourself to endless frustration. Hart would see it differently, arguing that to give up on the search for excellence is to condemn yourself to stagnation.

Afterwards, Hart accompanied the team to the Otago Supporters' Club clubrooms where the All Blacks received a warm welcome and he renewed acquaintance with fellow members of the Bastards Club. He'd met them earlier in the season after a Super 12 game at Carisbrook and was subsequently offered honorary membership. The invitation was open to several interpretations; Hart took it as a sign that he was making some headway in the Deep South.

When *National Business Review* chose Hart as its New Zealander of the Year, he got a note from the club congratulating him on being the first bastard to be New Zealander of the Year. Given the nature of such awards, it's unlikely he'll be the last.

That night's selection meeting featured some intense debate although the need to finalise the second test team there and then for an announcement first thing in the morning gave the panel less scope for analysis than they would have liked. Although they'd been disappointed with some aspects of the performance, particularly defence and scrummaging, the discussion narrowed down to one position: second-five-eighth. Little was now fully fit; his refusal to be deviated or embittered by his setbacks had only increased the panel's admiration for him. Scott McLeod had had a good debut but a curate's egg of a second test; he'd thrown a superb pass to send Cullen on his way to the most spectacular of his swag of tries but at times the pace of the game had found him out, both with ball in hand and on defence when he'd tended to rush up ahead of the line.

Hart: "That's always the issue when players go up a level, especially if the next level is test rugby – the extra speed of the game allows you less reaction time. Selectors must have the ability to visualise players at a higher level than the one they're watching them in and when they promote a player, they must track his progress carefully. I'd come to the view that McLeod still had a way to go and, now that Little was available, we should pull back on him and develop him further.

"It was a difficult decision, some might say an unfair one, but I believe that when a player who's missed a test through injury is restored to form and fitness, you must be just as fair to him as his replacement when weighing their claims. Apart from the issue of fairness, if players think that once someone else gets their spot, that's it, it's just an incentive to play with injuries."

Sunday morning's programme – breakfast at 7, team debrief at 7.30, on the bus to the airport at 8.30, press conference at 9.15 – didn't leave much time for one-on-ones and Hart only managed a short chat with McLeod before the team was announced to the media in the Koru Club lounge. He told McLeod that he'd done much of what the panel had expected of him but they had concerns about his ability to step up to test level and his accuracy on defence. They were relatively minor things in the context of a young player's development but Hart wanted him to understand which aspects of his play needed improvement.

McLeod took it on the chin and dealt with the media well. Hart sought to support him publicly by presenting the decision as more a case of restoring Little than detecting weaknesses in McLeod. That the panel didn't see McLeod as having failed was demonstrated by his retention in the squad as midfield back reserve.

"It's a matter of record that Scott didn't handle it that well in the longer term," says Hart. "He found it difficult to come to grips with and I must accept some degree of blame for not working through the process of reassessment. He drifted somewhat in South Africa, missed the Barbarians tour after some average performances for Waikato, and wasn't picked for the All Blacks' 1997 pre-season camp, which he took very badly because he'd done a lot of hard work. He came back a better player and a better person for the experience. He was outstanding in the Super 12 and, despite missing a number of games because of a serious back injury, his form propelled him back into the test squad."

There was strong emphasis on scrummaging in the preparation for Eden Park. The All Black scrum had been unimpressive in Dunedin, much less imposing than it would need to be against the Wallabies and Springboks if the strike runners were to be given room to move. The physical and mental approach had to change from settling for parity to striving for dominance.

Late in the game at Carisbrook, Lomu had left the field with a knee injury and was replaced by Eric Rush. The medical team's diagnosis was that he'd be right for Eden Park but the injury continued to hamper him and Rush took his place at training. On Friday, the panel decided that it wasn't worth the risk; the priority was to have Lomu operating at full throttle in the opening Tri-Nations series match against Australia two weeks hence. That brought in Rush, whose engaging personality had made him an important part of the All Black scene, with Adrian Cashmore moving onto the bench. The choice of Cashmore reflected the panel's view that they didn't have another specialist test-class wing to call on. McLeod had had one Super 12 game on the wing but Cashmore was better suited there and, if necessary, could swap positions with Cullen.

"Cashmore's a very talented player who was to suffer a big blow when he had to return from South Africa without playing a game," says Hart. "He possesses many of the attributes a fullback needs in the modern game and has the pace and developing defensive qualities to handle the wing. The way the game's going, there are increasing opportunities for players to utilise their skills in different positions – the key is not to push them into positions for which they lack the fundamental attributes. There are a lot of similarities in wing and fullback play, notably punting ability and counter-attacking. The main difference is in the defensive lines."

Cullen's extraordinary feats – seven tries in his first two tests following three in the trial – had rocketed him into the stratosphere on a flight path similar to Lomu's the year before. Hart was worried that expectations were running wild and pulled him out of the media spotlight that week.

There's something about Scottish tests at Eden Park that brings out the worst in Auckland's weather. It had happened in 1975 and 1990 and June 22, 1996, was another abysmal day; rain was driving in on a gale blowing straight down the ground and it was very cold. That 1975 test was the last word in wet weather football – Hart remembered marvelling at the All Blacks' skill and efficiency while questioning the wisdom of going ahead with the game with so much surface water on the pitch.

With the wind behind them, the All Blacks started well enough. In the third minute, the Scots took down a defensive scrum and conceded a penalty try. But for the rest of the first half, the 1996 All Blacks failed to match the skills and tactical awareness of the 1975 vintage. They tried to play expansive, dry-weather football and mistakes came thick and fast. Scrum power produced another try to Zinzan Brooke but that was immediately cancelled out by a defensive howler straight out of an "It's Moments Like These You Need Minties" advertisement. Acting on the principle of when in doubt, stick it up in the air, Shepherd launched an inoffensive up-and-under towards the New Zealand line. He set off after it, probably as much to keep warm as in the expectation that anything would come of it, and was gifted a try when no fewer than four All Blacks found something better to do than catch the ball.

Mehrtens kicked a penalty right on halftime and the All Blacks turned into the gale ten points ahead. If ever the Scots were going to beat the All Blacks, this was it. The game was being handed to them on a plate.

Bristling with anger, Hart stormed on to Eden Park to deliver what was probably the most emotional halftime speech of his career although the Richter Scale was to get another good shake in Brisbane five weeks later. The All Blacks' option-taking had been wilfully inappropriate. Avoiding defeat was going to require immaculate ball retention, denying the Scots field position from where they could lay siege to the All Black line, and a monumental defensive effort.

The second half was a test of character and composure and the All Blacks rose to it, lifting significantly from the careless defensive display at Carisbrook. Little and Bunce shut down the midfield; Michael Jones, already recognised as one of the greatest-ever openside flankers, demonstrated his mastery of the blindside flank, producing tackle after thumping, all-enveloping, repulsing tackle. The Scots cracked under the relentless defensive pressure, making errors and providing the All Blacks with scoring opportunities on which they capitalised through an utterly dominant scrum.

Scotland had plenty of ball but managed only one try with the wind compared with the All Blacks' three into it. The second half was won 19-5, the game was won 36-12. Under the gun, the All Blacks had marched through the mud to a decisive victory.

For Hart, there were three major pluses in the performance. The first was the form of his blindside flanker: "Michael Jones was a revelation. Remembering how he'd hobbled around in Napier, I was amazed that he'd come through three tests in three weeks, let alone played so strongly. When he scored, he threw the ball up and looked heavenwards – I wondered if he was savouring scoring a try in what would be his last test on Eden Park." That premonition became virtual reality 51 weeks later when Jones was stretchered off Albany Stadium with the second terrible knee injury of his remarkable career.

Number two was the continued development of his halfback: "Justin Marshall was now showing the qualities of a genuine test halfback, particularly in his ability to snipe and break with speed and strength. No player had taken up the challenge better – he'd worked assiduously to improve his body position and kicking. He wanted to be an All Black and a very good one and he was well on the way. He was to prove equally at home in wet or dry conditions and his self-confidence became an important element in the team's development. Early on, he'd sat back and taken it in, absorbing the collective wisdom. From Eden Park on, we watched him grow."

Number three was the team's steely resolve in the second half: "We'd put ourselves under pressure and had to get out of it. That performance did more for us than we realised at the time and the wet weather experience would stand us in good stead for Athletic Park."

Clearly, there were minuses. Cullen had found out the hard way that there was more to test rugby than just doing what came naturally. Above all, it was about concentration. For the back three, it was a forgettable afternoon all round; Rush's hands had let him down and Wilson had been forced from the field. Cashmore will always remember his test debut but didn't look comfortable during his 20-odd minutes on the field. No doubt he would have preferred blue sky, a dry track, and being at fullback.

When the All Black party arrived at the Carlton Hotel for the test dinner, Hart was informed that the Australian match commissioner had cited a player from each side: Frank Bunce and Mighty Mouse Mark Two, the Scots' nuggety hooker Kevin McKenzie. The citing came as a surprise since no-one could remember any incident. Instead of going to the test dinner, Bunce had to appear before a judicial hearing. Hart fast-forwarded through the match video to see what everyone except the eagle-eyed commissioner had missed. There it was: McKenzie goes in on the wrong side of a ruck; Bunce comes in to try to blow him out of it; they have what could be called an altercation. This baby of all altercations was over and done with in a couple of seconds and devoid of malice.

Normally the manager would accompany the player to the hearing but Hart was hot under the collar. As far as he was concerned, it was a non-event and he wanted to show his support. He spoke to the Scots' management who saw it in the same light. Bunce departed from the script by pleading not guilty to striking. The commissioner was obviously looking for a guilty plea to justify the whole exercise; then he could proceed to assess the seriousness of the offence. Bunce was eventually found guilty but the incident was deemed insufficiently serious to warrant a penalty.

As Hart later pointed out to the team, they could see something which happened on the field in a certain light but others might see it differently and it might be their view that mattered. Next time around, Bunce would take pains to ensure that the other guy took the rap.

10

RUNNING HOT
IN A COLD TOWN

THREE down, seven to go. There'd been the odd hiccup but the campaign was on track. It had been a demanding month – counting the trial, four big games in four weeks. For Auckland's All Black forwards, the Super 12 semi-final and final made it six in six. Players and management alike were grateful for a week off before heading into Phase Two – the Tri-Nations series.

It seemed to John Hart that in their anxiety to recoup the start-up costs of professionalism, administrators were treating players like robots: "It's critical that we get the right balance between the financial and marketing imperatives and the players' physical and mental well-being. Test matches put a lot of stress on players – they're draining affairs, no matter who the opposition is. When you play for your country, you must be at your peak – you can't take the risk of having an off-day. It doesn't worry me if the All Blacks play 12 tests a year as long as the schedule gives them reasonable breaks between games and takes into account what else is expected of them."

The All Blacks had come through Phase One unscathed except for the knee injury which had kept Jonah Lomu out of the second Scottish test. The squad to play Australia was the same as that named for Eden Park: with Lomu mended and Andrew Mehrtens and Josh Kronfeld now completely match-fit, a refreshed and fully fit squad assembled in Wellington – eventually.

The miserable weather which covered most of the country and had closed in on Wellington for the duration delayed the arrival of the Dunedin contingent – Kronfeld, Jeff Wilson, and Gordon Hunter. Hart put off the first training session in the hope that they'd get through but a further flight delay forced him to go ahead without them. It wasn't a good start. The All Blacks trained at the Poneke Rugby Club in front of a large and enthusiastic audience. The field was wet, the ball slippery, and the crowd-control non-existent – children encroached on the field to risk being run over by the high-speed threshing machine which is an All Black squad at full stretch.

Tuesday's training was merely disrupted. Wednesday's – probably the most important session of all – was a disaster. First Frank Bunce strained a hamstring. Scott McLeod took his place and promptly pulled up with the same problem only more so. They were taken out of the run and iced. Rehabilitation, in the form of extensive physiotherapy and stretching exercises, got under way immediately. John Mayhew and David Abercrombie earned their keep that week.

When is a mind game not a mind game and does it really matter if it distracts the opposition? The new Australian coach Greg Smith – like Hart, facing his first real test after a solid build-up against lesser opposition – reckoned the All Blacks were playing games. Bunce would play, Smith told the Australian media – they could put the ring around it.

Meanwhile, back at Psychological Warfare HQ, the selectors were reviewing their options. Alama Ieremia was in Napier preparing to play for a Hawke's Bay Invitation XV against Otago; he was pulled out of the game and put on a plane to Wellington. Ieremia was an ideal back-up; he'd been part of the shadow All Black squad at Napier and had come on for Bunce during the trial, plus he knew Athletic Park well. He gave the panel another option at centre if McLeod recovered but Bunce didn't. McLeod had played most of his rugby at second-five but Hart was beginning to think that, with his long legs and the extra space one out, he might be better suited to centre.

On the Tuesday night, the panel had been to Palmerston North to watch a Manawatu Invitation XV play the Colts. Hart didn't like leaving the team so close to a test match but it was part

of the ongoing selection process for South Africa. Tabai Matson
was returning from his second lengthy injury break of the season
but he was nowhere near match-fit. The next night, Hunter
watched Eroni Clarke in Napier. Clarke was experienced, in good
form, and could cover second-five at a pinch; he was pencilled in
as a reserve if neither Bunce nor McLeod came through.

The decision on Bunce was put off until Saturday morning.
Hart prefers to have these issues settled by Friday night but Bunce
was the cornerstone of the All Blacks' pattern. Furthermore, he'd
be marking Joe Roff, a young man who normally played wing and
whose inexperience was seen as a potential Wallaby weakness.
Bunce himself was very keen to play.

The Wellington Rugby Union (WRU) had forced Thursday's
training session to be shifted away from Athletic Park. At late
notice, the All Black management was advised that Friday's
scheduled light run couldn't take place there either. The WRU
weren't exactly going out of their way to ensure that the All Blacks'
preparation went smoothly. Mike Banks dug his heels in – a run on
the match pitch is an important element in the build-up – and got
the veto lifted. The private half-hour run was mainly devoted to
kick-offs with the coaches dusting off the All Black tactic of recent
years of splitting the forwards to disrupt the opposition.

That session was Mehrtens' reintroduction to the joys of place
kicking on Athletic Park. He didn't have fond memories of his
only previous appearance there and this was deja vu: the wind
whistling straight down the field, the goalposts swaying, not too
many kicks hitting the mark. Jon Preston, who was punching his
kicks low and hard with better results, gave Mehrtens the benefit
of his local knowledge and Zinzan 'The Boot' Brooke advised him
on the finer points of technique. Since Brooke had long coveted
the goal-kicking role, it was magnanimous of him to share his
expertise with the man barring his way.

The WRU struck again on Saturday morning. Hart and his
assistant coaches went to Athletic Park where they were staggered
to discover that the local union was still intent on staging a curtain-
raiser even though the ground was water-logged and the rain
continued to fall.

"Mike Banks protested but to no avail," says Hart. "We
approached the NZRFU who must've been getting sick of hearing
from us. They got involved and the curtain-raiser was transferred.
Obviously, the players and their supporters would've been
disappointed but, at the end of the day, they were the support act,

not the main event. It's pointless billing test matches as the ultimate spectacle if you provide an inadequate surface for the players and a curtain-raiser would've churned the pitch up badly.

"It was yet another example of the WRU's inflexibility and reflected the managerial and financial problems they were having at the time. It is important for New Zealand rugby that we have a strong Wellington on and off the field."

The Wallabies had been impressive in their three warm-up games. They'd thrashed Canada and their two easy wins over Wales had included 40 minutes of quite outstanding rugby in the Sydney match. Rather like Laurie Mains in 1992, Smith had come into the job wielding a new broom and declaring that the days of players getting picked on reputation were over; he was going to be ruthless in making form the sole criterion. He was as good as his word, continuing to make changes, notably in the inside backs, even though the team was winning well.

Conversely, having vowed not to pick players out of position, Smith chose Roff at outside centre ahead of an in-form specialist in Queensland's Daniel Herbert. The decision to replace Bob Dwyer with New South Welshman Smith rather than long-serving Queensland coach John Connolly had involved some hard-nosed politics. The deep-seated mutual antipathy between Queensland and New South Wales makes the sometimes testy relationship between Auckland and the South Island seem like a raging love affair and Herbert's omission gave Queenslanders all the excuse they needed to start sniping.

Hart considered the Wallabies talented but potentially vulnerable in some areas: "Even out of position, Roff was a formidable player – strong, fast, decisive. Ben Tune was an exciting prospect who'd done a good job on Lomu when Queensland thumped the Auckland Blues and no team containing Tim Horan can be dismissed lightly. I did feel the balance of their loose forwards wasn't quite right; Owen Finegan had looked useful for ACT but I wondered if he was a little cumbersome to handle blindside defence in a high-speed game – blindside flanker has become a highly specialised position.

"The scrum would be important. The Wallaby scrum hadn't been tested and the All Black forwards had a huge edge in experience – 300-odd caps to less than a hundred, half of which belonged to John Eales. We put a heavy emphasis on scrummaging all week; it's important to scrum well on wet grounds and we wanted to get their scrum going backwards to put pressure on their inexperienced inside backs. The experience mix is more important at the scrum than anywhere else – Zinzan Brooke has played a big part in Marshall's emergence by being a superb exponent of the art of delivering the ball at exactly the right time. I thought their loosehead prop Richard Harry had a big heart and a big future but felt they'd miss Phil Kearns' experience and leadership. That was no reflection on Eales, a consummate footballer who was making a good fist of the captaincy."

The Australians' preparation was a little different: it included a private session and was wound up on Wednesday. Hart's comment that private training runs were inappropriate in the professional environment was interpreted as another round in his private psychological slugfest with Smith: "Perhaps he saw it that way because our relationship never really got off the ground. I was really talking about the All Blacks and their place in New Zealand. I recognise that there's a place for private training runs but I thought the All Blacks had overdone it on tour in recent years. Their biggest benefit is that they give you a break from the public. Our Friday run lasted all of half an hour and wouldn't have revealed much – the main purpose of keeping it private was to get the team focused without a crowd to distract them."

The Wallabies had won the three previous encounters at Athletic Park, all of which had been played in foul weather. They talked about it being their lucky ground and made frequent references to the 1990 match when they'd ended the All Blacks' unbeaten run dating back to the 1987 World Cup. The confidence in their camp was evident in Smith's explanation for curtailing training: his boys were ready to go.

Hart was a little surprised but not disturbed by their confidence. He felt the analogy with 1990 ignored the fact that the Athletic Park test that year concluded a full-scale tour which had been dogged by bad weather. Then they'd had weeks to get used to it; this time, they'd jetted in from more clement climes – seven of the Wallabies were Queenslanders – a few days beforehand. The fact that the All Blacks had just played a test in terrible conditions was also worth bearing in mind.

During the Super 12 championship, Hart had publicly criticised the appointment of northern hemisphere referees to handle the Tri-Nations matches. His reasoning was that the series would be played under the new rules which hadn't been in force during the northern winter so the referees concerned wouldn't have administered them at club, let alone international, level.

Secondly, the changes had sped the game up considerably which required referees to be fitter than before.

His comments had been widely reported so it was with some slight trepidation that Hart, accompanied by Sean Fitzpatrick, went to the pre-game meeting with the English referee Ed Morrison and his compatriotic touch judges.

Morrison, a charming man, was swift to raise Hart's comments. After Hart had soothed ruffled feathers, they moved on to the question of whether the players could wear the vests with soft shoulder pads which were gaining popularity among southern hemisphere players. Both Tappe Henning and Wayne Erickson had approved them, in Erickson's case providing they were taped to the body. Morrison vetoed them and made no bones about his reason for doing so, saying he'd be criticised by the International Rugby Board's refereeing hierarchy if he didn't. It wasn't that big a deal – only three or four All Blacks would be affected – but it was an example of the inconsistency which bugs coaches and players. If referees can't agree on what protective gear is permissible, it's not surprising that their on-field interpretations vary so much. Morrison's explanation also provided a dispiriting insight into the politics of refereeing appointments.

He advised the New Zealanders that he'd be wired for sound and linked to his touch judges via an ear-piece. That was fine by Hart: he was all for touch judges alerting the referee to things like offside on the blindside and forward passes as long as they didn't dominate the game. As for his overall approach, Morrison was looking to apply advantage and let the game flow. He'd refereed a club match since arriving in the country and seemed to have a good grasp of the new rules.

Hart came away from the meeting feeling that the whistle was in good hands. It was; so much so that Hart was made to look something of an alarmist. Unfortunately, not all British referees are in Morrison's class and it wouldn't be long before Hart's worst fears were realised. Morrison, though, made such an impression that when Hart was asked for his views on who should referee the New Zealand Barbarians game against England at Twickenham, he suggested that Morrison would be the ideal man for the occasion.

Saturday morning was crunch time for Bunce and McLeod. The coaching staff, the medical team, and the hamstrung duo trooped over to the entertainment centre opposite the Park Royal Hotel for fitness trials. After some stretches and a warm-up, Abercrombie put them through a thorough test. Hart expected to lose one of them; if they lost both, it would've meant rushing Clarke to Wellington, a nerve-racking little logistical exercise which they could have done without. They'd held off summoning the Auckland centre on the basis of the medical team's confidence that Bunce would be okay.

"Both players passed the test," says Hart. "McLeod was grimly determined to take his place on the bench but, deep down, I felt he might've struggled if called upon. In hindsight, we should've gone with Ieremia. It would've been a desperately tough call on McLeod who'd taken a few knocks but it was a case of the heart ruling the head."

On the eve of a test match, it's traditional for the All Black captain to hold a team meeting which the management doesn't attend. Hart had thought about changing it but decided not to: "It was important for Sean and, besides, a coach must know when to let go – if captains aren't given the opportunity to lead off the field, it's hard for them to do so on the field. We talk about it beforehand but it's his meeting."

Hart also tends to take a back seat on the morning of the game. The players eat at different times; some have brunch, some have lunch, some have next to nothing. The players get together in the team room then the forwards and backs split, the forwards to go over lineout drills, the backs to put a ball through the hands. Then it's up to the manager's room to collect their gear. Like the post-match presentation of test ties to debutants, this little ceremony has lost none of its tradition.

Around 1pm, Hart talks to the team. The only others present are the manager and the other selector/coaches; the medical team are putting the gear on the team bus. NZRFU Chairman Richie Guy used to pop in to wish the team luck. When he and Hart had talked about it at the start of the season, Guy undertook to steer clear of the motivational stuff.

"I speak for quarter of an hour attempting to bring together what we've practised and talked about during the week. I saw that game as the opportunity to establish the 1996 All Blacks – that was the theme. It's not always the great motivational speech people imagine. Sometimes emotions are running high and you might bring them back a little; at other times you might go the other way and get them up. There was no need to do that this time – they were up against a heavyweight foe and it was the first game of the Tri-Nations. After that, my role is pretty much limited to the odd word with individuals rather than the team. In the dressing room,

Fitzpatrick and the senior players take over."

Fitzpatrick remembers Hart having "real doubts about whether we were up to this level of opposition because we hadn't really been tested. After that, he was okay, he knew he was going to be successful. I was less worried – I knew what the team was capable of after 1995. We had the talent so it was just a question of moulding the team and creating an environment in which we could express ourselves and he was doing that. In terms of the team's development, Hart came along at exactly the right time. We were mature enough to train without having someone jumping down our throat the whole time – it was just a matter of getting the top two inches right."

That afternoon, Athletic Park was one of the less inviting places on the planet. The good news was that the gale which had blown earlier in the week had eased to what was – by Wellington standards – no more than a stiff wind; the bad news was that it was a bone-chilling southerly. It was also very wet. It wasn't going to be pleasant for spectators but they were the lucky ones – they were outside.

Hart: "The Athletic Park dressing rooms – or dungeons as we used to call them when I was coaching Auckland – simply weren't suitable for international matches. They were very cramped and the shower and toilet facilities were abominable. I don't think Ed Morrison could believe what he'd seen. He must've thought he was in the third world and a pretty run-down corner of it at that."

Eales won the toss. The Wallabies delayed announcing their decision as long as possible, then took the wind. That didn't bother the All Blacks. "I think there's too much emphasis put on the wind," says Hart. "Sides often play with the wind thinking it'll do the job for them – it doesn't. We'd learned that lesson at Eden Park. Playing into the wind means you must eliminate mistakes and get into the game early. We had to produce a power-packed first half to stop them racking up a big lead. We set out to play the ball in hand game, mixing it with kicks in behind the opposition when they were flat in defence."

The mind games continued right to the opening whistle; the Wallabies ignored the haka, preferring to go through warm-up routines down in their 22.

As they'd practised the previous day, the All Blacks split the kick-off with half the forwards on one side of the field and half on the other. The best laid plans of mice and men . . . they got the first touch but it was a knock-on. The Wallabies conceded a short-arm penalty for not engaging at the scrum and the juggernaut rolled. "What it comes down to is: attitude is everything," says Fitzpatrick. "It's getting that white-hot attitude and having it explode at the right time."

The All Blacks tapped and charged, re-cycled the ball quickly and moved it. Bunce zipped past Horan and Wilson went close to scoring in the corner. Sitting in the grandstand, Smith must have felt that his scepticism about Bunce's injury had been vindicated.

The pack drove on a superb line-out take by Robin Brooke. As they would be all afternoon, the body positions were exemplary, the drive irresistible. The distinction of scoring the first try in the Tri-Nations series fell to Michael Jones, as it had done at two World Cups. This was the first rugby match on which Kiwis could bet. Hart, who'd made a few quid when Jones scored the first try at the 1991 tournament – back in the days when players and coaches were allowed to bet – wondered how many punters had studied the Iceman's track record. Television viewers who assumed from the All Blacks' rampaging start that the wind wasn't such a factor after all wouldn't have laboured under that misapprehension for long: Mehrtens' conversion attempt barely made the goal-line.

The Wallabies had a chance to get into the game a few minutes later but Tune, with no-one in front of him but the photographers, muffed the opportunity created by Scott Bowen's clever kick. They wouldn't get a second chance.

The All Black forwards came at the Wallabies like a wolf pack and the Wallabies never knew what hit them. They were shell-shocked; it showed in their glazed, disbelieving expressions. Denied territory and possession, all they had to show for their 40 minutes with the wind was two Matthew Burke penalties. When the Wallabies got their hands on the ball and tried to go forward, they were hurled back by brutal defence led by Michael Jones and Zinzan Brooke. Midway through the second half, they laid seige to the All Black line, battering away with a series of scrums and driving mauls from tap penalties. It was hand-to-hand combat. Even though the match was in the bag, the All Blacks prevailed.

"They had a lot of pride in defending their line," says Hart. "They wanted to defend more than the Wallabies wanted to score. The emphasis we'd put on the tackle, on never compromising on defence, had borne fruit."

A curious incident occurred early in the second half. Play stopped for several minutes while Foley was attended to by the Australian medical team. Fitzpatrick went to see what the problem was and became visibly annoyed as the stoppage dragged on. When the scrum finally went down, the All Blacks smashed forward, sending the Wallaby scrum skidding backwards. A black arm could be seen burrowing in the front row; a bit of tape was tossed away. As the scrum broke up, Foley stood there shaking his head at Fitzpatrick who said a few words and turned away wearing a satisfied smile.

So what was that all about? "Every time the game gets a bit hot for them or the Springboks, they pull a tactical injury," says Fitzpatrick. "It's usually a frontrower at scrumtime so the ref can't restart play without them. Foley went down and it was just to get his headband put back on. I said a few words to him about it and made the point at the next scrum by pulling it off."

It was a cameo to be savoured by aficionados of the black art of opponent-baiting, of which Fitzpatrick is the acknowledged master. Says Abercrombie, "I think that gave Fitzy as much pleasure as anything else that day."

Shortly before the close, something even more unusual happened: Fitzpatrick failed to go the distance for the first time in 77 tests. His departure from the field prompted the stalwart Norm Hewitt's first appearance in a home test.

The Wallabies had their moments in the second half but the All Blacks finished the stronger. With the crowd baying for 50 points and Justin Marshall about to feed an attacking five metre scrum, Morrison blew fulltime. According to the TV stopwatch, there were still three and a half minutes to go.

It had been a definitive performance. "Despite the conditions and the ball being like soap, the All Blacks made a total of five handling errors," says Hart. "Given their dominance of possession and the ambition of their attack, that sums up the game. Everyone played to his potential. Kronfeld had one of his greatest games, keeping his feet, keeping the ball alive, getting his body into positions no-one else could match to get the ball into the backs' hands. I'd wondered if his ball skills and vision were quite good enough – he made me eat humble pie."

Mehrtens created two tries with beautifully weighted attacking kicks. Zinzan Brooke, the hard man with the magician's touch, scored a try, set up two others, and flattened any Wallaby who attempted to cross the advantage line. In what was to be the highpoint of his frustrating year, Lomu plunged through the Wallaby defence trailing would-be tacklers like a fireman evacuating a burning orphanage.

Hart: "It was a resounding victory which was savoured by all those associated with the team. It's important to keep your feet on the ground and be humble in victory because the way a winning team behaves after the game can easily diminish their performance. These All Blacks had that under control. They've been described as arrogant which they're not; they are proud but they have every reason to be."

The aftermath to this supreme performance was a disgrace to New Zealand rugby. Chaos reigned under the grandstand. The showers were cold; the corridors, dressing rooms, and shower areas were flooded. Hart spoke to journalists with water lapping around their feet while the players had to stand on seats to get dry. Not even this epic shambles could dampen the All Blacks' exhilaration but, for the Wallabies, it was literally a case of adding insult to injury.

The NZRFU had brought the players' and management team's wives and partners to Wellington. Their presence was an extra incentive: a win would set up a big night out, a loss would kill it stone dead. It was clear at the after-match function that the Wallabies weren't going to be much fun to be around.

"There are always winners and losers but they'd been humiliated and Smith looked a forlorn figure," recalls Hart. "He wasn't easy to engage in conversation – we'd met at the parliamentary reception on the Wednesday and I'd found him quite tense, as he was to be again in Brisbane. In retrospect, he'd probably taken exception to my comments about private training sessions. I also understood the pressure he was under – there but for the grace of God went I."

The winners celebrated in a manner befitting their victory. Later, Hart slept more soundly than the night before when the injury situation had weighed heavily on his mind. But it's a coach's lot that even the greatest triumphs induce twinges of anxiety. Hart couldn't escape the suspicion that the style and scale of the victory would make what lay ahead even more difficult. The All Blacks had thrown down the gauntlet; the Springboks would relish taking up the challenge.

The world champions were in Sydney, preparing to play Australia the following week. François Pienaar professed to be unworried by the All Blacks' performance. He predicted, "They won't play like that again."

He was right.

11

MANY ARE CALLED, A FEW DOZEN ARE CHOSEN

THE players got another week off after Wellington. The panel didn't; they had one more week to finalise the squad for South Africa, one more week of criss-crossing the country. They were also working on a programme to ensure that, once the tour got under way, the 15 extra players integrated quickly with the test squad.

It wasn't simply a matter of picking the 36 best players. The rationale for the 36-man squad was quite specific: to keep the test XV out of the midweek games. The other 21 players, therefore, had to form a midweek XV plus reserves which included the six test reserves. It didn't necessarily follow that a test reserve was the second-best player in a particular position; Jon Preston's place on the test bench was more a reflection of his versatility – he covered halfback, first-five-eighth, and goal-kicker – than his ranking in the pecking order of specialist halfbacks.

A major problem was the lack of opportunities for fringe players to press their claims or, for that matter, maintain match fitness. At Napier, the panel had worked out how much on-field time each of the 45 trialists could expect before the touring team's departure. Leaving aside the test XV, the short answer was very little. Some would get opportunities with the Maori team or the

Colts but, aside from that, there was a real dearth. Aucklanders like Eroni Clarke, Lee Stensness, and Ofisa Tonu'u who weren't current All Blacks and weren't eligible for the Maoris or Colts would get only one game. Others wouldn't even get that. Unless something was done to get them games, the panel would end up having to gamble on both form and fitness.

"Harty's attention to detail and planning was unbelievable," says Ross Cooper. "We spent a whole day and half the night just looking at how we could give players outside the test fifteen games in the lead-up to the tour. We went through every player in the frame looking at how many games he'd get and what we needed to do, then went about getting the provinces' co-operation."

They approached a number of provincial unions which had fixtures in the next six weeks to see if they'd be prepared to turn them into invitation matches and include players from outside their unions. The response was gratifying. As a result of this initiative and the various provinces' co-operation, the Poverty Bay Invitation XV whch played Fiji on June 19 included Alama Ieremia, Tonu'u, Richard Fromont, Con Barrell, and Kevin Nepia; the Northland Invitation XV which played Auckland on June 26 included Norm Hewitt, Barrell, Preston, Blair Larsen, Simon Culhane, Scott McLeod, and Glen Osborne on the wing; the Manawatu Invitation XV which played the New Zealand Colts on July 2 included Adrian Cashmore, Tabai Matson, Phil Coffin, Mark Cooksley, and Culhane; the Hawke's Bay Invitation XV which played Otago on July 3 included Clarke, Barrell, Nepia, and Todd Blackadder; and the Canterbury Crusaders who played Canterbury on July 9 included Preston at first-five, Paul Thomson, Liam Barry, and Dylan Mika.

The next step was to try to tinker with the make-up of the New Zealand Divisional team, comprising Division Two and Three players, which had a three-match internal tour in July. The team had been chosen at the end of the 1995 season by the previous panel following a directive from the NZRFU to pick players who were in Divisions Two and Three in 1995. This created the anomaly that players from Southland, which had been demoted from Division One, weren't eligible while those from Taranaki, now in Division One, were.

John Hart approached the NZRFU board, pointing out that there were vacancies in the Divisional team because of injuries and the Colts taking priority. He argued that Culhane and Hewitt should be eligible since they were now second division players and, furthermore, needed the rugby.

"I wouldn't have got a hearing from the old council," says Hart. "The new board saw the logic of it and gave me the go-ahead."

The New Zealand Maori team's two-match internal tour which followed the trial was valuable for the panel. They could watch the likes of Rhys Duggan, Coffin, Nepia, and Carlos Spencer although the latter's knee injury sustained in the Bay of Plenty game took him out of the Colts. They got another look at Osborne on the wing and Taine Randell as a captain.

The panel had worked closely with the Maori selector-coach Matt Te Pou although Hart didn't use him as a fourth selector as Laurie Mains had used his predecessor, Chas Ferris. They'd signed off on Te Pou's squad which was criticised over the omission of the Waikato number 8 Deon Muir who'd made an impact in the Super 12 playing for the Canterbury Crusaders. Muir had actually been picked in the original squad but was the unlucky player when it was reduced from 22 to 21 at the insistence of NZRFU Chairman Richie Guy. It seemed to Hart that the culling had very little to do with rugby and a lot to do with bureaucracy.

At the beginning of July, the New Zealand Colts embarked on a short internal tour as a build-up to the Southern Hemisphere Under-21 quadrangular tournament with South Africa, Australia and Argentina. Six members of the team for South Africa would be on development contracts rather than full All Black contracts although, in this context, development didn't necessarily imply youth; the players concerned would be the six who wouldn't have made it if the NZRFU had stuck to the traditional 30-strong touring party. The selectors approached the three Colts who were in line for selection on that basis to make sure that they'd accept the lesser contracts.

"It was obviously a strong signal to Andrew Blowers, Chresten Davis, and Anton Oliver although we stressed we'd be having the same conversation with others," says Hart. "Those others weren't in the Colts – we saw the likes of James Kerr, Isotolo Maka, Mark Robinson, and Norm Maxwell as good prospects but it was too soon for them. The trio didn't take long to make up their minds – they'd take whatever contract was on offer. Blowers said he'd go for nothing, which is the attitude you look for in an aspiring All Black."

Hart got a similar response when he informed Osborne that he wanted him to play on the wing for the Northland Invitation XV: "He obviously had doubts but he took up the challenge, saying he didn't mind where he played as long as he got on the field. He had an outstanding game, showing some wonderful touches, and Ross and I came away feeling we had the answer to the question of who would be the fourth wing."

Although North Harbour coach Brad Meurant still preferred Osborne at fullback, he chose him as a wing for the game against Wairarapa Bush on July 10. As Hart couldn't get to Masterton, he asked former All Black selector Lane Penn to cast an eye over Osborne. Penn had been a winger himself and Hart respected his judgment. Penn's feedback was very positive and reinforced the panel's thinking.

In contrast, the selectors weren't making much headway in the search for a fifth prop. Because Mark Allen couldn't play tighthead and Barrell, who was firming as the likely fourth prop, could handle loosehead, the fifth prop – who'd be the reserve for the midweek team – had to be a tighthead. That effectively eliminated Nepia whose deficiencies at tighthead had been exposed at the 1995 All Black trial. The panel had reservations about Coffin so the spotlight went back on Otago's Nick Moore.

The panel had brought Coffin into the trial to ensure that the shadow All Blacks' opponents fielded a competitive scrum. Hart had learned from Alex Wyllie that mis-matched front rows can reduce trials to meaningless exercises. Coffin had been around a long time without gaining much recognition; he'd made his debut for King Country in 1985 and had played more games for the province than anyone, Colin Meads included. Under Frank Oliver's tutelage, he'd blossomed with the Wellington Hurricanes; the disciplines of professional rugby and daily training had got him fitter than ever before. However, the panel had concerns about his mobility, ball skills, and discipline on and off the field – he had a reputation for being a hard man in both settings. Total discipline would be the watchword in South Africa. With a large squad, abrasive opponents, and relentless media scrutiny, there was plenty of potential for the sort of bitter controversies and public relations disasters which can distract and destabilise touring teams. Hart was hell-bent on ensuring that that didn't happen to the 1996 All Blacks.

"Our one-on-one session with Coffin was enlightening," says Hart. "We told him that the trial was important for him, that he wasn't without a hope of making the touring team but he needed to perform really well and get into an intensive training programme after the trial because he wouldn't have much opportunity to improve his match fitness. We were worried that he'd drift now that the Super 12 was over. He'd been guarded to begin with but when I asked him how much he wanted to be an All Black, his eyes lit up: 'You tell me to jump, I'll say "how high?"' It was heartening to see this provincial veteran's burning desire to wear the black jersey. That session caused us to start thinking more seriously about him as a contender for the fifth propping spot. The issue was whether he could handle the discipline of touring, especially since the fifth prop could only expect to play two games in six weeks."

The conversation was filed away and the search for a third tighthead continued.

When the All Blacks were in Wellington preparing to play Australia, the panel brought the 1995 Colt Paul Thomson down from Auckland to play for a Wellington Invitation XV against the Colts on a freezing afternoon at Petone. Thomson was also slotted into the Canterbury Crusaders.

The to-ing and fro-ing over Dylan Mika's eligibility kept the panel on tenterhooks during this period. Initially, he wasn't considered. Then the selectors were given an indication that he was eligible and pencilled him in for the trial. Then it was, as you were – he was still on stand-down after playing for Western Samoa. With confusion surrounding both the IRB ruling and exactly when Mika had played for Western Samoa – a point on which the player himself was unhelpfully vague – it became a matter of watch this space. After the trial, opinion swung back in favour of Mika's eligibility so he was included in a couple of invitation teams. At the eleventh hour, the simple facts of the matter, which had eluded rugby's bureaucrats for two months, were finally rounded up: it was official – Mika's stand-down would extend until 1998.

The touring team was to be announced on July 14, the Sunday between the Wellington test and the clash with the Springboks at Lancaster Park. Hart had intended flying to Sydney to watch the Springboks play the Wallabies but the Divisional team's game against the North Otago Invitation XV at Oamaru on July 13 had taken on the dimensions of a trial. Peter Sloane went to Sydney in his place.

The invitation team included Cashmore, Rush, Matson, McLeod, Osborne, Preston, Tonu'u, Randell, Barry, Mika, Cooksley, Larsen, and Moore. The Divisional team included Culhane, Glenn Taylor, Allen, and Hewitt.

The panel arrived in Oamaru with their collective mind largely made up. It had been a methodical and thorough process. "We knew the skill sets and disciplines we were looking for and eliminated players who didn't have them," says Cooper. "After that, it was just a matter of form and fitness and growing people for 1999."

The fifth propping spot was still up for grabs though. Thomson had been discounted; he was a fine prospect but his body shape made him far better suited to the loosehead.

The game was a useful exercise in both a positive and negative sense as is usually the way with trials. It was galling to watch Mika play so strongly – he was a loss. Moore ruled himself out of contention; his potential was apparent but his fitness still wasn't up to the mark. Having just worked himself back to fitness, Matson was disconsolate at having to leave the field with a minor calf muscle injury. On the plus side, Osborne showed he was rapidly coming to terms with his new position while the most significant head-to-head contest was at lock where Taylor outplayed Cooksley.

"We'd decided to take only four locks," says Hart. "With Charles Riechelmann out, the search had narrowed down to Cooksley, Larsen, and Taylor who were competing for two places. Cooksley was to show what he's capable of in Waikato's Ranfurly Shield defence against North Harbour late in the season but inconsistency has been his problem. When the crunch came, Taylor measured up in the area of mental hardness and Cooksley didn't. He remains a prospect though; as the panel had hoped he would, he made real progress under Frank Oliver during the 1997 Super 12 and showed signs of coming to terms with the black and white nature of the game. His inclusion in the 1997 Tri-Nations squad showed just how far he'd come."

The panel deliberated one last time. Hart explains the thinking behind their conclusions: "The fullbacks were straightforward – Cullen had cemented himself and Cashmore was the up-and-comer making ground fast. Osborne had grabbed the fourth wing spot and he and Wilson could also cover fullback. We backed our hunch at centre, adding Matson to Bunce and McLeod. Matson had been plagued by injuries and played when he would've been better off resting. As a result, he'd never really found the form we were looking for and was probably fortunate to be chosen – he was one of the very few who was picked on potential rather than form. His selection was subject to him proving his fitness.

"Little and Ieremia were the clear candidates at second-five, with Ieremia and McLeod able to cover alternative positions in the midfield as well as the wing. We gave ourselves the luxury of three first-fives with Preston as a back-up. We could've left one at home and taken an extra outside back but our assessment of the injury risk and desire to invest in Spencer swayed the issue. Tonu'u had had a sound Super 12 and he and Preston were ahead of Duggan.

"The imperative of ensuring that the test players didn't play midweek games required versatility and we also wanted to invest in guys we saw as potential test players. Our loose forward stocks had taken a hammering after the World Cup with the loss of Brewer, Carter, Joseph, Pene, and Schuler and with Zinzan Brooke and Michael Jones both turning 31, there was a pressing need to bring on the young loose forward talent. Blowers had had an excellent Super 12 while Davis had started it sensationally and then had a knee operation. His form with the Colts on his return wasn't that good but we saw him as an investment.

"The flanker mix was two specialist opensiders – Blowers and Kronfeld – and three blindsiders – Blackadder, Davis, and Michael Jones. Blackadder and Davis could play lock if the need arose while Jones could cover his original position – openside – and number 8 where he also had test experience. Randell was picked as a number 8 but could cover all three loose forward positions. That degree of versatility is useful on the bench but utility players run the risk of not accumulating the specialist expertise needed to make the test line-up. That was a danger for Randell. He was our choice to lead the midweek team. It was asking a lot of a 21-year-old who was still learning the game but there'd be a lot of experience in that team to take the pressure off him and we had other options if he struggled.

"Blackadder brought hardness and commitment – I still remembered his dedication to the 1991 Colts. He might've lacked the speed and skill of some of his rivals but he had an enormous heart – he'd be a vital member of the midweek side who'd never let you down if he had to play a test.

"There was a temptation to take five locks and if there was a common critical thread to the media comment it was that the squad contained only four locks, two of whom had played a lot of their football as blindside flankers. We felt that with the new rules allowing support for the jumper, Davis and Blackadder could provide adequate coverage and Cooksley, the only real candidate for a fifth locking spot, hadn't done enough. Larsen had a big-match temperament and Taylor's performances with the

Divisional team had confirmed that he had a lot of heart.

"At prop, Brown, Dowd and Allen were out on their own. We persisted with Barrell and the logic which dictated that the fifth prop be a specialist tighthead ruled out Nepia. It was tough on Nepia, who's a strong scrummager and mobile for a big man, because it effectively meant he was competing with Allen. Nepia's career has suffered from his loyalty to Auckland; perhaps he should've moved a few years ago but he came under pressure from Graham Henry. His move to Canterbury will be good for him but age might start to count against him now, given the young propping talent that's coming through.

"We kept coming back to Coffin as the only realistic option. He'd trained well since the trial and we knew he was an excellent scrummager, good at ruck and maul, and had the hardness. His age was a factor – he was about to turn 32 – but, in the absence of an outstanding young prospect, the need for a stable scrum to provide a platform for the young loose forwards overrode that. It was the only decision I worried about – how would he fit in? In retrospect, I was being unfair to the guy and should've trusted the reaction I felt in Napier.

"The hookers were clearcut. We had to take three to ensure that one injury wouldn't force Fitzpatrick to play a midweek game. While there were some promising ones around, Oliver stood out even though he'd been handicapped by a disjointed Otago scrum."

There were six new All Blacks: Tonu'u, Coffin, Barrell, Blowers, Davis, and Oliver. Tonu'u had been picked for the 1995 French tour but injury prevented him from getting on the plane. Oliver had been called up as a reserve for the 1995 Bledisloe Cup match in Sydney which must have been an eye-opening experience for a 19-year-old, given that the WRC intrigue was then at its height.

Hart rang the two unluckiest players: "Liam Barry had fought back from injury and played well in Oamaru but Blowers was an investment for the future and his power and athleticism offered more under the new rules. It was a difficult phone call to make; we went back to the 1991 Colts and had kept in contact during my time in the wilderness and I knew his family well.

"Stensness had had a good Super 12 but seemed to carry the can for the Blues' loss to Transvaal. John Ngauamo added physical presence to the midfield but Stensness showed his class when he came on for Spencer in that must-win game at Durban and again in the semi-final. When Spencer recovered, Stensness went back to the bench for the final. It was a hard call, both for the coach who wanted to stiffen his defence and the player who'd played well. Lee's a confidence player; I encouraged him to keep working. He did so, earning a place on the Barbarians tour and returning to the All Blacks in 1997."

Those who got the nod were informed in advance although Hart didn't bother with the test squad – the fact that they'd been chosen to play the Springboks made them certainties. In Palmerston North, Mike Banks delivered the news in person to Blowers, Davis, and Oliver to prepare them for the media onslaught they'd face when they came off the field after playing for the Colts against Argentina.

Coffin was difficult to track down. They finally connected just before Hart had to leave for Eden Park for the team announcement and Coffin took the field in a club match: "I said I had some good news based on the fact that he'd give me 100 per cent on and off the field. He was humble and proud – I heard later he forgot the lineout calls during the game and had a big night. His selection was an important statement: a player may be seen as nearing the end of his career but he can still have a lot to offer, he can still do a job. It was nice to be able to reward commitment. I really enjoyed my association with Phil Coffin."

12
TWO TRIBES GO BACK TO WAR

THE All Blacks now prepared for the first of five confronta-
tions with the most uncompromising foe of all: the
Springboks.

Some felt that five All Black-Springbok tests in the space of six
weeks was too much of a good thing. The situation had come
about because, before the establishment of the Tri-Nations Series
under the News Corporation-SANZAR deal, the All Blacks were
scheduled to undertake a full tour of South Africa in 1996. With
the new competition in place, the NZRFU wanted to scale down
the tour; SARFU didn't. There was a battle of wills between the two
national unions in which, as John Hart puts it, "Louis Luyt's
negotiating skills and dominant personality carried the day. You
have to hand it to Luyt – he seems to get his way in most things."

After watching the match in Oamaru, the panel had hurried to
Christchurch to catch the South Africa-Australia match from Sydney.
The Wallabies bounced back from the blitzing at Athletic Park to win
21-16, ending the Springboks' run of 16 consecutive victories. Along
with the glory and the Webb Ellis trophy, the World Cup winners get
the extra pressure that goes with their world champion status. Like
the All Blacks and Wallabies before them, the Springboks were
starting to find out that getting to the top is easier than staying there.

"After Wellington, the Aussies were written off, especially at home," says Hart. "But as most coaches know, a lot of resolve comes out of adversity so I wasn't surprised by their stoic performance. The Springboks were clearly underdone. Andre Joubert was unfit, Joost van der Westhuizen didn't have a great night, and the pace of the game found some of their forwards out. They'd had one warm-up match against Fiji compared to Australia and New Zealand's three. I think our build-up was probably the best – the Samoans had tested us physically and Scotland had tested our set pieces and tactical nous."

The Springboks were without the coach who'd guided them to the World Cup – Kitch Christie. Hart had met Christie in early March when he'd come to New Zealand with the Transvaal team. At that stage, Christie was both Transvaal and Springbok coach; within a matter of weeks, he was neither. Having supplied 13 of South Africa's World Cup squad, Transvaal were a formidable side on paper. Within a fortnight of the Super 12 kicking off, they were looking like a paper tiger; they began their campaign with four matches in Australia and New Zealand and lost the lot. On his return to South Africa, Christie announced he was standing down as Transvaal coach to concentrate on the Springboks.

"Christie struck me as very shrewd and an impressive operator," says Hart. "As Springbok coach, he'd put together a simple but effective game plan which was implemented with great commitment. He clearly had health problems though, and it wasn't long before he was gone from the Springboks too. While ill-health was undoubtedly a factor, I sensed that not all was well between him and Luyt."

Christie was replaced by Andre Markgraaff, the coming man in South African rugby. Markgraaff had been a highly successful coach of Griqualand West and was now Chairman of the Griqualand West union and a SARFU board member. The talk in South Africa was that coaching the Springboks was only a stepping-stone to greater things: many people, including the big boss man himself, Louis Luyt, saw Markgraaff as a future SARFU president. He seemed destined to be one of the major figures in the game as it headed into the 21st century.

While losing to Australia wasn't the ideal preparation, Hart took little comfort from it – a wounded Springbok is a dangerous animal. When the All Blacks gathered in Christchurch, he detected an even more pronounced mood of excitement and anticipation than before the Australian game. The most intense rivalry in world rugby was about to be resumed.

Bitter memories of the World Cup final loss 13 months previously also contributed to the edginess. Only three All Blacks – Christian Cullen, Justin Marshall, and Michael Jones – hadn't played in that game. The team didn't talk about it much. Sean Fitzpatrick and others downplayed the payback theme when it was raised by the media but there was no doubt that the defeat was still gnawing away at some of them.

"I didn't refer to it," says Hart. "I wasn't part of it. Besides, victory at Lancaster Park wouldn't change a thing – South Africa would still hold the World Cup. When the subject did come up, it was pointed out that when emotions take over, teams lose the plot."

But was anyone listening?

Only eight of the side who won the World Cup would take the field at Lancaster Park. Injury had removed Kobus Wiese, Chester Williams, and Hennie le Roux while the selectors' axe had accounted for Balie Swart, Chris Rossouw, Hannes Strydom, and Joost van der Westhuizen.

Markgraaff chose to play tricks over who his halfback would be so van der Westhuizen's demotion wasn't confirmed until the day of the game. He was named in the starting line-up but the buzz was that Johan Roux would play instead. At training, they took it turn and turn about.

Hart told the All Blacks that Roux would play: "I thought the slippery conditions would suit his kicking game. Although he didn't have van der Westhuizen's speed and elusiveness, he was more solid and van der Westhuizen had shown some frailty in Sydney. He's an effervescent player, always putting pressure on you, but he's susceptible to pressure himself as Auckland found in an early Super 12 game.

"I'm not sure that holding back selections is in the best interests of the team although the players probably knew – Markgraaff told me later that he'd told van der Westhuizen after the Sydney game he wouldn't play in Christchurch. I suppose it kept us guessing, though. Now that substitutions are permitted, coaches have to think beyond the opposition's starting fifteen when planning tactics."

There were no such dramas with the All Black team; the starting line-up and reserves were unchanged. Hart felt that the preparation went well although, yet again, the weather turned ugly. They trained at Lancaster Park on the Thursday and it was very wet around the cricket pitch area.

The night before the game, Hart and Fitzpatrick had a meeting with the Scottish referee Ray Megson and his touch judges, Jim Fleming and Ken McCartney. Hart knew Fleming from the 1991 World Cup but not the others. He was hoping for a repeat of the pleasant experience with Ed Morrison in Wellington but his instincts told him things might not run so smoothly this time. The three Scots were staying in the All Blacks' hotel and Hart couldn't help noticing that they seemed quite nervous. Pretty soon, they weren't the only ones.

"Megson sent shivers down my spine," says Hart. "He was very authoritarian – it was his meeting, not ours. He wouldn't allow the vests – we were resigned to that – but what staggered me was his comment that the South Africans had complained about our lineout tactics which had been used throughout the Super 12 and by the All Blacks in four tests without anyone having a problem. He said he wouldn't be allowing players to change positions once the lineout had formed. I said I didn't consider that illegal; he replied that it wasn't just the South Africans' view, it was his view."

A compromise was reached: if a player didn't totally enter the lineout, he could move before the ball was thrown in. That was a relief – it meant the tactics could be persisted with, albeit in a modified form. Hart suggested to Megson that seeing he'd watched the All Blacks play and formed the view that the lineout tactics were illegal, it would have been helpful if he'd said so earlier to give them time to make the necessary adjustments at training. That fell on deaf ears; being helpful obviously wasn't part of the deal. Hart also expressed concern over the Springboks' habit of charging at the scrum engagements, suggesting that they would need to be carefully policed. It wasn't altogether clear whether Megson thought he had a point.

Hart: "I found it disturbing that he'd taken the South African case on board holus-bolus – was this to be the first of many South African attempts to unsettle us on and off the field? Fitzpatrick showed a lot of maturity in that meeting. We left without saying much to one another, knowing we'd have to handle it carefully when we reported back to the team."

First scrum: the Springbok front row charges, John Allan head-butts Fitzpatrick. New Zealand get a penalty and three points but Allan stays on the field. The message seemed to be, if you're going to have a crack at someone, do it early. Perhaps because they half-expect a bit of aggro early on or don't want to spoil the contest by leaving one side a man short for the whole game, referees seem to have a higher tolerance for violent play at the start of the game than thereafter. The message wasn't lost on Wallaby number 8 Michael Brial. As for the Springboks, conceding three points had no discernible effect on the intensity of their scrummaging.

First lineout: the All Blacks do exactly what Megson had agreed to under the compromise agreement. He penalises them, instantly negating a key component of their lineout play – having jumpers move up and down the line, switching positions. They were now in a straight lifting and jumping contest against bigger men who'd had years of lifting experience in their domestic rugby.

Joel Stransky matched Mehrtens' second minute penalty. The Springboks were showing more urgency and it was no real surprise when Joubert scored from a clever switch after they'd sucked the All Blacks into a ruck on the left. It was an authoritative piece of play. The All Blacks managed just one clean break in the half, via Walter Little; seven points beckoned but Joubert knocked down Little's pass to Frank Bunce. It looked every bit a professional foul but the term didn't spring so readily to commentators' lips in those days. The Springboks led 8-6 at the break; the All Blacks were just hanging in.

Both sides turned up the pressure in the second half. Things looked bad for the All Blacks when Wilson made a mess of an up-and-under and conceded a five metre scrum. The Springboks were calling the shots in the scrums but luck went the All Blacks' way and they scrambled out of it. The pressure was getting to Mehrtens who was looking less and less assured. He put two 22-metre dropouts out on the full, handing the Springboks prime attacking opportunities.

But it was Megson who continued to be the game's dominant personality. Ironically, after all the headaches he'd caused them, his biggest call of the afternoon may well have saved the All Blacks' skin. With five minutes to go and New Zealand ahead 12-11, the Boks had a scrum-feed 15 metres out from the All Black posts. It was the perfect set-up: the opposition scrum was creaking, they could go left or right, or Stransky could take the Ellis Park option and slot another match-winning dropped goal. The front rows collapsed; the whistle went. Hart took it for granted that the call would be "penalty green" but it was "penalty black". The All Blacks cleared their line.

In the final five minutes, Ian Jones made a string of tremendous lineout takes, snaffling several South African throw-ins and giving the All Blacks that element of control which they'd lacked for most of the game. Right on fulltime, Mehrtens lined up his ninth penalty attempt while François Pienaar looked on, frustration etched on his face. The kick went over and the game was won 15-11.

Megson had awarded 37 penalties, six of them at the instigation of the touch judges. There'd been 15 New Zealanders and 15 South Africans out on the field but it felt like the game had been hijacked by three Scotsmen. Fleming was refereeing the All Blacks' next game so there was some sorting out to do if a re-run of the lineout debacle was to be avoided. Hart would be seeking an audience much earlier in the week. The refereeing was the focus of much of the media coverage, the recurrent theme being that Megson had ruined the game. On Sunday morning, Hart saw the three Scots in the hotel studying a newspaper; they wouldn't have found much for the scrapbook.

"It was a performance which raised the whole question of the appointment of test referees," says Hart. "The IRB appoints a national union which then decides which of its referees will take the game. Megson was only ranked third or fourth in Scotland and was also short of recent matches – you'd have thought that a replay of the World Cup final deserved one of the world's best referees. In the professional era, we need professional referees and an appointments system which ensures that the best officials – regardless of where they're from – take the biggest games."

The refereeing controversy couldn't alter the fact that the All Blacks hadn't played well. Athletic Park was intoxicating but now the hangover had kicked in.

Hart: "We never came to terms with a very flat defence – Mulder and Venter spent most of the afternoon in our backline. Roux had a good match, tormenting us with his kicking game and continually driving us into the corners. Although still not a hundred per cent, Joubert showed what a wonderful player he is before his hamstring forced him off. And the Springboks were a desperate side – they hit us with everything but we didn't crack, we held our composure. And, at the end of the day, any win against South Africa is a good win.

"A couple of players hadn't covered themselves in glory. Wilson got few opportunities but seriously mucked up two defensive situations. Mehrtens' lack of composure, inconsistency, and decision-making under pressure were more worrying. Watching the tape that night, I was disturbed by his performance as I had been by his laissez-faire attitude after the game. It wasn't a happy dressing room but Mehrtens was the exception. He's different – an intelligent, exuberant character whose exuberance sometimes makes him less than acutely aware of others' sensitivities. I felt it was time that was pointed out to him."

Hart did so first thing next morning, before the team debrief: "He was taken aback, which reflected his innocence and youthful lack of awareness of how others were feeling. It was important that the team understood that the blasé attitude was his way of coping with and covering up his disappointment so I suggested he said something to them. The upshot was that I got to understand him better, as did the team, and he was galvanised into producing a superb performance under pressure at Brisbane."

A post-match talking-point for the team was the way the Springboks had homed in on Jonah Lomu whenever he was caught in a ruck. To an extent, that went with the territory of superstardom and Hart admired the way Lomu coped with the physical and verbal provocation. He was more worried about Lomu's knee which still wasn't right. An MRI scan conducted before the team left for Brisbane showed a slight cartilage tear. An operation would have sidelined him for two or three weeks and the medical team's feeling was that it might settle so it was decided to soldier on.

The defeat had done nothing to undermine the Springboks' belief in their superiority. As the teams left the field, Mark Andrews told Fitzpatrick, "Wait till we get you on the high veldt." At the after-match function, Markgraaff was disappointed but far from despondent: he thought his side had deserved to win but derived solace from their scrummaging. Expanding on Andrews' comment, he told Hart: "Wait till you get to South Africa – we'll show you what scrumming really is."

"He obviously believed that on a dry track they'd murder us in the scrums," says Hart. "The comments revealed their absolute confidence in themselves at home as well as how central the scrum was to their whole game. I wasn't worried about our scrum. It hadn't gone well that afternoon – we'd been high – but the front row were far from happy with their performance. It became a real focus in our ongoing preparation."

In the post-mortem, the pre-occupation with getting even for the World Cup final was pin-pointed as a major factor in the sluggish performance. "I had guys wanting massages at one o'clock on the morning of the game," says Marty Toomey. "Some of them got so hyped up – whether they admitted it or not, they saw it as revenge. Most of them had played the game in their minds so many times, they'd used up a lot of mental energy and it left them flat. Most of our opponents run at the same level physically so it comes down to the mental approach."

Fitzpatrick agrees: "It was a hangover from the World Cup final. We thought about it being a re-run too much and got exposed in a few areas – they taught us a few things that day. It all comes back to attitude: you know beforehand if it's right, you can feel it in the team during the week, you can feel it running onto the field. You can certainly feel it at the first scrum. Christchurch was the opposite of Wellington – we weren't physically and mentally right and they got into us from the first scrum and intimidated us."

A star is born – Christian Cullen scores on debut against Western Samoa at McLean Park.

New Zealand is lucky to have two outstanding first-fives – Andrew Mehrtens (above) and Carlos Spencer (opposite page) whose goal-kicking proved a revelation in 1997.

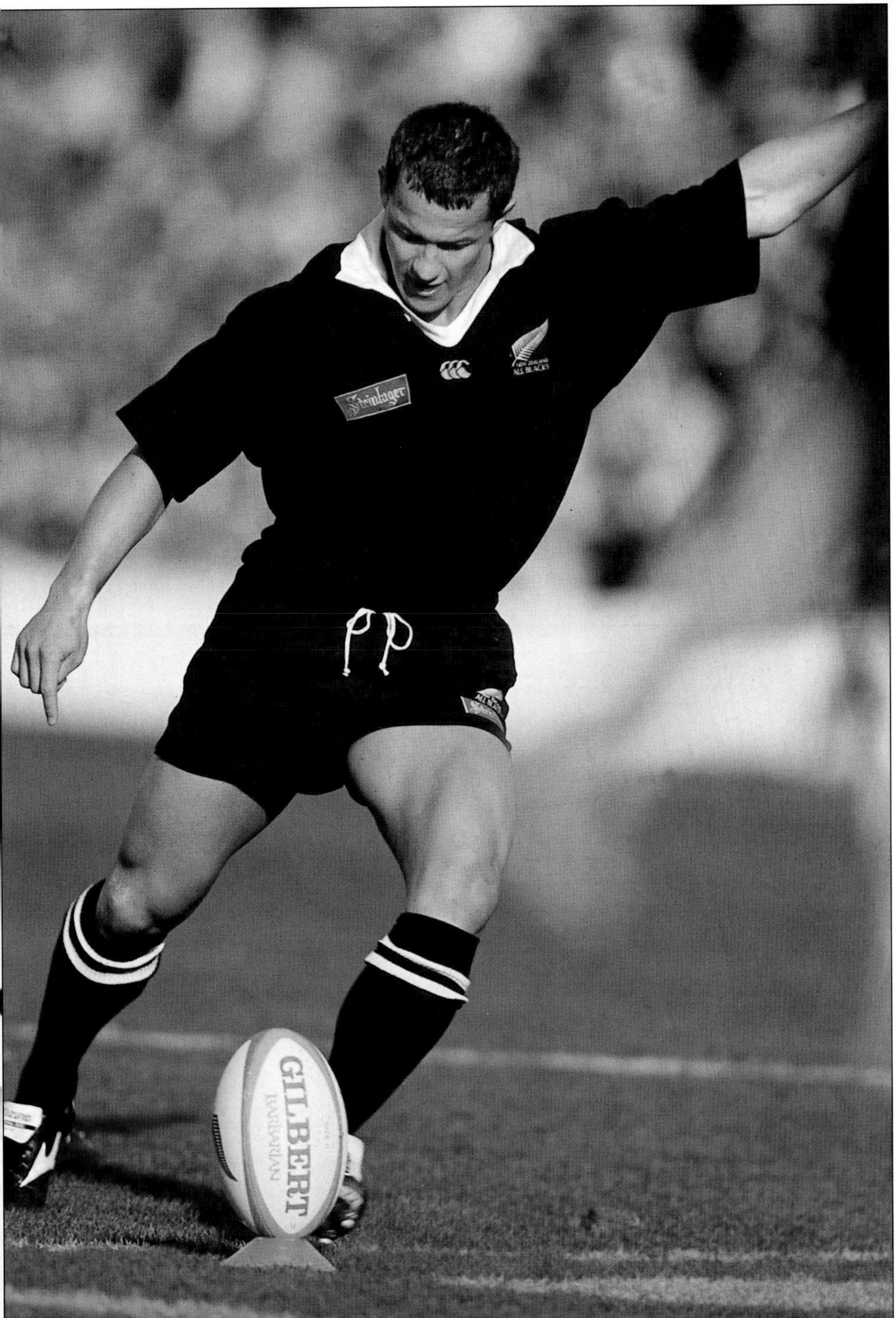

Photosport

The front row have been the All Blacks' Rock of Gibraltar. From left, Olo Brown, Sean Fitzpatrick and Craig Dowd.

Frank Bunce defied the years and the critics to provide the All Blacks' midfield cutting edge in 1997.

Taine Randell made huge strides in 1997 filling the gap left by Michael Jones' injury.

The All Blacks may not be the greatest singers of the national anthem but their pride in representing their country is second to none: Zinzan Brooke grasps the silver fern, Eden Park, 1997.

Peter Bush

A special moment – John Hart makes a presentation to Michael Jones to mark the great flanker's 50 test matches.

Peter Bush

13

THE GREAT ESCAPE

O N the Tuesday morning after the Lancaster Park test, the panel decided to take an extra player to Brisbane as cover for Jonah Lomu whose knee had flared up again. The only problem was that they were flying out at 3.45 that afternoon and the player in question – Glen Osborne – was in Wanganui, about to go pig-hunting. It was helter-skelter but he made it. Nobody noticed that he had his shirt on inside-out until he tried to put his passport in his shirt pocket.

Having got Osborne on board, the panel decided to bring him into the reserves at the expense of Eric Rush. Rush had been disappointing against Scotland while Osborne was playing well. In fact, with Lomu hampered by his knee and Wilson having an off-day in Christchurch, Osborne had strong claims to being the form winger. The "If it ain't broke, don't fix it" school of thought wouldn't have agreed but the panel felt that it made sense to have the in-form player on the bench given the distinct possibility that Lomu wouldn't last the 80 minutes.

"It was a good way to bring Osborne back in," says John Hart. "Earlier, we'd thought he'd struggle to even make the tour but the way he responded and handled the transition to wing made the selection process worthwhile. Rush had given Lomu a lot of support and did likewise for Osborne even when Osborne overtook him which shows the calibre of the individual."

As a first step towards bringing the non-test squad tourists into the fold, it was decided to fly them to Brisbane to watch the match and join the squad afterwards. To ensure that the management team wasn't distracted from the immediate task of preparing for the re-match with Australia, Hart enlisted the help of Neil Gray, a former NZRFU councillor and All Black manager. Gray cut short his holiday to oversee the outfitting and medical checks of the 14 extra players and bring them to Brisbane.

These pre-tour medical checks are something of a minefield. In the past, they've been criticised for erring on the side of stringency – as in 1991 when Mike Brewer was ruled out of the World Cup and played for Otago a week later – and laxity, as in 1995 when Josh Kronfeld was cleared to tour and proceeded to limp from one injury to another. Above all, they needed to be thorough – there would be no room for passengers in South Africa. It was therefore acutely embarrassing for everyone concerned that Adrian Cashmore could get all the way to South Africa before it was discovered that he had a stress fracture of the leg which would prevent him from taking any part in the tour.

Gray's group arrived in Brisbane on the morning of the test. The management team welcomed them and spelt out what would be expected of them in South Africa: to be totally disciplined both as individuals and team members and to make a contribution rather than just make up the numbers. Marty Toomey took them for a training run at Ballymore and subsequently reported that they were very enthusiastic though Cashmore and Phil Coffin hadn't moved too freely.

In Brisbane, Hart had wasted no time in contacting referee Jim Fleming. After the Lancaster Park game, Hart had aired his dissatisfaction with Ray Megson's lineout rulings without going into the details of the compromise agreement which had unravelled at the first lineout. He wanted to know exactly where Fleming stood before the All Blacks began their preparation.

"Fleming was in a difficult position," says Hart, "because to let us go back to the tactic of changing positions at the lineout would mean publicly parting company with his colleague and fellow Scot. He gave the impression that he didn't agree with Megson's interpretation so the issue was more a personal one. I put it to him that, as one of the world's leading referees, he really didn't want to be identified with what had been an ordinary display. It was a relief when he gave us the go-ahead; our lineout isn't as big as the other teams, so we rely on tactical variations, accuracy, and timing."

Neither side would lack incentive at Suncorp Stadium. The All Blacks led the Tri-Nations Series with nine points which included a four-try bonus point from Athletic Park; Australia had four points and South Africa two. If the All Blacks won, they'd go to South Africa with the Tri-Nations wrapped up; if the Wallabies won, they'd be in with a real chance of winning the series. An even more powerful motivation would have been their desire to redeem themselves in the eyes of the Australian public.

Hart noticed some sloppiness at training which he put down to the difficulty of switching back on within a few days of such a physically and mentally draining match. Whether it was a touch of tiredness, the humid conditions, lingering tetchiness over a disappointing performance, or all of the above, things came to the boil at an opposed training session in front of a large Australian media contingent.

Hart unleashed the reserves on the test team and they made the most of it. Norm Hewitt stormed in on the side of a ruck and rattled Ian Jones' rib-cage. Jones objected and punches flew. When the dust settled, Hewitt was on his way to get patched up. Hart tried to laugh it off, telling the journalists that it was a dispute over who got the double bed, but he feared the Aussie media would have a field day. No doubt they would have done if they'd had the footage but, amazingly, the television cameras missed all the action.

"There was no bad blood," says Hart. "It was a spur of the moment thing which happens at training from time to time. The Scots had a big one when they were in New Zealand and I understand the Wallabies had an altercation of their own that week. Maybe that's why their media didn't make more of it."

The Australian Rugby Union had moved the game from Ballymore, the home of Queensland rugby, to Suncorp Stadium, formerly Lang Park. As the venue for many torrid State of Origin league matches, Lang Park was synonymous with rabid crowd support for the Maroons artfully orchestrated and exploited by 'King' Wally Lewis. The switch was revenue-driven – Suncorp had almost twice the capacity of Ballymore – but perhaps the ARU was hoping to revive that intimidating Lang Park atmosphere. If so, they forgot to take into account the number of Kiwis living in and around Brisbane and on the Gold Coast. They turned out in force.

"As the bus made its way to the ground, we couldn't believe the number of black and white scarves and flags and the response the team got," says Hart. "The crowd was pretty quiet when the Wallabies were on top but came to life with a vengeance when the All Blacks began their comeback. I think the Australian administrators were as surprised as we were at the tremendous support for the All Blacks."

Coach Greg Smith and his fellow selectors had rung the changes following the demolition at Athletic Park. They'd gone back to their original inside back choices of George Gregan and Pat Howard, brought in Andrew Heath at tighthead prop, and replaced Owen Finegan with Daniel Manu at blindside flanker. They were forced into a significant last-minute change when Tim Horan suffered a badly broken nose at training. He was replaced by Richard Tombs.

It was clear from the opening whistle that this was a very different Wallaby team. They were fired up, determined not to be caught cold or take a backward step. But there's a fine line between refusing to be intimidated and getting your retaliation in first and the Wallabies weren't always on the right side of it. The first scrum turned into a shoving match. It was re-set but trouble flared again and the referee called out and duly penalised Wallaby hooker Michael Foley for nuzzling Sean Fitzpatrick with malicious intent. Foley's headband was already in tatters so perhaps Fitzpatrick had attempted a repeat of his Wellington sleight-of-hand. The battle of wills and words was on in earnest.

Judging by his wild-eyed mouthing and gesticulating, Wallaby number 8 Michael Brial had taken the field with a virulent dose of white line fever. In a pre-game television interview, he claimed that he'd been "belted and cheap-shotted" every time he'd gone into a ruck or maul in Wellington and vowed there'd be no more Mr Nice Guy. Sure enough, when Frank Bunce brought up his elbow in a tackle, Brial exploded. Although he can handle himself better than most and isn't naturally inclined to turn the other cheek, Bunce showed his discipline by covering up while Brial flailed away. Bunce's aunt wasn't impressed; she phoned after the game to tell him that on no account was he to stand there and take it next time.

Fleming had sent players off in test matches before so Wallaby supporters must have feared the worst as he spoke to Brial. He settled for reversing a penalty against Lomu for not releasing in a tackle. Unchastened by Fleming's lecture or costing his side an eminently kickable penalty opportunity, Brial gave his teammates the thumbs-up as he ran back to join them.

Once the red mist lifted, the Wallabies played some impressive rugby. It was Athletic Park in reverse; they were more aggressive, hungrier for the ball, and swifter to capitalise on mistakes, almost scoring in the tenth minute after Walter Little spilled the ball in mid-field. The All Blacks didn't get away with their next turnover; Zinzan Brooke released Andrew Mehrtens with a backhand pass from a lineout and Michael Jones drove forward. But when he went to ground, Brial pried the ball loose, Joe Roff and Ben Tune poured through a defence that was slow to reorganise, and Gregan scored a breakaway try.

Matthew Burke kept his side in front with two booming penalties from beyond halfway as a prelude to a sensational try just before the break. Howard and Tombs mucked up a move just outside their 22. Some referees would have called it a knock-on, scrum-feed to the All Blacks; Fleming let it go. Tombs flicked the ball up to Burke who took off from a standing start. He bustled through three innocuous tackles and suddenly there were wide open spaces in front of him – everyone had forgotten their defensive lines. Christian Cullen bought his dummy with the eagerness of a bargain-hunter at the Christmas sales and Burke pranced all the way to the line.

Hart: "I wasn't too worried at that stage because we hadn't got into any sort of attacking rhythm and their tries had come from our mistakes. After 17 minutes of the second half, I was very definitely worried – two more penalties had taken them out to 22-9 and we still hadn't put much together. If they'd scored again, we would've been on the ropes, but they went on the defensive and started to make mistakes and concede penalties."

Two sweetly struck Mehrtens penalties got the All Blacks to within striking distance with plenty of time left on the clock. Then Burke kicked his fifth penalty, pushing the deficit back out to ten. Two steps forward, one step back.

The Wallabies controlled the kick-off and Howard hoofed a wobbly left-footer down the field. Cullen snaked back up the middle to set up a quickly won ruck. The ball went to Lomu. He'd had a quiet afternoon but now he had space to wind up. He thundered down the left flank into the Wallaby 22 where a posse of defenders finally dragged him down. Again, the ball came back quickly. Halting the big man had left Australia short-handed on the blind and Justin Marshall scooted through the hole to score without a hand being laid on him. Mehrtens converted: 25-22.

Australia won the re-start. Howard launched a perfect up-and-under but Cullen held firm, making a superb catch under the crossbar and David Campese's nose.

With four minutes to go, the All Blacks got a centrefield penalty on halfway. Mehrtens' kick was majestic, clearing the crossbar with plenty to spare – 25-all. The next score would clinch it; the game had entered the dropped goal zone. The Wallabies got ideal field position. Looking to go out in a blaze of glory in his last game against the All Blacks, Campese went for it but the drop was awry and the kick never had a chance. Mehrtens slammed the drop-out deep into Wallaby territory; Tune tried to run it back without support in depth and was monstered by Lomu. Scrum black.

With everyone expecting a droppie, especially after Zinzan Brooke had picked up and driven a few metres closer to the posts, Mehrtens called a double-round move. He hared through a gap and found Cullen who'd managed to shake free of Roff's clutches. Jeff Wilson was unmarked on the outside and, with Gregan hurtling across in cover-defence, probably having an unnerving flashback to the Sydney Football Stadium, 1994. Instead, Cullen chopped inside. Hopelessly wrong-footed, Gregan flung out an arm. Cullen ducked it and lost his footing a couple of metres short of the line as Brial arrived on the scene. Hart thought the try had been butchered but Cullen had the presence of mind to plant the ball for Bunce who scooped it up and was driven over the line by Kronfeld. Making absolutely sure of it, a low-flying Fitzpatrick crash-landed on the pile of bodies. Right on the bell, the All Blacks had landed the killer punch.

Hart: "Overall, it was quite a solid All Black performance but the Wallabies had lifted a hundred per cent and to lose at the last gasp must have been heartbreaking. Their dressing room was barred to all outsiders for some time afterwards.

"Mehrtens had bounced back brilliantly. He was always in control and his goal-kicking under extreme pressure as we tried to claw our way back into the game was the stuff champions are made of – we simply had to keep clicking up those three-pointers to maintain some sort of momentum. For such a young player, the way he produced the rabbit out of the hat at the death was quite exceptional."

Fitzpatrick wasn't surprised by the Wallabies' startling turnaround: "They hadn't suddenly become a 50-point better team but their whole attitude was right, they were focused. They'd probably seen the South Africans, whom they'd just beaten, get into us the week before and realised that the gap wasn't so big, we weren't supermen. The difference between us, South Africa, and Australia is minimal so it comes down to preparation and attitude on the day."

The All Blacks had been rocked by a highly motivated opponent, they'd made mistakes, and they'd taken a long, long time to get into the game. But having got out of jail once, they knew they could do it again.

"After Brisbane, the team started to believe in itself a lot more," says Fitzpatrick. "We knew that if we held our composure, we could come back from those situations."

When he'd finished with the media, Hart went out onto the field to ring his family who hadn't enjoyed the first 70 minutes any more than he had. It was encouraging to see the test reserves out there holding a private training session while the team recovered in the dressing room. It was even more encouraging to hear later from the old hands that some of the inspiration for the fightback had come from seeing the tense faces of the young All Blacks sitting in the stand and hating the thought of their coming into a losing side. With that attitude at the top, there was no danger of a pernicious divide between the senior players and the rest in this All Black team.

14
TIME OUT

THE exhilaration of the great escape wore off quickly. Next morning, the All Blacks dispassionately reviewed their performance and found it deficient. There was no getting away from the fact that they'd been lucky – the Wallabies should have won. No-one kidded themselves that they could give the Springboks that sort of head start on their home turf.

For the new boys, that Sunday morning debrief was something of a crash course in the All Black culture. Says John Hart: "They saw the very high expectations the test players had of themselves and the analysis and soul-searching they went through before moving on."

The touring party unwound for a few hours at the Hyatt Regency resort hotel at Coolum before flying to Sydney. Hart and Sean Fitzpatrick took on Richard Fry and Ian Jones on the demanding golf course: at stake, shirts worth up to $80 from the pro shop. The North Harbour pairing won. Jones chose a shirt worth $79.95; Hart was surprised he didn't pocket the change. Ever the wily campaigner, Fitzpatrick talked Fry into choosing a shirt which, unbeknownst to him, was on special.

They overnighted in Sydney and flew out to Johannesburg on Monday morning. Although business class and Doctor Mayhew's sleeping pills took some of the sting out of the 16-hour flight, long-haul air travel can still be an ordeal for the big men, especially Jonah Lomu whose knees and ankles tend to swell up. Mike Banks had received a fax saying they'd be met off the plane by SARFU officials; in fact, the welcoming committee consisted of their liaison officer and baggage manager. Neither SARFU's President nor the Chief Executive deigned to put in an appearance. It was the first of many such breaches of the traditional courtesies.

The press conference at an airport hotel was relatively low-key. Hart had expected a grilling on his predecessor's claim that the All Blacks were nobbled before the 1995 World Cup final. It didn't eventuate. In a one-on-one interview afterwards, he was asked to give a rationale for the 36-man squad; tongue-in-cheek, he replied that the breakdown was 30 players and six chefs. The words were scarcely out of his mouth before he was imagining the provocative headline a literal-minded or mischievious sub-editor could conjure up from that throwaway line. Luckily, the journalist recognised it as such.

It was an uncharacteristic lapse, especially given his determination to avoid the controversies and sour relations with the local media which had intensified the pressure on previous All Black teams in the republic. Jane Dent had compiled a dossier identifying both the issues likely to come up in the media during the tour and the South African journalists with whom they'd need to establish relationships. Nor could the New Zealand press group travelling with the team be taken for granted. Things had gone well on the home media front since the All Black show had been on the road but they'd be looking for even more co-operation to ease the deadline pressures caused by the ten-hour time difference.

The first week would be mainly devoted to rest and relaxation, immersing the new men in the All Black culture, and team-building. Given the itinerary and the fact that the test side had now been together for the best part of two months, there was a real risk of the party splitting into two teams with different leaderships, cultures, and even agendas.

"It's important that you get the balance right on tour," says Hart. "Intensity has to be balanced with fun and relaxation." To generate some fun and togetherness, the squad was divided into four teams who'd compete across a range of disciplines. In consultation with Fry, the captains – Andrew Mehrtens, Eric Rush, Zinzan Brooke, and Mark Allen – chose names for their teams.

Rush's team was North Otarbour, named after the new provincial union unveiled by Richie Guy when he announced the test team to play Western Samoa. The team included a real bolter: North Otarbour's unobtrusive midfield back Scott Bunce. Rush's team wore red t-shirts bearing the legend "The All Blacks proudly sponsored by the All Blacks," another gem from *The Sayings of Chairman Richie*.

Mehrtens named his team Big Mex in homage to his hero, former All Black Murray Mexted. Naturally, their t-shirts were black with the number 8 on the back. Allen chose No Mercy, which had some tenuous connection with the running of the bulls in Pamplona, and Brooke's team were the Perfs. At first, this was thought to be an acronym for Playing Excellent Rugby Football Sometimes but it actually stood for Police Employment Rehabilitation Fund. Brooke's source of inspiration was Blair Larsen who'd recently announced that he was seeking an early release from the police force because of stress, a course of action known in police jargon as perfing.

The captains chose their teams by pick-up, the sole proviso being that the four carpenters in the squad – Fitzpatrick, Simon Culhane, Craig Dowd, and Robin Brooke – had to be shared around. Zinzan Brooke snapped up Fitzpatrick, signalling that the Perfs' strategy would rely heavily on gamesmanship, while Mehrtens elected to surround himself with fellow Cantabrians.

After a flight to Port Elizabeth and a three-hour bus trip, the All Blacks arrived at the Beacon Isle Hotel at Plettenberg Bay where they were welcomed by the hotel staff in black t-shirts performing the haka. It was an ideal location for the management's purposes: isolated, devoid of media, but with plenty to do.

They trained at the local rugby club. The pitch, which hadn't been much to look at when Banks checked it out on his reconnaissance visit, was now in superb condition. The coaches thought about holding integrated training sessions but decided that the immediate priority was to develop some cohesion in the midweek side. The test players also needed a break from the physical stuff like scrummaging and defence, the very things to which the midweek team had to knuckle down.

Hart laid it on the line for the new All Blacks: "I warned them that, for various reasons, there are a few failures on every tour. Some guys can't handle being in the midweek side and not getting much rugby; some can't handle being away from home; some can't handle the disciplines or resist the temptations. The challenge was to return to New Zealand with 36 players who'd been successful and would continue to be All Black contenders.

"Realistically, not all of them would be test players – some, in fact, had been selected to do a specific job for the midweek team. Their goal had to be to prove themselves worthy All Blacks and stake a claim for future selection, especially if 36-man touring squads were to become the norm. It wasn't necessarily a question of whether they could force their way into the test side on this tour; it was more whether they could establish themselves as long-term All Blacks in line with the panel's goal of building an expanded squad of genuine test-quality players for the future."

Phil Coffin couldn't train because of a damaged calf and was finding the enforced inactivity enormously frustrating. Hart drummed into him that he had to follow the medical team's instructions to the letter – if he pushed too hard and did further damage, he'd be on the next plane home, following in Adrian Cashmore's flight-path. The Aucklander had been invalided out after an MRI scan showed he had a stress fracture which would need six weeks' recovery time.

The panel had a number of players on standby but, with Glen Osborne and Jeff Wilson in the squad, hadn't expected to need another fullback. Lomu's knee had changed the equation: they didn't want to play Osborne at fullback in the midweek team while there was a real possibility he'd have to be drafted into the test side on the wing.

Matthew Cooper had had a mixed Super 12 for the Otago Highlanders who'd used him as an impact player at centre as much as at fullback. However, Gordon Hunter was a strong advocate, not that Hart needed much convincing. In 1987, he'd taken Cooper, fresh from the Colts, on the All Blacks' tour of Japan and remembered him as a good tourist. Cooper didn't have quite the speed the panel wanted in a fullback but he still had a lot going for him; he was solidity personified, one of the best goal-kickers in the country, and a good team man who'd come in and make a contribution straightaway.

When Hart rang, Cooper thought it was his brother having him on. He was guarded until it sank in that it really was the All Black coach at the other end of the line, offering him a recall to the ranks. He was all for it and joined the party on the second-to-last day at Plettenberg Bay, in time to make the team to play Boland.

At a barbecue put on by the local rugby club, Hart saw Lomu-mania at first-hand: "Jonah was absolutely beseiged. Witnessing the abuse he got from people who behaved as if he had some sort of obligation to respond directly to them – and who ruined it for the 95 per cent who simply wanted to express their admiration – really brought home to me how much pressure he was under. Afterwards, we congratulated him on the way he'd handled it. Overall though, he was lack-lustre. He was missing his wife and the knee was continuing to lock."

The Plettenberg Bay mini-Olympics got under way. Disdaining a run-up, Lomu threw the javelin – a corner flag with a nail in it – 15 metres further than anyone else and Jon Preston burned off the field in the three kilometre run. Fitzpatrick displayed a hitherto well-concealed sensitive touch in the egg-catching event which took place at a training session watched by about 500 black children. It wasn't until many eggs had bitten the dust that it dawned on them that they were wasting food in front of a bunch of kids for whom hunger was probably more than an abstract concept. The players signed a lot of autographs that day.

Two scrum and two ruck machines had been brought from New Zealand in kit-set form. One of the events was a race to assemble them, hence the need for a carpenter in each team. Their approaches varied: Fitzpatrick stood back and gave orders, Culhane and Dowd decided it was easier to just do it all themselves, and Robin Brooke tried a bit of both.

The ease of the Perfs' victory reflected the fact that they'd left nothing to chance. Dowd found himself short of a vital bolt which – surprise, surprise – turned up in Zinzan Brooke's pocket. That wasn't all. While in Hart's room, Fitzpatrick had spotted a document intended for management's eyes only – a list of events on which the machine assembly race featured prominently. The Perfs discovered where the machines were stored and slipped out to the training ground at the crack of dawn for a practice run to get the hang of it. Fitzpatrick denied it of course but his long list of "priors" meant that no-one was listening.

It seemed the Perfs would stop at nothing. They were cleaning up in the sports trivia quiz until Hart realised there'd been a leak from within the management team who'd drawn up the questions. Big Mex went to the other extreme: their obsession with getting "eight" into every answer was a self-imposed handicap which they utterly failed to overcome.

The Perfs and North Otarbour were neck and neck going into the final event, a theatrical performance judged by the management. North Otarbour performed a satirical song which, while not without merit, hardly deserved the maximum points it was awarded by some judges. Bribery and corruption were now rife. A protest walk-out was narrowly averted when the Perfs' take-off of the All Black dressing room before a test, complete with Walter Little being told to put his cigarette out and Osborne cleaning his teeth, didn't receive the high marks they felt it cried out for.

Predictably, Big Mex's self-absorbed offering was of interest to no-one but themselves but the No Mercy team came up with a dramatic re-enactment of the training paddock fracas in Brisbane. Cooper convincingly portrayed the coach although one of the judges felt that the towels inside the tracksuit were way overdone. Culhane and Glenn Taylor were the combatants and Norm Hewitt played the part of Grant Batty, the former All Black now resident in Queensland, who'd been at the session and told a TV reporter that a punch-up at training was a healthy sign – it showed the boys were ready.

When the votes were tallied, North Otarbour won the right to wear the yellow jersey for the rest of the tour. The Perfs bitterly denounced the judging but gained little sympathy. Those who live by the sword . . .

From the outside, the stay at Plettenberg Bay might have seemed an indulgence and some of the activities bordering on childish. To Hart, it was "an important phase of the tour when we bonded together for what lay ahead. It was us against a nation and we had to be united."

A thousand-strong crowd, mostly young and black or coloured, welcomed the All Blacks to the Lord Charles hotel at Stellenbosch. The New Zealand media contingent was also waiting for them and Hart had to drag himself through a round of interviews which was the last thing he felt like after the four-and-a-half hour bus trip. He was exhausted; he'd worked hard at Plettenberg Bay, keeping the fun going and ensuring that everyone was mixing in, and wasn't sleeping well – he seldom does away from home. The indefatigable Fitzpatrick led the charm offensive, mixing with the crowd and responding to the youngsters.

Before leaving New Zealand, the panel had undertaken to give every player at least two games. It wasn't an issue at lock – with only four locks in the party, Taylor and Larsen were going to get plenty of work – or for Allen and Taine Randell whom the panel wanted to give as many games as possible. But it meant that halfbacks, hookers, first-fives, and tighthead props would have to share and there'd also have to be some juggling with the midfield backs and loose forwards. For players like Chresten Davis and Anton Oliver though, the learning experience was as much off the field as on it.

The team to play Boland had Scott McLeod at centre outside Ieremia with Osborne and Rush on the wings and Cooper at fullback. It was a big day for Ofisa Tonu'u, Andrew Blowers, and Con Barrell who were making their All Black debuts as well as for Randell, a 21-year-old captaining a team containing a lot of experienced players, several of whom skippered their provinces.

Hart: "We swapped McLeod and Ieremia because we felt McLeod was perhaps a little leggy for second-five and might go better wider out. We also wondered if Ieremia had the vision we were looking for at centre. I think the jury's still out on whether McLeod's a better second-five or centre but during the season we concluded that Ieremia was well-suited to both positions.

"With that pair, there may even be a case for playing the two-centre game. We need to think more about who can kick off which foot and who's more comfortable and effective on which side of the field. Andre Joubert's left boot gave South Africa an extra dimension and they utilised his kicking skills the way the Australians have used David Campese's. Ieremia kicks well off his left foot so you might bring him in to second-five in defence to give yourself an extra kicking option."

The day before the Boland match, Banks and Hunter went to Worcester to inspect the ground. SARFU had allocated the fixture to Worcester as part of its development programme in the black and coloured communities but the ground was sub-standard, pitted with potholes and drains. They were also worried about crowd control; with the test team sitting in the middle of a sell-out crowd, it was easy to imagine Lomu in particular having a hellish afternoon. He was given the option of staying at the hotel with Michael Jones but chose to go to the game.

Everyone was conscious of South Africa's chilling reputation for violent crime. An All Black custom is for the Dirty Dirties – the players not involved in the next game, even as reserves – to go out for dinner the night before. In this case, the DDs were the test fifteen. Shortly after they left for a restaurant, someone rang the Lord Charles to say they were being followed by a column of cars. There are easier ways to make a buck than kidnapping the All Blacks but this was the wild west – anything was possible. A frantic call went through to Fitzpatrick who explained that they'd been escorted rather than pursued; the fans who hung around outside the hotel had seen the team bus depart and decided to tag along.

Boland was bolstered by two Western Province players and coached by Nick Mallett, one of South Africa's leading coaches. Later in the year, he was drafted in by Andre Markgraaff to help with the Springbok forwards. Looking at the performances on their end-of-year tour, Hart got the impression that Mallett and the assistant back coach Hugh Reece-Edwards had brought a lot of organisation to the Springboks so he was surprised when their services were dispensed with in the aftermath of the taped conversation affair which brought down Markgraaff. Perhaps it was another example of English backgrounds being a drawback within the Afrikaner-dominated SARFU.

The All Blacks started well. The lead was 24-0 at the break and could've been a lot more. Then with everything set up for a romp, they lost their way. Most of them hadn't played for several weeks – five or six weeks in some cases – and the lack of recent match play started to tell. Continuity dried up and some dreadfully sloppy defence handed Boland three simple tries before Tonu'u sealed an unconvincing 32-21 victory with a late try.

Davis' athleticism proved valuable when he replaced Larsen to become the fourth debutant. Blowers and Randell had strong games while Ieremia and McLeod ruled the midfield. Tonu'u was lively, although his defence let him down a couple of times when Boland lifted their attack, and the scrum went well. But there was at least as big an entry on the other side of the ledger. The midweek team had a long way to go.

15

CAPE OF GOOD HOPE

A FTER two trouble-free months, the three-coach system had a slight malfunction in the build-up to the Cape Town test. Because of the midweek team's game against Boland, John Hart missed the test XV's Tuesday practice which was taken by Ross Cooper and Gordon Hunter. Wednesday morning's run began with a grid devised by Cooper which left most of the players exhausted. The subsequent contact session against opposition from the local university was highly physical but less than satisfactory with a lot of mishandling. With Hart back on deck and the assistants carrying on from where they'd left off the day before, there were too many voices and too little direction.

"We got feedback through Sean Fitzpatrick that it wasn't what the players wanted," says Cooper. "After that, Harty had to be more hands-on."

"The three-coach system needs a very defined line of command," says Hart. "I'd probably taken one step too many back because of the demands of the first week and a half, the need to focus on the midweek team, and wanting to give Ross and Gordon opportunities."

Managing and coaching two teams was proving just as difficult as Hart had expected. Clearly, the hardest part would be maintaining a focus on the midweek team once the countdown to a test match had started. Richard Fry was able to shoulder some of the management load by taking responsibility for signing sessions, school visits, team dinners, and preparing the daily team sheets. On test day, Fry would take charge of the DDs; after they'd trained with Cooper and Hunter, he'd keep them away from the hotel to ensure that the test team's build-up wasn't disrupted.

On Wednesday afternoon, the All Blacks moved down from Stellenbosch to Cape Town where Jonah Lomu had an MRI scan on his knee. It was supposed to be private but there was a crowd waiting for Lomu and John Mayhew at the hospital and the results of the scan were in the public domain before the management team had even had a chance to discuss the matter. Since the leak didn't come from the Western Province union officials attached to the team, there had to be a question mark over the confidentiality of the All Black management's communications with SARFU and its medical people.

Lomu's knee hadn't got any worse since the previous scan in Auckland; then again, it hadn't got any better. It was continuing to lock and he wasn't running strongly. Although the Tri-Nations was already decided, the game at Newlands had huge psychological significance for the series to follow. Hart decided he wasn't going in with players who weren't 100 per cent fit so Glen Osborne replaced Lomu on the left wing in the only change to the team who'd played in Brisbane. By hauling himself out of a rut and playing his way back into the test team in a new position, Osborne had shown what he was made of, both in terms of character and rugby ability.

The deliberations over the composition of the reserves bench were complicated by the restrictiveness of the six-substitutes rule. Blair Larsen still had the edge over Glenn Taylor at lock but the panel weren't convinced that he could handle playing blindside flanker against the Springboks. They were also keen to have Andrew Blowers in the reserves. Jon Preston's ability to cover both inside back positions gave them the option of a two back/four forward bench which wasn't a huge gamble given how rarely three backs get injured in a game. Alama Ieremia's powerful performance against Boland had pushed him ahead of Scott McLeod; he'd cover the midfield and the back three with Jeff Wilson or Osborne going to fullback if Christian Cullen got injured.

Paul Holmes was doing his show from Cape Town. His lead-in to an interview with Hart was classic Holmes: he told the nation that this was a crucial game for the coach who had yet to prove himself. Six wins out of six and still an unknown quantity – it's tough at the top. Hart preferred to see the game as an opportunity for the All Blacks to create a launch-pad for their mission. With the final two tests at altitude, it would be important to go into the series with the momentum.

Prime Minister Jim Bolger was also in town. Mike Banks and Hart were invited to a state dinner – to be attended by Nelson Mandela – on the night before the test. Having previously had the privilege of meeting Mandela, Hart passed his invitation to Cooper. Hart and Bolger spoke by phone. A senior politician once told Hart that one should never underestimate the impact of All Black victories on public morale; as an avid All Black supporter and a Prime Minister facing a watershed election, Bolger had two reasons for hoping the coach had got it right.

At Bloemfontein the previous Saturday, the Springboks had eked out a slightly fortunate 25-19 win over Australia. Victory came at a price: Johan Ackerman, the huge young lock who'd impressed Hart at Christchurch, out for the season with a wrecked knee. Apart from replacing Ackerman with the more cumbersome Steve Atherton, Andre Markgraaff had kept faith with the pack which, in his eyes, had decisively won the forward battle at Lancaster Park. Behind the scrum, however, the comings and goings continued. With Andre Joubert injured again, James Small was shifted to fullback and Justin Swart came in on the wing. Hennie le Roux and Joost van der Westhuizen were back, the latter because Johan Roux was down with 'flu. With Swart having shortcomings and Small playing out of position, Hart and his fellow coaches felt the Springbok back three might be vulnerable.

Word had reached the All Blacks that not all was sweetness and light within the Springbok camp: apparently the mercurial James Small was getting on his teammates' nerves. It later emerged that, on the eve of the game, Small had been nightclubbing into the wee small hours. He was called to account by SARFU and didn't reappear in Springbok colours during the tour. Somewhat surprisingly, South African public opinion seemed to be on the bad boy's side.

The All Blacks spent a lot of time revisiting Lancaster Park and setting themselves for a big scrummaging performance. Markgraaff had telegraphed the fact that he saw the scrum as his side's trump card but then there's probably never been a Springbok coach who didn't see the scrum as the key to establishing psychological and physical domination. He'd have to wait for a dry track though – the sun was out when the All Blacks walked Newlands on Friday afternoon but the ground was soft and slippery from recent rain and heavy use.

Hart and Fitzpatrick came away from their meeting with the Irish referee David McHugh feeling that refereeing wouldn't be a major issue. In Hart's view, McHugh was to have a satisfactory day at the office but the South African referees who assessed his peformance saw it otherwise. Early in 1997, McHugh rang Hart to ask if the NZRFU had expressed an opinion on his performance at Newlands. He explained that the assessors had delivered a damning report which had led to him being downgraded in the referees' rankings to the extent that he hadn't been appointed to any European Cup fixtures.

Hart: "I told him that, as far as I knew, we hadn't been asked to comment and that apart from feeling that he'd overdone the penalties early on, we'd been pretty happy with his performance. One had to wonder if other forces were at work – the South Africans took that defeat very hard. Referees also tend to be very technical in their assessment of each other so there's a good case for having coaches and captains, who may have more feel for the game, involved in the assessment process to bring in a little balance."

With the Tri-Nations decided, there was some debate over whether the game at Cape Town was the first in a four-test series or a "nothing" game. The official position was that the Tri-Nations and the three-test series were two separate entities with no overlap but the public didn't necessarily see it that way.

Taking their cue from Markgraaff who was claiming that the Springboks' focus was firmly on the three-test series, the South African press pushed the line that there was nothing on the game. Call him cynical but Hart had no doubt that if South Africa won in Cape Town, there would be an edict from on high altitude designating the match as the first in a four-test series.

Luckily, no-one told the players that there was nothing on the game. They produced a pulsating encounter which totally overshadowed the war of attrition at Lancaster Park.

For the second game running, the All Blacks were slow out of the blocks and their opponents correspondingly swift to capitalise on their mistakes. In the 12th minute, Justin Marshall kicked out on the full from a good All Black scrum, giving the Springboks a throw-in on the New Zealand ten-metre mark. Joel Stransky's up-and-under was tapped down to Japie Mulder who doubled back through traffic, before straightening the attack and finding Mark Andrews steaming down the left touchline. Andrew Mehrtens and Michael Jones brought him down but the ball came back quickly. With le Roux running interference, Stransky put Mulder over behind the posts.

Quarter of an hour later, Mehrtens had a drop-out charged down, then failed to find touch. The Springboks ran it back; van der Westhuizen sniped down the blindside and nudged through an inch-perfect kick, forcing the All Blacks to concede a throw-in a metre from the corner flag. They knew what was coming but stopping it was another matter altogether; they couldn't and Os du Randt rumbled over from Atherton's take. The Boks had been sharp, strong, and efficient and deserved their 12-point lead; the All Blacks had been tentative and error-prone and looked like being played right out of the game before halftime.

There wasn't the hint of a crack in Fitzpatrick's granite-like self-possession but, deep-down, he was beginning to fear the worst: "We'd lost the World Cup final, we should've lost at Lancaster Park, we hadn't scored a try against them for God knows how long, they'd crucified us in the scrums at the World Cup and at Lancaster Park . . . I was having real doubts that we were up to beating them. Before we left New Zealand, someone told me I had the opportunity to be the most successful All Black captain ever to visit South Africa. As I trudged up the field to a lineout and looked up at the scoreboard, which showed us 15-3 behind, I can remember thinking that I could be the most unsuccessful All Black captain ever to visit South Africa."

On the half-hour, three offensive tackles in quick succession by Michael Jones and the Brooke brothers followed by a Bok turnover seemed to bring the All Blacks to life. The attack from the ensuing scrum almost produced a try and the Springboks needed the benefit of a couple of marginal refereeing decisions to clear their line. Five minutes later, a sweeping movement which began with Olo Brown on the Willie Away ended with Cullen being dragged down a metre short of the line. But the Springboks had got off-side in the middle of the field giving Mehrtens an easy penalty kick. The forwards went on the rampage from the kick-off, bullocking into Springbok territory to set up another surging attack which broke down ten metres from the line.

Hart sensed that the tide was turning: "Our scrum was holding up well. Van der Westhuizen had started brilliantly but the mounting pressure on his scrum and the attention from our loose forwards was preventing him from setting the Springboks alight. At halftime, I told the side they had to stay calm, improve their ball retention, and keep the pressure on and the tempo up – the Springboks weren't handling being moved around all that well."

Two minutes into the second half came one of the game's critical moments: as Walter Little went to fire off a wipers kick, he went over on his ankle and the resultant mis-kick ricocheted off advancing Springboks. The All Black outside backs, including Cullen, were already in hot pursuit so there wasn't a defender between Mulder and the All Black posts as he went to scoop up the ball. There was the merest suspicion of a fumble but McHugh, who'd let a couple go earlier, called the knock-on.

Little was replaced by Ieremia who immediately made an impact with some no-nonsense straight running. "One of the keys to our success in South Africa was that every time a replacement had to go on, he added value," says Hart. "It didn't happen by accident – it reflected our preparation and their ability and commitment. We spent a lot of time talking to the reserves about how they needed to focus on the game as if they were in the starting line-up so they could get into it straightaway rather than feeling their way in."

Another Stransky penalty took the Springboks out to 18-6. Ieremia said afterwards that he'd been amazed at how composed the All Blacks were despite being 12 points behind. In Churchillian terms, they had not yet begun to fight.

Now they started to make up for lost time, hammering at the Springbok line in an all-out offensive which went through 15 phases. But the Springboks kept swarming forward to make tackles and finally the turnover came. The Springbok scrum was shunted backwards and Bunce charged down Mulder's attempted clearance. A try seemed certain as he pursued the ball into the vacant in-goal area but there's nothing certain about the bounce of a rugby ball.

"When that evil bounce deprived Bunce of a try, it was tempting to think, as Fitzpatrick said afterwards, that the gods were against us," says Hart. "I began to wonder if we'd ever score a try against them. Often when a side throws everything at the opposition but can't post points, the heads go down, the pressure lifts, and they quickly concede points at the other end."

But although they'd been denied, it was the All Blacks who were lifted by that astonishing passage of play. They could see on their opponents' faces how much the titanic defensive effort had taken out of them. It finished off François Pienaar who'd gone down shortly after halftime but played on in obvious distress. After a long delay, for which the Springboks must have been grateful, came the sad sight of Pienaar being stretchered off with his neck in a brace.

Six reserves covering 15 players doesn't compute so there's an element of gamble in the make-up of most benches. This time Markgraaff bet wrong. With no loose forward cover on the Springbok bench, Hannes Strydom, a lock, had to go on which forced Andrews to the side of the scrum. Gary Teichmann aside, mobility hadn't been the South African pack's strong suit to start with and was even less so now.

It still took the All Blacks twenty minutes to make a dent in the deficit. After another period of sustained pressure, Mehrtens kicked his third penalty and added a fourth five minutes later. He was repeating his nerveless display at Brisbane.

With ten minutes to go, the Springboks were penalised for coming up at a scrum on the All Black 22. The pack launched a steam-roller drive from the ensuing lineout, clearing space. Mehrtens hit the flying Cullen with a superb cut-out pass. He pulled the cover-defence towards the touchline then connected with Osborne coming on the inside cut. The Comeback Kid wrong-footed three men and scored handy to the posts.

The All Blacks had opened up a defence which had started to take on an air of impregnability. The try drought had lasted 390 minutes going back to the second test at Wellington in 1994. With the Springboks' confidence in their ability to stop the All Blacks scoring tries having almost reached the point of arrogance, the psychological reverberations of Osborne's touchdown would be felt beyond this game.

Going behind for the first time galvanised the Springboks but Andrew Blowers, who'd replaced Josh Kronfeld, and Michael Jones buried Mulder in a sandwich tackle in front of the All Blacks' posts, forcing a turnover. The scrum feed became a penalty when Fitzpatrick goaded Stransky into a petulant shove.

That was the Boks' last roll of the dice. The All Blacks got down the other end and the pounding resumed. Ian Jones won a lineout against the throw, Ieremia took it up the middle, Cullen and Wilson probed on the right, and Bunce muscled his way close to the line. When Craig Dowd picked up the ball at the back of the ruck, he found the short route unguarded and trundled over. The conversion put the All Blacks eight points clear with six minutes to go but the Boks were in no shape to mount a big finish. The All Blacks went back on the attack and Mehrtens rubbed salt in the wound with another penalty, his seventh goal from eight attempts.

After that passage of play, the hulking loosehead prop du Randt became the second Springbok forward to leave Newlands on a stretcher. But was The Ox knocked out or just knackered?

The All Black medical team were quite sure that he was concussed which, with the mandatory three week stand-down, would've put him out of the series. According to David Abercrombie, "du Randt was away with the fairies – he didn't know what was going on." Mayhew could see that he'd been knocked out and was concerned for his welfare: "I went to their team doctor to ask if he needed help; he told me, 'It's okay, he's coming round now.'"

But according to du Randt himself, there was nothing medically wrong with him – he'd just had enough. He used an Afrikaans term which meant either fed up or exhausted, depending on which version you read. The charade enabled du Randt to lumber out onto Kings Park a week later but it also gave the All Black sledgers – no prizes for guessing who – some A-grade ammunition which they didn't waste.

When the time came to present the winning skipper with the Tri-Nations Cup, Louis Luyt was nowhere to be seen. Even though the cup was roughly the size of the dome of St Paul's Cathedral, none of Fitzpatrick's teammates lifted a finger to help him when he attempted to raise the trophy aloft in time-honoured fashion.

"I was proud of the All Blacks," says Hart, "especially the way they'd maintained their composure and discipline under pressure and competed for eighty minutes to end up dominant. It wasn't doing much for my nerves though. They won the scrum battle hands-down with Dowd turning the tables on Marius Hurter who'd had a big influence on proceedings at Christchurch. The loose forwards, led by Michael Jones, had tackled resolutely and the power and ball retention going forward in the second half had brought the backline into the game.

"Marshall put on another commanding performance, making big tackles, making breaks to create momentum and get us going forward, and distributing coolly. To my mind, he was the stand-out player. Watching the video that night, I heard Bill McLaren compare him to Gareth Edwards, an immense compliment. Although it was premature, there was no doubt that he was fast becoming one of those players capable of stamping his personality on a test match. There are very few who do it regularly."

Pienaar had suffered a displaced vertebra and was out of the forthcoming series. As far as the All Blacks were concerned, that was a worse break for them than the Springboks.

Hart: "Pienaar's form in the Super 12 was average and he didn't really go up much when the Tri-Nations began. For all his PR skill, he was very much a captain in the traditional Springbok mould; he wanted field position and physical dominance based on the scrum. I thought Teichmann, being from Natal and under the influence of their coach Ian MacIntosh, might bring a more expansive style to their game."

"We knew there was a bit of friction within their team centred on Pienaar," says Fitzpatrick. "We thought Andre Venter would add a dimension – which he did – and we knew how highly their players respected Teichmann."

With some misgivings, Hart visited the Springbok dressing room to console Markgraaff and Pienaar. It was difficult to tell which was the stronger emotion in there – disappointment or resolve.

A huge night of celebrations got under way back at the team hotel. Wilson performed that strange ritual of marking great victories with a convict haircut. Hart, who couldn't believe that Wilson would sacrifice his trademark golden locks, failed to recognise him from the back.

At the Sunday morning debrief, Hart searched in vain for any signs of intelligent life in the 21 pairs of glazed eyes which looked back at him from under drooping lids. He began by asking Olo Brown to talk him through the scrummaging. A professor of linguistics would have had his work cut out deciphering the garbled, faltering monologue which followed. Perhaps remembering how he'd been left to grapple with the Tri-Nations

Cup on his own, Fitzpatrick took his time in coming to the rescue of his front row colleague.

Before the All Blacks left Cape Town, there was a sequel to Hart's unproductive conversation with Alex Wyllie in Pretoria earlier in the year: Zinzan Brooke and Fitzpatrick were coming out of the gym at Newlands when Wyllie pulled up in a big Mercedes. The Legend wasted no time bringing the conversation around to the Springbok front row.

"He asked me about [Springbok hooker John] Allan and the props," says Fitzpatrick. "I knew what he was up to – he wouldn't look me in the eye. After that conversation, it didn't surprise me when Allan was replaced by Henry Tromp."

16
FIRST BLOOD

THE All Blacks' luck with injuries had to run out sooner or later. It happened on the morning of the second midweek match: the test side were having a fun warm-up game between the backs and the forwards when Andrew Mehrtens and Jeff Wilson went down in quick succession. Wilson's knock wasn't overly serious but Mehrtens had suffered a torn knee cartilage. He was out of the next test and perhaps the rest of the tour.

SARFU's medical people were on the job and, within hours, Mehrtens was headed for Johannesburg and a date in an operating theatre. He was crestfallen as were the team – he'd played a vital part in the come-from-behind wins in Brisbane and Cape Town. The panel didn't contemplate summoning a replacement; counting Jon Preston, they still had three first-fives to choose from.

Jonah Lomu was making his tour debut against Eastern Province at Port Elizabeth knowing that he'd have to produce something spectacular to regain his test spot from Glen Osborne. Phil Coffin and Anton Oliver were making their All Black debuts. Coffin's calf injury had held him back but it would have taken a ball and chain to stop him getting on the field this time. Oliver's celebrated father Frank had also made his All Black debut at the Boet Erasmus Stadium which, for the 20-year-old hooker, must have added to the thrill of entering the All Black brotherhood. With Tabai Matson, Carlos Spencer, and Preston having their first outings and Chresten Davis used as a replacement against Boland, the selectors would have given everyone a run in the space of three games.

A problem for the midweek side was the fact that the test reserves weren't able to train with them until the last minute. Preston, Andrew Blowers, Blair Larsen, and Mark Allen were in the starting line-up for the Eastern Province match but because the test preparation took priority, their only full session with the midweekers was on the Sunday before a game.

Eastern Province had been an afternoon match in the original itinerary. SARFU then informed the NZRFU that they were considering staging it at night to attract a bigger gate. At the request of the All Black management, the NZRFU objected; a night game would make it impossible to get to Durban for the vital Wednesday morning training run. The alternative – splitting the party and sending the test team to Durban early – was even less acceptable. SARFU went ahead and re-scheduled the game anyway, undertaking to put on a charter flight to get the All Blacks to Durban by midnight Tuesday.

The Eastern Province union had lured Alex Wyllie to South Africa but he'd moved on – obviously to higher things – and his replacement hadn't lasted long. Despite instability on the coaching front, the indications were that Eastern Province would push the midweek side hard. The weather made a tough assignment even more difficult; by nightfall, the strong winds which habitually buffet Port Elizabeth were accompanied by heavy rain.

The All Blacks produced another schizophrenic performance. "We settled well but, once again, the second half blues took hold," says John Hart. "EP climbed all over us, getting as close as 26-23 before a late Matthew Cooper try got us home. Eric Rush had a good game, Cooper was solid and timed his runs well, the two debutants came through a difficult game in credit, and Preston goal-kicked well in the tricky wind. After that, there wasn't a whole lot to enthuse about. The defence was average, Spencer had a horror game, and the forwards knew they'd been in a contest which they failed to dominate."

The game had jangled a few nerves in the All Black camp. Before the night was much older, their nervous systems were going to get a real working-over. After a perfunctory aftermatch function, they were bused to the airport for the flight to Durban. They were expecting a jet. What they got was a propellor-driven Hawker Siddeley which looked as if it had just been de-mothballed from some vintage aircraft museum. As for the pilot of this museum piece, he looked old enough to have learned his stuff from the Wright brothers.

It was an invidious choice: chocks away on Air Doom or compromise the test build-up by not getting to Durban until the following afternoon.

Richard Fry was all for hitch-hiking to Durban. Shortly before the tour, he and three friends had boarded a private flight for a fishing trip to Great Barrier Island. The plane crashed on take-off from North Shore Airport; miraculously, everyone on board walked away. The experience had greatly increased Fry's respect for the laws of gravity and his knuckles were whiter than most that night.

Hart: "I'm sure Hawker Siddeleys are safe aircraft but that particular plane didn't inspire confidence – if anything, the interior was even worse than the exterior. It was a hair-raising experience which took an hour longer than it was meant to so we didn't reach Durban until the early hours of Wednesday morning. SARFU had done us no favours by insisting on a night game."

Meanwhile, the Springboks were also experiencing a little turbulence. Their main strategic weapon – the scrum – had been neutralised at Cape Town and the fall-out from James Small's adventures in clubland continued. After SARFU had taken disciplinary action against Small, Springbok manager Morne du Plessis expressed regret that the matter hadn't been left to him and his management team. The implication was that if they'd been allowed to deal with it in-house, Small wouldn't have been banished from the fold. Even as du Plessis was distancing himself from SARFU's action, rumours persisted that the entire Springbok camp had had a gutsful of Small and his big night out was just a convenient excuse to show him the door. Still marching to a different drum, Small promptly jetted off for a European holiday.

The unconcussed Os du Randt, by contrast, had been forgiven for throwing in the towel but that was over-shadowed by the choice of the Northern Transvaal hooker Henry Tromp to replace John Allan. In 1992, Tromp and his father had punished a black farm worker accused of stealing by thrashing him with a fan-belt; the man later died. Even by the old regime's standards, this was regarded as somewhat heavy-handed and Tromp went to jail, serving four months of a two-year sentence.

While white South Africans had been outraged to learn that a black cabinet minister had cheered his head off when Craig Dowd scored his match-sealing try at Newlands, Tromp's selection was hardly the way to generate support for the Springboks among the black and coloured communities. The old South African flag had reappeared at the Wallabies-Springboks test at Bloemfontein in the Orange Free State, the Boer heartland. It all suggested that, far from being the catalyst for national unity it had appeared at the World Cup, rugby was reverting to its traditional role of being a fundamental expression of Afrikaner culture.

Less contentiously, Steve Atherton had been replaced by Hannes Strydom at lock and the tall Free State flanker Andre Venter had come in for François Pienaar with the impressive Gary Teichmann taking over the captaincy. Venter would add mobility but faced a big step up in intensity given that his province hadn't taken part in the Super 12. The musical chairs continued at halfback; Johan Roux had recovered from 'flu and was preferred to Joost van der Westhuizen. This time, though, Andre Markgraaff would manage to have it both ways.

Injuries at training deprived the Springboks of their Transvaal centres Hennie le Roux and Japie Mulder. Mulder was a big loss – he was the hub of their midfield defence and, in Hart's estimation, a world-class player. According to the rumour mill, which scored highly for productivity if nothing else, le Roux's absence had more to do with his financial dispute with SARFU than his physical condition. They were replaced by the youthful Northern Transvaal pair of Danie van Schalkwyk and Andre Snyman whose inexperience was a major topic in the All Blacks' tactical discussions. Despite the return of Andre Joubert, making it seven changes in all, the Springbok backline looked low on strike-power.

With all that to contend with, it couldn't have been an easy build-up for the Springboks. Hart didn't take too much comfort from that: he was sure they'd draw motivation from adversity and come out breathing fire. And as the media kept reminding everyone, the Springboks had lost only once in 15 tests at Kings Park – to Australia in 1933.

Hart and his fellow selectors didn't hesitate to replace Mehrtens with Simon 'Nibs' Culhane despite the fact that he'd had very little rugby in 1996 – two Super 12 matches, two invitational games, a couple of outings for the Divisional team, and the tour opener.

"He's an excellent trainer, very committed, and one of the

better tackling first-fives," says Hart. "The question was, would he have the sharpness for this level given his lack of match time? A late change in a pivotal position can have a negative impact but the team had a lot of confidence in him."

Lomu had dispatched his opposite number with a piston-like fend on his way to a try at Port Elizabeth but still wasn't stretching out. He was, however, included in the reserves to cover for Wilson. With the panel going back to the conventional three back/three forward formula, there was no room among the reserves for Blowers who'd done well at Newlands. Lomu would also cover the loose forwards and going by the amazing lift-off he achieved at the pre-game lineout practice on the beach, he'd certainly add something to the lineout if he got on the field. He was one jumper who didn't need a lift.

It would be Sean Fitzpatrick's 81st test, making him the most-capped forward of all time. Fittingly, he was overtaking the legendary Willie John McBride, another indestructible warrior who led a team to glory in South Africa. Fitzpatrick had left the field once – with ten minutes to go and the opposition crushed – and missed only one test since 1986 – when he was rested from the slaughter of the innocents, the 1995 World Cup pool game against Japan. It's a record which speaks volumes for his consistency and durability as well as testifying to the existence of an implacable will.

The All Black management enlisted the aid of Ian Borthwick, a New Zealand-born journalist who works for the French sporting paper, L'Equipe, to act as an interpreter in their discussions with the French referee Patrick Thomas. Although lacking on-field experience of the new rules, Thomas seemed to be on the right wavelength.

"Both he and his compatriot Didier Mene, who took the Pretoria test, proved very good, particularly in applying the advantage," says Hart. "Being young men as international referees go, they weren't fazed by the speed of the game. One can't help but think that some of the older, less athletic referees will struggle to meet the increased fitness demands imposed by the pace and continuity of the modern game."

Starting with the Western Samoan game in Napier, the panel had got into the ritual of going out for a Chinese meal on the eve of a test. There was no particular superstition involved; Hart just happened to like Chinese food and was sure that, in time, Ross Cooper and Gordon Hunter would come to share his enthusiasm.

In Durban, however, the trio arrived at the recommended restaurant to find it was a Mecca for every All Black supporters group in the republic. Not wanting an ear-bashing with their wontons, they headed back to the hotel. They passed another Chinese restaurant which was about to close; with a little help from his police card, Hunter managed to persuade them to stay open a bit longer.

An alarm woke Hart at 4am that morning. It was what Dame Edna Everidge might call 'a spooky coincidence': the night before the Cape Town test, a car alarm had gone off not far from the All Blacks' hotel and wailed through the night. It came from a rental van parked on the street. This time, Hart decided to investigate. He went for a walk and found that it was a waterfront kiosk's burglar alarm which had been set off by the wind. Hart got a phone number off the kiosk and asked the hotel staff to contact the owner to get the alarm turned off. The racket ceased an hour later. South African schemes to disrupt touring All Black teams are the stuff of legend and range from the sinister to the lurid. The kiosk burglar alarm seemed to be an accident; Hart wasn't so sure about the rental van.

At Kings Park, the All Blacks started well for a change – the coach's nerves would be stretched later in the game. After the Springboks had been penalised for hurling themselves into a ruck and then marched ten metres for lip, Justin Marshall ran a tap penalty in his own half. He transferred to Zinzan Brooke who found Osborne in space on the left. He went round Roux, sat Joubert on his backside, and set up a ruck inside the Springbok 22. The ball was flipped along the chain to Wilson who finished in style. A few minutes later, Culhane found the mark after another ruck infringement – 8-0.

With a quarter of the game gone, Stransky pulled three points back but then the All Black veterans showed their class. After Josh Kronfeld had bolted up the middle, Frank Bunce showed eye-popping speed off the mark before taking out two defenders with a pass. Zinzan Brooke's hands were a blur as he made the transfer to Christian Cullen who wormed under Joubert's tackle. This time, Culhane drilled it from the right touchline. Twenty-two minutes gone, 15-3 up – sweet dreams are made of this.

Stransky kept the Springboks in touch but he could have done better than that – he managed only three goals from seven attempts in the half. Perhaps the gashed forehead he suffered early on scrambled his radar because the misses included two of the worst shanks of all time. It was 15-9 at halftime.

After an exchange of penalties, the All Blacks scored what proved to be the decisive try. They attacked on the left with the forwards doing most of the work, then Walter Little exposed the Springboks with a precise crossfield kick. Wilson harassed Pieter Hendricks and freed the ball to Fitzpatrick who thoughtfully delegated the 20-metre sprint to the corner to his lieutenant Zinzan Brooke. Never one to shirk a challenge, Brooke got there in style, holding off the cover-defending Roux with an imperious fend.

It was time to go for the jugular. Perhaps the moment came and went when Little charged down a kick and gathered the ball with a clear field in front of him only for Zinzan Brooke to be penalised for detaching early from the scrum. It was uncomfortably reminiscent of Mulder's miniscule knock-on at Newlands when he blew the opportunity which might well have nailed it for the Springboks.

The All Blacks went through a flat patch and the Boks cranked it up. They ran into heavy defence – Zinzan Brooke almost cutting the luckless Stransky in half – but eventually van Schalkwyk scored from a tap penalty move. The conversion made it 23-19 with twenty minutes to go. The match was wide open.

As they'd done all season, the All Blacks finished strongly and looked like outlasting their opponents. Perhaps frustrated by the stalemate as the game wound down, Markgraaff threw caution and decorum to the winds. Hart watched in disbelief as the South Africans made two blatant tactical substitutions, flouting the strict requirement that players must be examined by a doctor and deemed unable to continue before they can be replaced. First, Kobus Wiese came on for Strydom who rather spoilt the effect of his assisted hobble to the sideline by hurdling an advertising billboard. The return to the arena of the gigantic Wiese, a powerhouse lock and influential figure in South African rugby, was a significant event in the context of the series.

Secondly and inevitably, van der Westhuizen replaced Roux. Far from bothering to feign injury, Roux emphasised the brazenness of it all by jogging off the field. Perhaps it was meant as a protest.

"Roux was clearly upset at being pulled off," says Hart. "He told me afterwards that he'd let his management know exactly how he felt about it. It was evident that they weren't exactly clear on what they were trying to do at halfback. They had a choice between

Fotopress

Meet the media: the All Black selection panel of Ross Cooper (left), Hart and Gordon Hunter conduct another press conference. In the background, Jane Dent keeps an eye on things.

John Selkirk

Pep talk – the coach delivers his halftime message.

Before the deluge. Hart talks tactics with Jonah Lomu at Athletic Park before the 1996 Bledisloe Cup clash.

John Hart sees the funny side of the All Blacks' scrummaging at training before meeting South Africa at Lancaster Park in 1996. It gave the Springboks something to think about, too.

Jeff Wilson touches down for his sublime chip and chase try at Pretoria, 1996.

Injury and fatigue complicated the All Blacks' preparation for their final test in South Africa. Here Hart looks on as Zinzan Brooke receives attention.

Fulltime at Loftus Versfeld, Justin Marshall and Zinzan Brooke are elated; Andre Venter and Joost van der Westhuizen take defeat hard.

The Dirty Dirties perform their celebratory haka in the grandstand. The white-shirted gentleman in the right foreground is a study in contrast.

John Selkirk

Manager Mike Banks (left) and the coaching team of Hunter, Hart and Cooper go onto Loftus Versfeld to greet the All Blacks.

Winners are grinners: John Hart and Sean Fitzpatrick savour the historic series win in South Africa.

Fruits of victory... coach and captain show off the silverware during the Queen Street tickertape parade.

brittle brilliance and predictable solidity, between a runner and a kicker. Seeing they didn't have a player who combined both, I guess they decided substitution was the next best thing."

Although they couldn't put the Springboks away, the All Blacks held on. It was all going according to plan.

Hart: "It was a crucial win. From the outset, we'd been desperate to avoid having to play a decider at Ellis Park at the end of the tour when the odds would be stacked against us. We'd also been very keen to maintain the psychological edge we'd gained at Newlands. That we'd done – they'd thrown everything at us but we were still standing and in fact had finished the stronger.

"One South African writer described the Springboks as 'manly and competitive but boring.' I didn't think they were boring at all – they didn't chance their arm that much but then Bunce did a great job of shutting down Joubert, their most potent attacker. Without le Roux, Mulder, Small, and – for most of the game – van der Westhuizen, we could focus on Joubert as the only real attacking threat. The inexperience of the Northern Transvaal midfield backs had been exposed under pressure – they'd dropped passes at critical times. The Boks had fielded a huge scrum but failed to put us under pressure. Now we were headed up to the high veldt where Markgraaff had promised we'd learn what scrummaging was all about. I'm not sure that they still believed they had much to teach us."

Tromp's performance hadn't compensated for the damage done by his selection. He'd been brought in to bolster the scrum but the All Blacks had maintained their edge there. They'd gone out to pressure the Springbok lineout in order to put the heat on Tromp's throwing-in; he wasn't as accurate as the man he'd replaced so what little they'd gained at the scrum, they lost at the lineout.

For the media, the hot item was South Africa's tactical substitutions. Hart happily stirred the pot: "I complained that what they'd done was illegal. I supported the principle of tactical substitutions but the rules didn't allow it and, until they were changed, we had to abide by them."

Wiese's introduction was in fact a salutary lesson in the dangers of tactical substitutions. Four points behind and pressing hard, South Africa had the put-in to a scrum just outside the All Black 22. The scrum was delayed while South Africa changed their locks. Sensing that the Boks might take time to reorganise, the All Blacks ploughed into them. Wiese's high and ineffective body position amidst the tangled wreckage of the Springbok scrum indicated that he wasn't prepared, either in terms of technique or concentration, for a confrontation of such intensity. With their scrum disintegrating, the Boks infringed, losing possession and momentum.

Fitzpatrick considered that that scrum settled the outcome. Markgraaff learned the hard way that making a tactical substitution is like proposing marriage – you've got to choose your moment carefully.

17

HOLY GRAIL

J ONAH Lomu and Carlos Spencer had a lot riding on the third midweek game, against Western Transvaal at Potchefstroom. Lomu was running out of opportunities to salvage something from a tour which was shaping as a major come-down from his larger-than-life deeds at the World Cup. For Spencer, it was a chance to get back on track and rebuild his confidence after his wretched experience at Port Elizabeth.

John Hart spoke to Spencer in Durban: "Even with Andrew Mehrtens injured, Carlos had taken himself out of the test frame. He was quite dejected, a little homesick, and his mind wasn't really on the job so we had to get him back on the field as quickly as possible. He has huge natural talent but I stressed the importance of developing his goal-kicking. Touring can be lonely when things aren't going your way: management and senior players have to be alert to individuals becoming disenchanted and move quickly to bring them back into the fold. Young guys striving to succeed but not managing to do so can quickly get it into their heads that the world's against them."

This match would be a test of character for the midweek side. The tourists were now on the high veldt and conventional wisdom is that you need six days' preparation to get used to altitude. The alternative is the hit-and-run: going up the night before or even on the morning of the game. The All Blacks had gone up to Pretoria on the Sunday which gave the test side time to adjust but left the midweekers betwixt and between.

There was also the motivation factor. Given the test team's success, it was unrealistic for many of the midweekers to aspire to higher things. The panel kept reminding them that they could still stake a claim for the future. Whatever their aspirations, the first step was to lift their collective game and eradicate the lapses into mediocrity which had marred their displays to date.

With Potchefstroom lacking a suitable hotel, the team faced a two-hour bus trip from Pretoria on the morning of the match. Not wanting to subject the test side to four hours on a bus, the management decided to make an exception to the rule and split the tour party; when the wagon-train left for Potchefstroom, the test XV stayed behind.

Western Transvaal were meant to be easy meat but the omens weren't good. The hotel where the team had brunch had a distinct Fawlty Towers feel about it but even Basil Fawlty's brow-beaten guests would have downed utensils when the food finally arrived. Strictly speaking, it was what had been ordered but the proof of the pudding is in the eating and there was no rush to perform the role of food-taster. It was an awkward scene; most of the players decided to go without. Doctor John Mayhew – whose brief included nutrition – was embarrassed, and the hotel's banqueting manageress was in tears.

Perhaps because the coach has never let him forget it, Mayhew becomes a touch defensive when the words "inedible" and "Potchefstroom" are mentioned in the same sentence: "It was the midweek team's best win so the food can't have been that bad."

Stomachs rumbling, the players got back on the bus and went looking for a pitch where they could stretch their legs and put a ball through the hands. Potchefstroom isn't exactly a teeming metropolis but it took forever to find the ground. When they got there, Murphy's Law was still in force; Lomu's knee was locking and he couldn't run freely.

It was overcast but unlikely to rain, according to the local experts. They were right. To say it rained in Potchefstroom that afternoon is like saying it gets a bit nippy in Siberia. It was pelting down when the All Blacks got to the ground but that was just a prelude to a torrential downpour, accompanied by hail, lightning, and a plunge in the temperature. The pitch was flooded and there was talk of delaying, if not cancelling, the game. The All Blacks wanted to play, though, and Mike Banks persuaded the match officials to go ahead.

It was a strange sort of day and about to get stranger. Keith Quinn takes up the story: "If I don't know the players in one of the teams, I'm not satisfied just going off the jersey numbers – I like to go down when they arrive in their blazers and get someone to put names to faces. It was lashing down with rain so about 45 minutes before kick-off, Wayne Graham and I went under the stand and knocked on the door of the Western Transvaal dressing room. I told them who we were and asked if we could come in and check the faces. That was fine. It was a small dressing room and there were eight or nine players in various states of undress. The manager introduced them and I made a few notes – moustache, knobbly knees, headband, that sort of thing. I asked where the rest of them were. The manager took us through to a room off the dressing room where four or five players were lined up in front of a guy who looked like a doctor – he had a medical bag. He was giving them injections in the backside. The stuff in the syringe was a sort of light ale colour. No-one objected to us being there and the manager just carried on introducing the players. Meanwhile, I'm wondering why they're getting jabs in the backside this late in the day."

Mayhew had long harboured reservations about the seriousness of South African rugby's commitment to stamping out drugs, given their refusal to act on positive drug tests from 1992 to 1995 on the grounds that they wouldn't stand up in court. Nothing he'd seen on tour had allayed his fears; he was appalled by the sloppiness of the procedures which were wide-open to abuse. He's bemused by what Quinn witnessed in the Western Transvaal dressing room: "It could have been quite innocuous but it's unusual to say the least."

Fitness expert Marty Toomey offers this perspective on what's going on over there: "You see a lot of pretty normal guys in South Africa. They're not all huge."

Western Transvaal brought on new props at halftime and replaced their hooker a few minutes into the second half. One of the substituted props, Rocco Peddar, was later found to have failed the post-match drug test. A strange day indeed.

Ignoring these bizarre happenings and the truly awful conditions, the All Blacks played superbly, winning 31-0. Eric Rush mudlarked productively, Alama Ieremia was assertive, Phil Coffin caught and passed with aplomb to send Spencer on his way to a try, and Chresten Davis came through his first full game satisfactorily. Although Lomu had another unmemorable afternoon, Spencer shone, mixing solidity with his trademark flair and finesse.

The test team had been given a couple of days off and had a gym session rather than full-blown training that Tuesday. When Hart got back to Pretoria, he was button-holed by Sean Fitzpatrick and a couple of senior players. They were bored; they missed the discipline of training. They wanted to get back to work.

Speaking of discipline, the previous day Hart had had a remarkable conversation with Lester Mills, rugby writer for the *Pretoria News*, who'd complimented him on the team's discipline. Mills knew what he was talking about; he admitted that he'd been on the All Blacks' trail for six weeks looking for dirt but hadn't found a speck. Perhaps it was pent-up frustration which caused him to burst into print a couple of days later, accusing the All Black management of being unhelpful to the South African media.

"On tour, there's always an issue over what extra privileges you give 'your' media – the Kiwi journalists accompanying the team – as opposed to the locals," says Hart. "Now and again, we held sessions solely for the New Zealand media: some were purely social, some involved extra briefing. While you want to be fair to everyone, surely all touring teams feel an extra responsibility to their own media who are, after all, their channel to the people at home."

Andrew Mehrtens had made a startling recovery from his knee operation. The arthroscopic surgery had revealed that the ligament wasn't damaged and he was on an exercycle within 48 hours. He was so frisky during the warm-up for Wednesday's training run that Hart asked him to do some kicking. He went through it quite freely but confessed afterwards that he wasn't entirely confident. That was enough to persuade the selectors that it would be too risky to rush him into the upcoming test although he'd definitely come into consideration for the series finale at Johannesburg.

That was the only issue in the starting line-up. The panel did make a change to the reserves, restoring Andrew Blowers to a two back/four forward bench. With his strength and athleticism, Blowers appealed as a player who could make a real impact in the closing stages of a game and with the wear and tear on the test loose forwards, it was likely that he'd be needed. Josh Kronfeld was visibly tired and Zinzan Brooke's chronic pelvic injury was seriously restricting his training.

Hart: "I never ceased to marvel at the way Zinzan always fronted up on the day. It was the most fundamental challenge facing any athlete: going through the pain barrier. It wasn't that he was aggravating his condition because playing wouldn't make it any worse but he could hardly walk after a game. I explained to Lomu why he was being left out of the reserves. He was coming right and keen to play but, as we now know, he was battling his kidney condition which was reflected in his mood swings."

As usual, the make-up of the Springbok team was generating plenty of speculation. The big questions were, would Japie Mulder play and would the two run-on subs at Kings Park – Joost van der Westhuizen and Kobus Wiese – be in the starting line-up this time? With Loftus Versfeld being van der Westhuizen's home ground and the Springboks having to win to keep the series alive, Hart was sure he'd be a starter and expected Wiese to be out there for the national anthems as well. In the event, the only change was at halfback.

Concerned by the firestorm of publicity over tactical substitutions, the Springbok manager Morne du Plessis suggested a meeting to take the heat out of the situation. On the Thursday, Banks and Hart met du Plessis and Markgraaff at a hotel between Pretoria and Johannesburg. They agreed that, while the law was an ass – how can a doctor tell from a cursory examination whether a player's feigning a muscle strain or a back injury? – it shouldn't be openly flouted. It amounted to a tacit agreement to have tactical substitutions but, for appearance's sake, only after the players being replaced had undergone a medical check. They also resolved to lobby the IRB to allow tactical substitutions and increase the number of reserves.

"Both men were under pressure," recalls Hart. "It was clear that du Plessis' days were numbered which was a pity because he's a fine man. Markgraaff and I had talked about going out for a meal together but it didn't happen – those relationships are very hard to get off the ground in an ultra-competitive environment."

Not surprisingly, the subject of substitutions also came up at the meeting with the French referee, Didier Mene. Hart promised to do it by the book. He was impressed when Patrick Thomas, who refereed the Durban test, asked for a meeting to review his performance: "I thought it showed humility, a drive to improve, and a readiness to listen to others."

The injured Springbok lock Johan Ackerman was among the observers at one All Black training session. He seemed particularly interested in the scrummaging; if he'd got much closer, the All Blacks would have had a nine-man scrum. That was taking openness too far and he was asked to keep his distance.

"Ackerman's a nice guy and I was sad to see him get caught in the drugs mire in 1997," says Hart. "I think he was just curious and wanted to say hello to the All Blacks but I'm not sure the Springboks would have welcomed Ian Jones at one of their training runs."

The All Blacks were confronted by the greatest challenge of all: the Springboks at altitude. Moreover, it was a Springbok team under phenomenal pressure to maintain their proud home record against New Zealand. Despite that and the momentousness of the occasion, the team was very relaxed. Hart believes that teams often get tense because the management has created a tense atmosphere. He and Fitzpatrick agreed that there was quite enough tension and expectation in the rarefied air without them adding to it.

"Hart did a superb job of preparing the test team for Loftus," says Fitzpatrick. "Maybe another coach would've thrashed us at training but he understood what we needed and respected our ability to know what was best for us. It was the philosophy of being accountable and represented a big change from the previous four years – the only time we were thrashed at training was when we needed it. The players knew what was expected of them and knew they had to do a lot of the hard work in their own time."

Hart had sensed fatigue start to set in after the Durban test. He feared that the relentless schedule was taking its toll and fretted that the team might not have enough gas left in the tank to complete the mission. Perhaps his fears partly reflected the shape he himself was in.

Says Ross Cooper, "Harty found it really hard and I don't know how he kept going. His mind raced. He didn't sleep well. I roomed next to him and I could hear him pacing up and down. I couldn't understand why he put himself under so much pressure – three hours of media a day, trying to organise everybody. We started trying to take the heat off, telling him, 'For Christ's sake, go and have a game of golf, we'll look after things.' The trouble was, all the media wanted to talk to him. He wanted everything to be right but he was getting tired."

Test day brought bad news for the Auckland contingent – Taranaki had lifted the Ranfurly Shield. Bull Allen wore an ear-to-ear grin but the senior Aucklanders, who stay in close touch with events at home while on tour, were disappointed. North Harbour had the first challenge and, as far as the North Harbour All Blacks were concerned, the shield was already in an open car making a triumphant progress through the streets of Takapuna. Hart felt obliged to point out that North Harbour had already had to cancel one tickertape parade when their shield challenge failed to bring home the bacon.

Destiny beckoned. Only the 1960 All Blacks had got this far – taking the field knowing that victory would secure a series win. But that prize had eluded them as it had eluded all those who'd gone before and since, many of them among the greatest names in New Zealand rugby. It had fallen to these men to erase this maddening blot on the All Blacks' stupendous record and lay the South African bogey once and for all. Perhaps it was just as well that the significance of it was largely lost on some of them.

"The history of it probably wasn't all that significant within the team," says Fitzpatrick. "Some of the young guys like Christian Cullen were only just born when the All Blacks last played a series in South Africa so they didn't really get it. It really brought home to me what it meant to the old All Blacks for us to beat them when I saw Murray Mexted with tears in his eyes after the Cape Town test."

It was a brilliantly sunny day, about 25 degrees. There was a small but vociferous group of Kiwis among the 51,000 at Loftus Versfeld which is yet another of the magnificent stadiums which grace South African rugby.

The need to start well had been a mantra in the All Blacks' preparation. Early points on the board would reinforce the doubt in the Springboks' minds. And with the heat, the altitude, and the fatigue factor to contend with, the last thing the All Blacks wanted was to have to play catch-up in the final quarter.

The game plan was to take it to the Springboks from the bell. They went out with the same attitude and the game started at a frenetic pace. The opening sequence went on and on but it was the Springboks who had field position; the All Blacks played into their hands by spurning chances to clear the danger zone and continuing to move the ball under pressure. Boxed in in the corner, Jeff Wilson brilliantly avoided conceding a lineout but the Springboks ran his kick straight back. Justin Marshall's desperation cover tackle on van der Westhuizen only delayed the inevitable. The Springbok pack sealed off the ball and heaved their way to the line. Joel Stransksy's kick hit the upright. Three minutes gone, 0-5. It wasn't meant to be this way.

But the setback hadn't dented the All Blacks' confidence with ball in hand. After some high-risk pass-the-parcel behind the forwards, Marshall broke the line and weaved his way up the middle with the locking partners ranged either side in support. They got the ball to Jeff Wilson who primly deposited it behind the posts. Robin Brooke's pass to Ian Jones looked forward but then so had Stransky's to Mark Andrews in the build-up to the Springboks' try. After twelve minutes of vibrant, passionate rugby, it was almost back to square one.

The Boks quickly regained the lead from a dubious late-charge penalty but the All Black counter-punch was a gem: Zinzan Brooke moved it blind off a strong scrum; Marshall fed Cullen who'd timed his run to perfection and put Wilson outside his man. Wilson chipped Joubert and burned off the chasers. Right on cue, the ball sat up perfectly for him. Simon Culhane converted from near the touchline. Twenty-three minutes gone, 14-8. Things were back on track.

"Wilson hadn't had a great season, falling short of his standards at Lancaster Park and Suncorp," says Hart. "We'd talked to him about the need for concentration and consistency – it was just a matter of the little things, the basics, letting him down. Once it all clicked, his immense talent would flower. We'd been delaying the ball at the back of the scrum too much, giving the defence a chance to organise. In this game we decided to go for quick release and Wilson's second try was a direct result of that tactical change."

The All Blacks continued to threaten. Shortly before halftime, Frank Bunce foreshadowed his bravura performance at Ellis Park a year later with a searing outside break from a lineout. He unloaded to Cullen who chose to go it alone with Glen Osborne unmarked outside him. Andre Snyman dragged him down a few metres short of the line but luckily for the All Blacks, especially number 15, the ball went dead off a Springbok boot to give them a five-metre scrum. Zinzan Brooke went to his bag of tricks and dusted off a scrum move last used against the Barbarians at Twickenham in 1989: Marshall on a lateral run flicked the ball to Walter Little cutting back against the tide; he made a lightning transfer to Brooke who surged through Stransky's tackle to score. The conversion made it 21-8.

After giving the Springboks a five-point start, Hart would have happily settled for a 13-point lead and the momentum going into the second half. But on the stroke of halftime, Michael Jones floored Andre Venter with a highish tackle. The crowd and Gary Teichmann reacted and Mene awarded a centrefield penalty which Stransky thumped over.

For the All Black management, the first forty minutes had been more trying than they needed to be; thoughtless ticketing had placed them slap-bang in the middle of a public area. The atmosphere was oppressive and Hart was spat on as he walked out to speak to the team.

"The big message was self-belief," he says. "I told the team that they had to keep taking it to the Boks because I sensed they were tired. I knew we were tired too but once you start talking about conserving and defending, you're effectively conceding the initiative. If we sat on the lead and let them back into the game, they'd really lift but if we kept the pressure on, they'd have to make the play. Perhaps we overdid it; there were a couple of instances in the second half when we kept moving the ball across the field looking for space until the movement broke down and we gave away a scrum. We'd have been better off taking the ball into a midfield ruck and getting some control."

There'd been a couple of health scares during the first half; Wilson had suffered a dizzy spell and Zinzan Brooke had collapsed while jogging back to halfway after a try.

"Zinzan has a condition known as atrial fibrillation," says Mayhew. "Erratic heartbeart in layman's terms – the heart can race to 200 beats a minute. It's controlled by medication provided he can be bothered taking it. I don't know what caused Jeff's dizziness. He came back from Argentina in 1993 below par and had some tests which were negative. He's a bit different – he needs a little more TLC than most."

When word of Wilson's dizziness came through from the medical team, Hart ruefully recalled the decision to take Lomu out of the reserves. The panel were confident that Ieremia would do a reasonable job on the wing but the reality was he couldn't foot it with the specialists over 50 metres. Wilson was still distressed at halftime so Hart told Ieremia to warm up.

Wiese had replaced Strydom after 26 minutes and in the second half the talented if volatile and injury-prone James Dalton came on for Henry Tromp. Ironically, given all the fuss, the injuries appeared to be genuine.

Which is more than the All Black medical team would say about many of the stoppages which punctuated the game. "Both

South Africa and Australia pulled fake injuries when they got tired or to reorganise their patterns on attack and defence," says David Abercrombie. "The referees didn't control it well but it's hard to detect. Look who gets injured – it's the halfback or frontrowers at scrum time so the ref can't just wave play on. Van der Westhuizen went down three or four times for things that weren't real. Zinny went over and slapped him on the back; on TV it would've looked like friendly concern but it was far from it – he was telling him, in very plain English, to get up and get on with it."

The verbal exchanges were almost as uncompromising as the physical ones that afternoon. "The Springboks are pretty good at sledging," says Abercrombie, "mostly along the lines of how they're harder than we are. Fitzy and Zinny do a lot too but it's to annoy people and put them off their game."

When Culhane kicked a penalty three minutes after halftime, it seemed, briefly, as if the second half would be a formality. No such luck. With their backs to the wall, the Springboks' desperation reached fever pitch. It was never going to be any other way: on television the night before, du Plessis had vowed that the game wouldn't be won before the final whistle, that his men would go all the way to the wire, that there was no way the All Blacks would win.

Midway through the half, the wheels fell off the black machine. The Springbok pack got up a head of steam and stormed the All Black line. There was nothing remotely subtle about it. They took a short-range tap penalty and it was a case of "here we come, stop us if you can." The All Blacks couldn't. Hart detected an ominous weariness and lack of urgency in their failure to hold back the dark-green avalanche.

The referee called the kick-off short, a line-ball decision. The Boks worked a back-row move off the scrum and battered their way upfield, maintaining the physical pressure. Van der Westhuizen popped a kick over the ruck and Cullen, unfathomably, let it bounce. The bounce wasn't kind. It was panic stations at the back as van der Westhuizen, as sharp-witted and swift a predator as there is in the game, stole in like a thief in the night. Stransky hit the woodwork for the second time to leave the All Blacks clinging to a one-point lead.

The glittering prize was starting to slip away. "We'd gone flat," says Hart. "Maybe we were burned out and used up; maybe we were going to struggle to compete in the final fifteen minutes. We'd squandered the lead, partly through our own mistakes, but you couldn't help but admire the grim ferocity of the Springbok onslaught. The hard-edged Ruben Kruger, who seemed a better player without Pienaar, was becoming a very influential figure."

Fitzpatrick: "It was a nightmare. As in Durban, we had them on the rack and should've put them away. We missed a kick which would've nailed it and they came right back at us. We could see that they were stuffed but they wouldn't give in."

Culhane had broken his wrist and was replaced by Jon Preston. The first time Preston touched the ball was to place it for a 38-metre kick at goal. In the grandstand, Hart was remembering the goal-kickers' practice session at Loftus 24 hours earlier: Wilson had landed a couple of monsters, Culhane had sprayed them around, Preston had been immaculate. That hadn't changed – 27-23.

Stransky brought it back to a one-point ballgame seven minutes later. The tension was becoming unbearable. It was test rugby stripped down to its physical and emotional essence – 30 players pushing themselves to the limits of their endurance for the emblem on their left breasts. The New Zealanders looked out on their feet when Michael Jones read a Springbok backline move and pulled off an interception. He was in the clear but there were almost 50 metres to go and this wasn't the 22-year-old openside flyer who'd bedazzled the rugby world in 1987. This was the patched-up, remodelled version whose specification didn't include runaway tries. Van der Westhuizen ran him down inside the 22, Kronfeld was penalised for leaving his feet, and the opportunity was lost.

Eight minutes to go: Hart made a double substitution to shore up the forward effort, sending on Blair Larsen for Ian Jones and Blowers for Kronfeld. Jones had injured his knee but Kronfeld justified his departure with a convincing portrayal of a man with a damaged shoulder.

Six minutes to go: Blowers set up a midfield ruck on halfway. The Springboks went off their feet and gave away a penalty.

"Before the game, I'd told Fitzpatrick to give Wilson a crack at any long-range penalty opportunities because of Culhane's lack of distance," says Hart. "But now Preston, who was striking it with precision, was out there. I was screaming at Gordon Hunter, who operated the communications link to the medical team, telling him to get a message down to the field that Preston should take the kick."

It's a wonder that Olo Brown wasn't given the job. Hunter was worried that the communications were being eavesdropped on so he'd devised a code which involved referring to individuals by the name of whoever had played in their position in the previous game – for example, if he meant Cullen, he'd say Cooper. Clearly, the code wasn't designed to cover the eventuality of Preston at first-five.

When Fitzpatrick offered him the kick, Preston didn't hesitate. He didn't have a reputation as a siege-gun goal-kicker but, at altitude, sweetly-struck kicks fly like migrating birds. Preston was a battler who trained harder than anyone and practised his goal-kicking religiously. It was as if he'd honed his body and skills knowing that some day the call would come. He made perfect contact and had range to burn – 30-26. It would take more than a penalty or a dropped goal to deny the All Blacks now.

Three minutes to go. Field position was everything. The All Blacks were at the end of their tethers, playing on instinct, but they clawed their way back into Springbok territory. Bunce set up a centrefield ruck on the 22. As Marshall stooped for the ball, he heard Zinzan Brooke call for it.

As Hart saw Brooke steady for the drop kick, a vision of a charge-down and runaway try flashed through his mind – there wasn't a black jersey behind the number 8. But Brooke doesn't contemplate failure. Whereas some shy away from taking responsibility, he revels in it. Where some see the risk of letting the team down, he sees the chance to be a hero.

Ahead 33-26, the All Blacks couldn't lose but a converted try would earn the Springboks a draw and the chance to level the series at Johannesburg. The mission could still fail. Even though Stransky's goal-kicking had been moderate at best, Fitzpatrick was stone-cold certain that he wouldn't miss if he got the chance to keep the series alive with a last-gasp conversion.

One minute to go. The Springboks had also played themselves to a standstill but they dredged up the energy for a final charge, winning a throw-in 15 metres from the All Black line. Here was danger. The Springboks loved this situation; they'd make a clean catch and use their bulk and strength to chug all the way to the try-line. Dalton connected with Andrews but the driving maul went to ground within a few metres – it looked as if the All Blacks took it down. Van der Westhuizen went to his backs. Joubert hit the line at pace but was ripped down by his nemesis Bunce. He still managed to get the ball away to Pieter Hendricks whose bounced pass deprived the unmarked Justin Swart of a precious second.

Seeing the cover coming, Swart doubled back to the left-hand touchline to link with his forwards. They drove. Mene missed

Venter's slight fumble at the back of the ruck. Venter made a couple of metres; when he was halted, Os du Randt took over. The All Blacks were penalised for killing the ball, Mene turning a Nelsonian eye to Kruger's after-the-whistle stomping spree. Van der Westhuizen tapped and darted for the corner. Robin Brooke bowled him into touch but was penalised for not retreating. During the Super 12, New Zealand referees had dished out penalty tries for similar offences.

Injury time. The Springboks were five metres short. Their pack huddled, planning the assault. Mene checked his watch. It was a carbon copy of the situation twenty minutes earlier which had produced Kruger's try: tap and roll, stop us if you can. Zinzan Brooke and the two props launched themselves at the Springboks, going low to stop the first wave in their tracks before the momentum became irresistible. The Boks peeled off and tried again, making another metre before Michael Jones enveloped the ball carrier. The colossus Wiese grabbed the ball and lunged for the line but was thrown back by Fitzpatrick and Blowers. It was stacks on the mill. With Marshall pleading with him to end it, Mene blew for trapped ball, scrum feed green. The scrum never packed. Mene decided enough was enough and blew fulltime. It was over. The series was won. The 1996 All Blacks had found New Zealand rugby's holy grail.

Slowly, the pile-up untangled. Andrews shoved aside an All Black's legs and made a bee-line for the dressing room. Fitzpatrick and Michael Jones were at the bottom of the heap. They lay still, waiting for the aches to recede. Craig Dowd sank to his knees. Zinzan Brooke flopped onto his back, arms outflung, eyes shut. Eventually, Fitzpatrick got to his knees and thumped the turf, a gesture which recalled David Kirk in the 1987 World Cup final. Then he climbed to his feet and began congratulating his players. When he met Zinzan Brooke, they embraced like brothers-in-arms when the guns have fallen silent.

"By this stage, the Springboks had real doubts in their minds but every game against them is a battle to the very last moment," says Fitzpatrick. "They just never stopped and they're so big and strong. We knew we had to really take the game to them and I think we surprised them with the way we got into them. They were very hard, physical games, probably the most physical I've ever played in. You were pretty sore afterwards.

"They were absolutely shattered at the end as you could see from the reaction of Venter and Andrews. But they were gracious losers afterwards and I couldn't believe how gracious the public was – I think they appreciated that it had been a good series in the true All Black-Springbok tradition. But their players still had amazing self-belief – as far as they were concerned, they'd just had another off-day and they'd still beat us at Ellis Park."

The coaches went down to the players' tunnel to await the team. "Ross Cooper urged me to go out onto the field to meet them," says Hart. "I was reluctant; we'd had the good fortune to help these guys achieve glory but it was their moment, not ours. In retrospect, I'm very glad he persuaded me to go.

"The players' eyes glowed with elation in their drawn, exhausted faces. Some of the least emotional men I know were in the grip of powerful emotions. It was nice to walk off with Michael Jones – he's a special player in my career and I was thrilled that he'd been there when history was made. As the team walked off, the Dirty Dirties performed a haka in the stand. Their commitment to the cause, their contribution to tour discipline, and their support for the test players had been vital to our success.

"I felt immense relief and pride in the players who'd given everything they had for the black jersey. The heat, the altitude, and the ferocity of the Springboks' second-half onslaught had taken their toll but they'd held the line. If anyone had said we'd leave Pretoria with nine wins out of nine, I would've laughed. It's only after you've worked with these guys for a while and seen their courage and commitment that you realise anything's possible.

"The front row had confronted South Africa where it really counts, knowing that if that battle was lost, we were finished. The locks were massively outweighed but never shaded in any other respect. Kronfeld was fearless and unflagging, Michael Jones was the defensive lion, and Zinzan Brooke the footballing genius who can be part of the team while remaining true to his own instincts. In the backs, Marshall had been creative without shirking the grinding duties – he was one of our best defenders. Wilson's display in the first half was a sublime blend of speed and skill while Bunce was a stand-out player in 1996; an absolute rock on defence whose pace on the outside break surprised many and who saw and exploited opposition defences' preoccupation with the threat of Cullen, Lomu, Wilson, and Osborne.

"In many ways, Preston's performance was the most remarkable of all. For those fifteen minutes, his decision-making and execution at first-five was coolly efficient. It was a fantastic display of temperament from someone who'd played very little rugby at first-five and only one match, five years earlier, of anything remotely approaching this intensity."

The dressing room is normally an inviolable sanctum but this was a moment in history to be shared with the nation. It was thrown open to the media so that they could breathe the atmosphere and convey the elation and deep sense of achievement to the people at home.

Half an hour after the game, Keith Quinn saw Zinzan Brooke trying to sign an autograph. His hand was shaking so much that he couldn't sign his name: "I remember him looking at his hand, watching it shake. It was just the release of tension."

For Hart, coaching the All Blacks to their first series win in South Africa was a supreme vindication. Many had been convinced he would never coach the All Blacks; some had made it their business to prevent him doing so. For an energetic, restless man imbued with self-belief, he'd had a long and sometimes painful wait to fulfil his destiny. Now that the moment had arrived, his thoughts were not of vindication, of having proved the doubters wrong. As he walked out onto Loftus Versfeld to ring his family, he was thinking how much sweeter it would have been if his dear, departed friend Peter Murdoch had been there to share the joy.

18

A BRIDGE TOO FAR

WHEN the All Blacks arrived in Kimberley for their game against Griqualand West, John Hart got a call from Springbok manager Morne du Plessis. He was upset about a tackle made by Sean Fitzpatrick on Gary Teichmann at Loftus Versfeld the previous Saturday. Du Plessis said he didn't intend to pursue the matter or make a public issue of it but he wanted Fitzpatrick disciplined. Hart remembered Teichmann going to the blood-bin and later leaving the field for good but hadn't seen the incident; he told du Plessis he'd watch the tape and get back to him. Given that the All Black management had heard that there was a story in the *Citizen* newspaper blaming the ten stitches in Teichmann's head on a punch thrown by Fitzpatrick, du Plessis' undertaking not to go public was taken care of.

Hart viewed the tape. He saw Teichmann come off a ruck and get crunched by Fitzpatrick, who slammed a heavy arm across his rival skipper's chest. A couple of Boks reacted angrily and Fitzpatrick was penalised. On the tape, referee Didier Mene could be clearly heard telling Fitzpatrick that the penalty was for offside, not for the tackle. Teichmann, meanwhile, was back on his feet – unbowed and, unquestionably, unbloodied. Hart was confused;

from what du Plessis had said and what he'd heard of the *Citizen* article, this was the incident they were up in arms about. He watched more of the tape. Several plays later, Teichmann emerged from a ruck bleeding from the head. Where was Fitzpatrick? Where else but out on the wing! After re-playing the sequence several times, Hart formed the strong impression that Teichmann was a victim of rugby's version of friendly fire. When forwards hurtle into rucks, feet flying – as the Springboks did more than once that afternoon – everyone on the deck, friend and foe alike, is at risk.

Hart told Fitzpatrick what was going on, then rang du Plessis to express surprise that he'd bothered to raise the issue; if the Springbok manager was concerned about over-vigorous play, Hart could refer him to a ruck in which two Springbok forwards had given Fitzpatrick a real working-over even though he was nowhere near the ball.

When the All Black management finally saw the *Citizen* article, they were outraged: it accused Fitzpatrick of an assault on Teichmann which had put him in doubt for Ellis Park. On the principle that management's obligation to discipline a transgressor is balanced by their right to support someone who's been wrongly accused, Hart asked Jane Dent to demand a retraction. The editor refused. Hart drafted a letter threatening legal action if a retraction wasn't published within 24 hours.

One appeared the next day. You had to look hard for it but it was there.

The *Johannesburg Star's* take on the affair was a cartoon showing Fitzpatrick, complete with halo, standing on a Springbok's head; Hart looks on, saying, "He won't hurt a fly, I swear." The original now hangs in Hart's office.

"Sean's the man they love to hate in South Africa," says Hart, "mainly because they wish he was in their team. He's got many of the attributes they admire, particularly the hard-nosed, physical approach. He may be a master sledger and niggler but there was a maturity in his play in 1996 which reflected his awareness that he had to demonstrate control if the team was going to maintain its composure."

With the series won, the captain was beginning to revel in his role as South Africa's public enemy number one: "I enjoyed that last week. I even enjoyed fronting them in public instead of ignoring them or walking away as I'd done before. They're very self-confident people, very blunt and brash, and maybe we take

"He won't hart a fly, I swear."

The Johannesburg Star's *view of the Gary Teichmann affair which put John Hart at odds with the Springbok management.*

them the wrong way. When you have them on about the way they come at you, maybe by telling them that we don't talk to people like that in New Zealand, they're quick to assure you they don't mean anything by it. Maybe we're not that different in our desire to win and our self-belief but we just hide it behind that sort of English politeness. You realise it's not personal, it's just that you're the captain of this horrible bunch who are beating them. I think after the second test they realised that we were a good team and the series was everything an All Black-Springbok series should be, complete with all that brute strength stuff they love."

The panel considered playing Andrew Mehrtens against Griqualand West to give him some matchplay. However, the commitment to giving everyone at least two games and the desire to continue Junior Tonu'u's development took priority and Jon Preston was picked at first-five. Scott McLeod and Alama Ieremia resumed their midfield partnership and Con Barrell came into the front row. Given the injury situation at first-five, it was pretty much what the panel regarded as the best midweek side.

The midweek team had been solid without managing to put together an 80-minute peformance. Matthew Cooper, Eric Rush, Ieremia, Glenn Taylor, and Mark Allen had all had their moments. So too had Taine Randell, even with the added pressure of the captaincy.

Griqualand West were going to be tough. It's hard-line Boer country, a place of long traditions and harsh attitudes. The province boasted a good record against touring teams and a rugged pack built around the notorious Bester brothers. Their notoriety took on a whole new dimension early in 1997 when Andre Bester stage-managed the downfall of Andre Markgraaff.

Full-scale Lomu-mania greeted the team at Kimberley airport. Kimberley is the home town of Jonah's wife Tanya whose family still lives there. Lomu had showed some of his old explosiveness at Sunday's training session in Pretoria and the panel sensed that he was aiming to turn it on at Kimberley. A big performance would put him in line for a test recall which would have been a reward for toughing it out and fighting back rather than a reflection on Glen Osborne, who'd done everything asked of him.

Hopes were high that the midweekers would wind up their tour in style and the real Jonah Lomu would finally be seen. It looked good early on; moving freely for the first time on tour, Lomu got off to a storming start and when McLeod dotted down under the bar it looked as if the All Blacks were taking control. But Lomu had been given the treatment in an early ruck and, as the half wore on, had increasing problems with his shoulder. When Osborne replaced him at halftime, it was the first time a test player had taken the field in a midweek match.

Even so, the midweekers seemed comfortably placed: four points ahead and turning with the wind at their backs. But their last 40 minutes of rugby in the republic were anything but comfortable.

Hart: "The second half was all Griqualand West, aided by what seemed to us to be some pretty marginal refereeing. They got a lot of latitude and took our lineout apart. I'd heard that Louis Luyt, Markgraaff, and the referee Tappe Henning had been in earnest conversation before the game. We knew Henning so I was fairly relaxed about it but I guess you should never underestimate the pressure that referees can come under in South Africa."

The Griquas notched a couple of tries to lead 18-10 midway through the half. The 13,000 spectators were in a frenzy. Hart was having a trying afternoon, not helped by the fact that the spectator sitting behind him kept donging him on the head with a plastic hammer.

A Preston penalty cut the deficit to five points with a few minutes to go. The midweekers were showing real grit and putting in a big finish. With time up on the clock, they poured down the left flank. Cooper's pass to Andrew Blowers lurking out wide looked forward but wasn't called. Unable to get the inside pass to McLeod who had a clear run to the line, Blowers set up a ruck. The All Blacks swung it back to the openside and Osborne latched onto a floated pass from Ieremia to outflank the defence. The conversion would win the game; who better to take on such an assignment than the hero of Loftus Versfeld? It wasn't an easy kick, though – about 15 metres in from touch on the "wrong" side of the field for a right-foot kicker and across a swirling wind. To make it a bit trickier, the All Blacks' kicking tee had disappeared.

David Abercrombie was out on the field tending an injured player: "I thought the try was scored midway between the posts and the corner but Henning's line was closer to the sideline which Preston complained about. His kicking tee was nowhere to be found so the ballboy gave him the opposition's tee. I noticed that one of the touch judges had the tee behind his back. I asked him for it but he wouldn't hand it over. Henning was telling Preston to hurry up. I ran over and grabbed the tee off the touch judge but, when I tried to give it to Preston, Henning told me to get lost or he'd blow fulltime without the kick being taken. At that stage, I figured it was a lost cause."

The kick drifted across the face of the goalposts and Henning blew fulltime. The match was drawn.

"The business with the tee was bizarre," says Hart. "We didn't really deserve to win but, under the circumstances, it would've been fitting. That last week was always going to be hard – now we realised just how hard."

Markgraaff had good reason to celebrate: his union had come very close to claiming the All Blacks' scalp and despite his modest results – two wins out of seven after taking over a team on a 16-game winning streak – he'd just been given a free hand with the Springboks. In future, he'd run the show like a soccer manager, exercising complete control over all aspects of management, selection, and training.

The All Blacks' departure from Kimberley was delayed for two hours due to electrical storms. That really made their night; it was midnight when they eventually got into Johannesburg.

The panel was still mulling over the make-up of the test team. Some of the forwards weren't in great shape: Josh Kronfeld was running on empty, Ian Jones' damaged knee ligament made him a 50/50 proposition, and Zinzan Brooke's pelvic condition had reached crisis point.

"Zinzan has a chronic inflammation of the pubic bone for which the only effective treatment is rest – six to twelve months' worth," says John Mayhew. "He'd played with it all year but had to have an injection for this game. He's terrified of needles."

On top of the various ailments – Jeff Wilson had been struck down by a severe dose of 'flu – was the fatigue factor; the team was bone-weary. "Early in the test programme, they'd recover from a game by Monday," says Hart. "After Durban, it took till Wednesday. They still hadn't fully recovered from the Pretoria game by Friday which is why I keep hammering away on the theme that it's not how many tests the players are expected to play, it's how much recovery time they get between them."

According to Marty Toomey, "tiredness is mental rather than physical, though they go hand in hand. Once we'd won the series, they relaxed mentally and started to feel all the bumps and bruises – we knew it was going to be hard to lift them. I thought they could recover. We didn't do a lot of physical work that week so I didn't have a gauge. If we'd known how tired they were, we might've done things differently."

With Ian Jones carrying an injury, Taylor's ability in the middle of the lineout earned him a place on the bench at Blair Larsen's expense. Jones was a key player so he'd be given every chance to make it; if he didn't, Taylor would take his place in the starting line-up.

"I'd had a lot of time for Taylor since I had him in the Colts," says Hart. "He'd worked hard on tour to improve his lineout play and concentration and was emerging as a test-quality lock. It was hard on Larsen who'd had a sound tour but, in the end, selections must be made for the right reasons and the heart can't rule the head. One of the lessons of this test was that we failed to adhere to that rule in other respects – we should've brought in some fresh legs."

The only pair of fresh legs belonged to Mehrtens. For the panel, the decision on who'd play first-five had been clearcut:

Mehrtens was fit, Simon Culhane wasn't, Carlos Spencer's goal-kicking wasn't good enough. Notwithstanding his admirable cameo in the previous test, it would have been a big ask of Preston to play a full game at first-five against the Boks at Ellis Park. The promotion of Ieremia and Taylor to the test bench during the tour showed the back-up players that it was possible to lift themselves in the pecking order.

The coaches took it easy at training, not stepping up the tempo until Thursday. The amount of dropped ball was an indicator of the team's lack of sharpness. Seeing the All Blacks struggle to come up again, some observers began to think the unthinkable. "They trained badly on the Wednesday," says Murray Deaker. "They were buggered. I said to Hart, 'They're gone, aren't they?' Harty said, 'I'll get them up.' That was the only time on the tour that I felt he was having doubts. I think deep-down he knew they were gone."

While the All Black selectors were sticking with the tried and trusted, the South Africans were ringing the changes. Joel Stransky's goal-kicking had been erratic and his confidence was down so it was no great surprise that he was replaced by Natal's Henry Honiball, an exciting runner and one of the best defensive first-fives in the game. Japie Mulder returned from injury to displace Andre Snyman while this time Kobus Wiese and James Dalton made the starting line-up. Dalton was a lot more mobile than Tromp and promised to inject some of the energy he'd shown in his dynamic display against Australia in the World Cup opener. Dawie Theron, who'd been pulled from the Griqualand West team which played the All Blacks and whom Markgraaff rated highly, replaced the injured Os du Randt at loosehead. For du Randt, who'd started the year with pretensions to being the best prop in the game, it was a disappointing end to a disappointing season.

The Springboks had five pairs of fresh legs to the All Blacks' one; in hindsight, that may well have been decisive. The All Blacks were tired but they'd known the score from the start and the opportunity to leave South Africa with an unbeaten record was a strong incentive. For the Springboks, a four-test whitewash at home would be a national disgrace, pure and simple. They had to win; the All Blacks didn't.

"It can't be denied that there was a sense of mission accomplished," says Hart. "The objective was to win a series in South Africa and we'd achieved that. The need to win had waned."

Not bringing in fresh legs was the first mistake. The second was the decision – made early in the piece – to fly out of South Africa on the Sunday morning after the test. They'd have to leave the hotel at 6am which meant packing well in advance. Some players had their minds more on souvenirs and reunions and getting their laundry back than on the game.

Hart rang home early on the morning of the test to learn that Taranaki had seen off North Harbour's shield challenge. That made it two NPC losses out of two for North Harbour. At this rate, observed Hart jokingly with the North Harbour contingent, there'd be some illustrious Harbour names in the 1997 Divisional team, chosen from second and third division players. As it turned out, North Harbour had a decisive win over Wellington at their next outing. By earning bonus points from their first five matches they were never in serious danger of relegation. They had two more opportunities to get their hands on the Log o' Wood but, alas, the 1996 season passed without a ticker-tape parade through the streets of Takapuna.

The referee for Ellis Park was the highly experienced Welshman and celebrated gold watch recipient, Derek Bevan. (After the 1995 World Cup final, Luyt presented Bevan, who'd refereed the Springboks' semi-final cliff-hanger against France, with an expensive gold watch. Bevan returned it.) Bevan opened the pre-game discussion by saying how disappointed he was that this test wouldn't decide the series. Hart could understand a promoter thinking that way, but not a referee; he replied that any All Blacks-Springboks clash at Ellis Park was a major rugby occasion. The comment made him nervous. Just how big a stage did Bevan want? Did he see himself as the leading man in the drama, rather than a supporting actor?

Abercrombie and Mayhew also had a disturbing pre-game encounter with Mr Bevan. "Doc and I have a tradition of going for a beer on the night before a test," says Abercrombie. "In the bar we ran into Bevan who was sitting with his linesmen and the liaison guy. We introduced ourselves. He came across as pretty arrogant. It was a striking contrast with the attitude of the two French referees who were happy to sit and talk; they obviously had a lot of respect for New Zealand rugby and were looking to learn something."

Honiball kicked two quick penalties before Mehrtens put the All Blacks on the board with a booming 64-metre penalty. Hart interpreted it as a sign that the young Cantabrian was going to have a big game but, sadly, it was a case of flattering to deceive.

Mehrtens was striking his kicks well enough – another attempt from a similar distance cleared the dead ball line – but his direction was astray. All told, he would miss five out of eight. By contrast the Springboks, who'd had the kicking blues in the earlier tests, were bang on target.

The first try of the match came in the 24th minute: the Springboks won a short lineout and Ruben Kruger chimed into the backline to put Joubert through a gap. Joubert, who was back to his Rolls Royce best in this game, hit the accelerator. He brushed off a tackle and flipped a reverse pass to Pieter Hendriks who had a couple of grabs at it before nudging it into Joost van der Westhuizen's path with his boot. Bevan was right on the spot; a less confident referee would have ruled a knock-on but he waved play on and van der Westhuizen loped in under the posts.

Bevan was spotting wrong-doing in every second ruck and a long-range Joubert penalty put the Boks out to 16-3 in the shadow of halftime. The All Blacks came back, Mehrtens carving through to send Cullen racing for the corner. Van der Westhuizen tipped him into touch with a magnificent cover tackle, preventing the try and earning his team the throw to the lineout. But Ian Jones got first touch, tapping the ball down to Fitzpatrick who collected a knee in the head from van der Westhuizen as he flopped over the line. It was 16-8 at halftime. That was as good as it got.

Hart felt that Bevan had indulged in some northern hemisphere nit-picking, especially at second phase. Fitzpatrick agrees: "When we had ball coming back from rucks and mauls, we always seemed to get pinged for something, unlike in the previous tests. Late in the game, I told Bevan he must be getting more than a gold watch for this. He said, 'You're bloody right, boyo.'"

Bevan might have also pointed out that if Mehrtens had kicked as well as Honiball and Joubert, the All Blacks would have been in front at halftime.

At the break, Zinzan Brooke told the team that half of them were already on the plane home. Hart told them to take the attack to the Springboks and eliminate mistakes. Mehrtens promptly put the restart out on the full. Shortly afterwards he missed a gift penalty and then, with the All Blacks hot on attack, turned the ball back inside with a huge overlap outside him. The movement broke down and the Boks hacked the ball clear. That was the All Blacks' last chance to get into the game and generate some momentum.

Another penalty made it 19-8, then van der Westhuizen miscued an up-and-under on halfway. When the ball came down, there wasn't much urgency in the All Blacks' attempts to secure it or to reinforce the thinly defended blindside when Stransky, who'd replaced Mulder, set off on a probing run. Stransky linked with Joubert who strode out majestically for the corner.

The Springboks sniffed blood. Five minutes later, van der Westhuizen burrowed over for a try which the All Blacks disputed. There were three dubious refereeing calls during the sequence of play leading up to the try; all of them went the home team's way. In reality, however, a heavy air of inevitability hung over Ellis Park. Joubert's third penalty made it 32-8 with 25 minutes to go. It was one-way traffic. The Springboks had gone into the game desperate to avoid humiliation; now it was the All Blacks' turn to face that prospect.

Hart feared the worst but his team dug deep. Showing great resolve, they launched a series of furious if disjointed attacks. Two converted tries, the first created by a deft Mehrtens chip-kick, reduced the margin to respectable proportions. Still they kept coming. With ten points the difference, the die-hard optimists in the grandstand were daring to think that another converted try would put the All Blacks within a penalty goal of a draw.

"We didn't deserve it," says Hart. "That loss was a valuable lesson in selection and preparation. It was a flat team which returned to the dressing room." Their dejection was deepened by the grim awareness that they'd failed to mark Michael Jones' 50th test in appropriate style.

The post-match press conference featured a rare appearance by the Greta Garbo of the front row, Olo Brown. Bevan's display was the hot topic; it was obvious that some of the journalists were itching to make an issue of it. When asked to comment, Hart prefaced his remarks by emphasising that the All Blacks weren't blaming the referee for the result.

"I said that the Boks had outplayed us and deserved to win and if anyone wrote that we were blaming the referee, he was on notice as to what my reaction would be. I didn't want 'we wuz robbed' headlines. I went on to say that I thought Bevan had been inconsistent, that we were disappointed with his display, and that he probably would be too when he looked at the tape. But there could be no excuses – the All Blacks didn't fire as they should have."

Still feeling the thump on the head which accompanied his try, Fitzpatrick missed the after-match function. Zinzan Brooke's deep-seated aversion to defeat meant he was in no mood for speech-making and Ian Jones' injury also prevented him from attending. It was left to Hart, on behalf of the team and management, to thank the people of South Africa and pay tribute to the Springbok victory.

Luyt responded. Victory had put him in an expansive state of mind. He began by saying that it was the second time he'd had to follow Hart (the first being Grant Fox's *This Is Your Life* which coincided with a celebration of Auckland's Ranfurly Shield era) and it wasn't an easy task. He went on to lavish praise on the All Blacks, declaring that they were the best team in the world and had taught the Springboks a lot. He was clearly seeking to make amends for his gracelessness after the World Cup final.

As the All Blacks left the function, Hart spotted Bevan across the room: "I hadn't had an opportunity to talk to him after the game and wanted to tell him to his face what I'd said to the media – if I wasn't prepared to do that, I shouldn't have said it. My parting shot was that I was glad we hadn't gone into the game all-square. Afterwards, I regretted saying it."

No doubt Bevan's defence would be that he called it as he saw it, just as he did at Eden Park almost a year later when he sent off Andre Venter and the Boks got a caning in the penalty count.

Meanwhile, back at the team hotel, Professor Fitzpatrick was continuing his anthropological research among the locals. As he and Mayhew walked out of the restaurant after having a bite to eat, he was button-holed by a young woman: "She was having a romantic candlelit dinner with a guy but she really started in on me – you're the guy we love to hate, all that stuff. I asked them if it was a special occasion. It was their first anniversary dinner. She said, 'If you were in a green jersey, we'd love you, but you're not, so we hate you.' I said, 'Enjoy the dinner,' and moved on. The guy hadn't said a word."

19
HERO PARADE

THE All Blacks were officially welcomed home at a reception at Eden Park which was shown live on a special one-hour edition of the *Holmes* show. John Hart had wondered how the players would scrub up for the cameras; they'd flown out of Johannesburg at 7am and the long-haul flight wasn't ideal therapy for the hangover from Ellis Park, a deflating combination of soreness, disappointment, and sleep deprivation. But the All Blacks' professionalism remained intact; they looked the part.

With an election at hand, it was no surprise to find politicians jostling for the best seats on the bandwagon: Jim Bolger, Helen Clark, and Jim Anderton were all there. Hart was miffed when a shot of himself with Anderton, taken at the reception, appeared in the Alliance's election advertising. Frank Bunce might've endorsed them but he certainly hadn't.

The following day, 250,000 people crammed into the centre of Auckland to salute their heroes as they made the slow journey up Queen Street. Some of the All Blacks hadn't been looking forward to it; they soon changed their minds.

"Whether out of shyness or cynicism, some of the players weren't that keen on a ticker-tape parade," says Hart. "They admitted afterwards that they'd been moved by the surge of goodwill. It gave them a real insight into the emotions they could stir in their fellow New Zealanders by performing well and showing humility in addition to pride in the black jersey."

Hart shared a float with Sean Fitzpatrick and some of the silverware the team had accumulated throughout the season. At one point during the parade, Fitzpatrick suggested that they ought to have a chat about 1997 and whether he should carry on. When Hart asked him if he wanted to, the skipper's eyes gleamed – it was obvious that the fire still burned.

"Sean's leadership was one of the successes of 1996," says Hart. "He was an outstanding leader on the field and a role model off it. Of all our rugby players, he is the most professional and he flourished in the new environment. His dedication to training is second-to-none; he realises that, at his age, he has to keep on top of his physical fitness. He did an enormous amount to assimilate young players into the All Black environment, having learned the lesson of 1991 when the older players became arrogant and the younger ones got disenchanted. He was the most responsive of the senior All Blacks to the needs of the media, putting himself out time and time again on their behalf. He also had the maturity to know when to back off to give himself time and space to prepare. And as a player pure and simple, he was superb. The Kel Tremain Memorial Trophy for rugby's Personality of the Year and his nomination for New Zealand Sportsman of the Year were richly deserved."

When they recalled that conversation later, Fitzpatrick observed that he'd contemplated retirement at the end of every year since 1991. Yet there he was at the beginning of September, thinking about 1997. Having gone into the coaching role wondering whether he'd be accepted by the captain and the team, Hart was enormously encouraged by the fact that Fitzpatrick was looking forward to doing it all over again.

On the morning of the Johannesburg test, Hart had breakfasted with Keith Parkinson and Ronnie Masson, Chairmen of the Natal and Western Province unions respectively and members of the SARFU executive. He'd told them that he was far from happy with the way the All Black party had been treated by SARFU, particularly the lack of protocol shown towards Mike Banks and NZRFU President Don Shuker, who'd been in South Africa for much of the tour.

"The New Zealand-South Africa relationship is unique and must be preserved and enhanced," says Hart. "That won't happen of its own accord. If an All Black touring team and senior representatives of the NZRFU aren't deemed worthy of respectful and considerate treatment, it suggests that those running South African rugby don't value the relationship all that highly and one-sided relationships don't last in any sphere. Perhaps the fact that Banks, Shuker, and I weren't All Blacks had something to do with it – a Meads or a Lochore probably would've been better treated. But, in this context, it's the office and what you represent that counts, not what you did in your playing days. I'd been disappointed for Mike and Don and was aware that they probably wouldn't raise the matter.

"I wanted the message understood and passed on. I saw SARFU Chief Executive Rian Oberholzer at breakfast but he was with other people and probably wouldn't have appreciated it. I knew Parkinson and Masson would be concerned because both of them go to great lengths to ensure that when touring parties are in their provinces, they're well looked after. The problem couldn't be rectified but I was trying to ensure it didn't recur."

Banks confirms that established protocol wasn't adhered to: "I'm fairly ambivalent about that sort of thing but some of my predecessors certainly would've taken umbrage. I was surprised that we weren't met on arrival and by the ongoing lack of contact with officialdom. Maybe the professional environment made them too focused on the issues of the moment and they forgot a tour was taking place.

"The first time I sighted Louis Luyt was in Cape Town when Ross Cooper and I went to a state banquet hosted by President Nelson Mandela. Dr Luyt was sitting at a table a few yards from us and at no time did he acknowledge our presence, let alone come over and say hello. Our next meeting was at the function after the Cape Town test where we spoke very briefly although he didn't introduce himself. After the Durban post-test function, I was walking to the bus with some players when I almost bumped into him – he had no option but to stick out his hand. After Loftus, he came across to shake hands and say, 'Well done, you've made history.' When I wandered into the South African dressing room after the Ellis Park test, he walked up to me, put his arm around me, and told me what a mighty guy I was."

Season of Glory, a book celebrating the achievements of the1996 All Blacks, was published a few days after the All Blacks' return. It contained the transcript of a Murray Deaker interview with Hart, conducted shortly before the Johannesburg test. Replying to a question about South African hospitality or the lack of it, Hart chided SARFU for not paying due respect to Banks and Shuker, talked of South African "arrogance", and wound up his answer with the comment that, "overall, the rugby union has treated us with a bit of disdain".

Throughout August, Oberholzer had seemed scarcely aware that a full-scale All Black tour was taking place but these comments certainly got his attention. He attacked Hart for waiting until he got home before voicing his complaints, adding, "that's the measure of the man." It was a textbook *ad hominem* response: don't address the criticism, abuse the critic. It was also inaccurate given that Hart had raised the issue face-to-face with two members of SARFU's executive. When the All Blacks were back in South Africa in 1997, Parkinson confirmed that he'd promptly passed Hart's concerns on to Oberholzer. Happily, the 1997 visit was a more enjoyable affair in terms of relations with the host union; SARFU's hospitality had improved out of sight.

Don Cameron, the *New Zealand Herald's* distinguished rugby and cricket writer, had dubbed the 1996 All Blacks *The Incomparables* and the honorific had been made official at the Eden Park reception. That was a red rag to a Buck – Shelford charged into the public arena, snorting indignantly that the 1996 All Blacks didn't deserve the title because the 1987 World Cup winners were a superior team.

Hart, who'd had a hand in selecting and coaching the 1987 team, wasn't sure that the facts justified Shelford's dogmatism: "The 1987 team's record of seven out of seven reads well but their opponents were Italy, at that stage a genuine minnow, Fiji, at that stage a declining force in the fifteen-man game, Wales ditto, Argentina, Scotland, France, and Australia. Seven of the 1996 team's ten matches were against top-quality opposition – Australia and South Africa. When all is said and done, however, I just don't think we should make comparisons between different teams from different eras playing under different rules.

"It's indisputable that the 1987 All Blacks were a great side and that the 1996 team didn't play to its maximum potential throughout the season – it really only hit the heights in Wellington. However, I'd argue that it's impossible for a team to produce ten utterly dominating performances in thirteen weeks, given that five games were against the most unyielding foe in international rugby and four of those five were on that foe's home turf where every previous All Black team had failed. Sublime performances occur when teams are at their mental and physical

Who'd be a coach? The strain shows on Greg Smith (above left), Ian McGeechan (above right) and Andre Markgraaff (below).

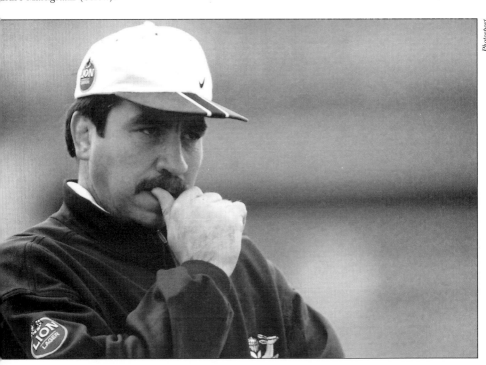

Who'd be a referee? The All Blacks have had contrasting experiences at the hands of Ed Morrison (above) and Derek Bevan in 1996 and 1997.

Ian Jones and Robin Brooke form one of the great locking partnerships in rugby history.

The rest and relaxation stints have been important in the All Blacks' 1996 and 1997 campaigns. Here the coach lays down the team tennis laws as Hewson's Heroes prepare to take on Dowdy's Freaks. The contestants, from left, Josh Kronfeld, Carlos Spencer, Mark Carter, Ian Brest, and Mard

The most important support team of all – Judy, Kay and Chris join John at his Fletcher Challenge retirement function.

Putting the Springboks on the rack at Eden Park, 1997. Above, Josh Kronfeld gets a pass away as Henry Honiball and a team mate make the tackle. Below, Justin Marshall, now a vital cog in the All Black machine, drives for the line.

Management and planning have been key factors in the All Blacks' success in 1996-97. The All Black management team in session: Clockwise, from left: Ross Cooper, David Abercrombie, Gordon Hunter, Mike Banks, John Hart, John Mayhew, Martin Toomey, Richard Fry and Jane Dent.

Three wise men? The All Black panel - from left, John Hart, Gordon Hunter and Ross Cooper - at Sun City.

peak and that won't happen too often under the current playing schedule."

It wasn't the first time that Shelford had declared himself underwhelmed by the 1996 All Blacks. In a series of columns in *Rugby News* ghosted by Bob Howitt, a tireless booster of the previous regime, Shelford had criticised what he regarded as a lack of pattern in their play.

Hart couldn't help but wonder if Shelford's bombshell dumping from the All Blacks in 1990 still rankled: "I wasn't questioning Buck's right to criticise but I was a little worried that, as someone who has great mana in the game, he was damaging himself in the eyes of the public."

When the fuss died down, he rang Shelford to express his disappointment and try to establish if there were other – personal – issues at work. Shelford said it was nothing personal, adding that he'd had many calls from ex-All Blacks and others supporting his stand. He mentioned some names, including that of Fred Allen. One would have thought that Allen, of all people, would appreciate the significance of victories on South African soil.

At the end of the season, Hart once again went in to bat for his team. This time, though, the sceptic was more open to persuasion.

"I made a shocking mistake," says Murray Deaker. "In response to a question, I said on air that Auckland was the team of the year. I was carried away. When I got home, the phone was ringing. Harty said, 'I know you're getting married but have you lost your marbles completely?' He went through it chapter and verse, pointing out that the Auckland Blues in the Super 12 and Auckland in the NPC weren't quite one and the same and quoting me back at myself to the effect that the 1996 All Blacks were the greatest ever – 'have you forgotten that already?' I went on air the next day and said the programme was being run by a man with Alzheimer's Disease."

But people will always disagree on the relative merits of teams and individuals, especially those from different eras. Hart had his own yardstick: measuring performance against the four goals he and the All Black management team had set early in the year.

• To win as many games as possible and to win in style: "The 1996 All Blacks won twelve and drew one out of fourteen games, winning nine out of ten tests. The Tri-Nations tournament and the series against Scotland and South Africa were won, the latter an historic achievement. In terms of style, the All Blacks scored tries playing imaginative, attacking rugby, except at Lancaster Park. We adhered to the rules and showed consistently good discipline. The avoidance of incidents and controversies is a key indicator of style, given the growing importance of players as role models. We came under pressure to take Richard Loe to South Africa because he was clearly the second-best tighthead prop in the country. We refused to compromise on our principles and I believe the lack of controversy – and a couple of incidents in the 1997 Super 12 – vindicated our stand."

• To achieve consistency of performance through consistency of selection: "The panel felt that we got most selections right first time and this was borne out by the fact that we used only 19 players in the tests. The players repaid our faith in them with consistent performances – when a team starts losing, pressure comes on selectors to make changes. The only form-driven change was Walter Little for Scott McLeod but if Little had been fit from the start, that issue mightn't have arisen. The others were injury-related: Eric Rush and then Glen Osborne for Jonah Lomu and Simon Culhane for Andrew Mehrtens. The fact that the same pack played in all ten tests was remarkable and a credit to their resilience and commitment. The relentlessness of the playing schedule in the professional era may mean selectors have to take hard-nosed decisions to rest players even though their performance may warrant re-selection."

• To establish the All Blacks as role models with the media and public: "The tremendous support we got from the New Zealand public while we were in South Africa, the public response to the team on its return, the results of the end-of-year media survey, and the winning of the Team of the Year award all testify to the All Blacks' high standards on and off the field. Jane Dent deserves much of the credit for helping the players become far more professional and polished in their dealings with the media."

• To create an enduring base for professional rugby: "It's far too early to make an assessment of our progress in this area. What can be said is so far, so good. We were confronted by a host of issues and weathered the storm. WRC gave the players the whip-hand but, while they took the opportunity to maximise the benefits, I didn't sense arrogance coming into the All Black set-up. They were grateful for the financial rewards. The challenge is to ensure that they don't become greedy and that they only take a share of what's in the pot, not the whole lot. The elite can only exist if the grassroots are nurtured and the amateur game remains healthy. If those of us at the top forget that, professionalism will fail.

"Today's stars, the likes of Zinzan Brooke and Carlos Spencer, started out bare-foot in the back-yard, kicking tatty old balls around and dreaming of being All Blacks one day. If we ever kill that dream, we'll halt the momentum of the game in New Zealand and undermine our position as world leader. Now that the elite have been taken care of, it's time to provide our youngsters with good facilities and coaching resources in clubs, schools, and provinces in order to produce the Super 12 players and All Blacks of tomorrow."

So what do other members of the All Black management team see as the key contributory factors to this highly satisfactory report card? Most of them would point to planning and organisation and cite the 36-man squad as the best example. Andre Markgraaff criticised SARFU for allowing the All Blacks to bring 36 players. He complained – and maybe only an Afrikaner would state it as bluntly as this – that it put the tourists on a level playing-field. He was absolutely right: none of the Springboks played midweek matches between the tests and, apart from Osborne's 40 minutes against Griqualand West, neither did the All Black test XV.

In sport as in commerce, you know that something's worked when your competitors copy it. Markgraaff took a 36-strong squad on South Africa's end-of-year tour of Argentina, France, and Wales. Greg Smith complained bitterly when he was restricted to 30 players for the Wallabies' tour of Italy and the UK. As it turned out, a rash of injuries saw Australian rugby players shuttling between London and Sydney like supermodels. In 1997, the Lions took 35 players to South Africa and their excellent manager Fran Cotton is now recommending 36 players for future Lions' tours.

It wasn't just big-picture stuff either; the same attention to detail was devoted to day-to-day activities. At the management team's morning meetings, meals, training, and the day's programme would be planned. After breakfast, there'd be a team meeting to outline and discuss the structure and objectives of that morning's training session. Each night, the team received a print-out of the next day's activities containing times, assembly points, dress codes, and functions.

"It was very structured, very orderly," says John Mayhew. "Harty's depth of planning is ahead of anything I've been involved with."

According to Marty Toomey, the only survivor from the 1995 management team, "The biggest difference was the greater organisation and the planning and thoroughness of Banks and Hart. You were told, 'this is your responsibility – do what you need to do and keep me informed.' Laurie Mains was more autocratic;

he liked to be in control which sometimes worked and sometimes didn't. He'd ask my opinion but wouldn't necessarily follow it."

There was quite some difference in the area of media relations as well. The 1995 All Blacks and management were pilloried in the media survey conducted at the beginning of the year, scoring five or less out of ten on virtually every count. The survey was repeated at the end of 1996 and widened to include the South African media and British rugby writers encountered on the Barbarians tour. This time, the average score was eight.

"I think the previous culture was that we don't need the media, they need us," says Dent. "John brought about a major change of thinking; a lot of it began with him saying that the media aren't the enemy and adopting a pro-active, co-operative approach. The players saw it working and followed suit.

"We never covered up anything that would've been an issue had the media known about it. Discipline was really emphasised – it wasn't heavy but it was there. I was amazed at how the players controlled themselves – they're not the beer-swilling oafs of legend. That came from the top but also from within and was reinforced by the knowledge that, if they didn't behave, there was someone else to take their place."

The policy of giving senior players responsibility for their specialist areas in order to develop a second tier of leadership supporting Fitzpatrick and improve individual and collective decision-making bore fruit. The confidence it generated was reflected in individuals being prepared to express themselves, even under pressure, and by the team's composure in tight situations. As Zinzan Brooke told Keith Quinn on the Kimberley golf course: "Under Hart, we seem to win the close ones."

"Compared with the late '80s, these guys are better thinkers on the field," says David Abercrombie. "That comes back to the Hart influence and the way he gave individuals responsibility rather than it all being left to Fitzpatrick. I couldn't get over the way guys like Zinzan and Robin Brooke, Michael Jones, and Bunce developed and the input they came to have. Guys who'd previously been a bit shy were now putting so much into attack organisation, defence organisation – they'd sit and talk about this option and that option."

"Harty spoke to the senior players a lot," says Fitzpatrick. "Laurie did everything and one of our downfalls was that we didn't develop other leaders. As a team we spoke about the fact that Hart wasn't going to be barking at us all the time so we had to take the responsibility ourselves. The guys enjoyed having an input and being asked their opinion on things rather than being scared to say what they thought.

"Some of the young guys like Mehrtens are different from their recent predecessors in that they're very confident, both in the team context and outside it. You saw that in the way they responded when Hart asked them to contribute. Previously, it was all follow the leader – they weren't able to make decisions themselves."

The All Blacks undoubtedly had a golden run with injuries compared with their Tri-Nations opponents. Was that good luck or good management?

"I guess you make your own luck," says Mayhew. "The training programme and the season was well-planned and the guys looked after themselves and were well-prepared."

"Mains was big on endurance," says Toomey. "There was a lot of emphasis on circuit stuff in gyms and getting out on the roads. They weren't tested for strength until the Queenstown camp late in 1994 and it was obvious that upper-body strength was a problem. We'd seen it against the French that year, the way they kept ripping the ball off our guys. Now we're making sure that all the components are worked on and the players have got significantly stronger."

And while Mayhew doubts that the All Blacks' training methods were significantly different from those used by, say, the Wallabies, observers everywhere were struck by the intensity of their training sessions. Former British Lions number 8 John Beattie was amazed when he watched the New Zealand Barbarians go through a reasonably intensive physical work-out during their short end-of-year visit to England. He'd never seen anything like it.

"The training was designed to put players under pressure all the time," says Gordon Hunter. "I think that helped us in the close games. We had people with the ability to develop the hard-nosed attitudes required at this level."

There was one other factor, one that shouldn't be underestimated: the 1996 All Blacks had fun.

"At the beginning of 1996," says Fitzpatrick, "Olo Brown said to me that he'd never enjoyed playing for the All Blacks and that he wished he could enjoy it like he enjoyed playing for Auckland. Being in the 1996 All Blacks was a hugely enjoyable experience and Hart deserves the credit for creating that happy environment. If you'd said in 1995 that when their contracts expired, senior All Blacks would be signing on for more rather than looking off-shore, I wouldn't have believed you."

20
WOLVES IN
SHEEP'S CLOTHING

THE Rugby Football Union [RFU], as England's national union rather grandly titles itself, had asked the NZRFU to contribute to its 125th anniversary celebrations by sending the All Blacks over to play a test at Twickenham in late November. So keen was the RFU to get the All Blacks that it was prepared to offer an inducement: a share of the gate receipts. It was an offer that the NZRFU, struggling to keep its head above the flood of red ink released by the sudden and hugely expensive transition to professionalism, would find hard to refuse.

Looking at it from a coach's point of view, John Hart tended to see the hook rather than the bait. He didn't think there was much to be gained from playing a one-off test out of season and without adequate preparation after such a demanding schedule. But conscious that he and the players couldn't simply shrug off the NZRFU's $6 million black hole as not their problem, he suggested a compromise: rather than a full All Black side, send a Barbarians team containing a mix of established and fringe All Blacks and emerging talent.

It was a neat and acceptable solution although it threw up the lesser issue of player payments. The Baa-baas epitomise rugby's amateur tradition. While the club accepted the shift to professionalism, they'd never paid players and weren't about to start. An agreement was reached whereby the NZRFU and the Barbarians would organise the tour, the NZRFU would pay the players, and the All Black panel would pick the team. As a senior vice-president of the Barbarians, Hart would carry out the dual roles of coach and, along with president John Sibun and club captain Bruce Gemmell, guardian of the club's interests.

The short trip would be a useful rehearsal for the All Blacks' 1997 UK tour so it made sense to involve some of the All Black management team. In addition to Mike Banks, Jane Dent, John Mayhew and David Abercrombie, Peter Sloane, a Barbarians club member of long standing, was the assistant coach and Peter White was appointed fitness trainer and masseur, a role he'd performed for North Harbour and the Waikato Chiefs.

Selecting the touring party became the panel's main focus during the NPC. As the championship progressed, it became apparent that some All Blacks either wanted or needed a rest: Josh Kronfeld, Jeff Wilson, and Frank Bunce came into that category. For Walter Little and Craig Dowd, the end of the domestic season cleared the way for long-delayed operations while Zinzan Brooke's pelvic problem demanded a decent break from the game.

Mindful of England's giant pack, the panel's blueprint specified a nucleus of battle-hardened All Blacks, particularly up front, complemented by second-stringers and contenders who showed good NPC form and a sprinkling of youngsters. Working from that plan, they settled on a pack built around Sean Fitzpatrick, Olo Brown, Robin Brooke, Ian Jones, and Michael Jones with Justin Marshall, Andrew Mehrtens, Jonah Lomu, Glen Osborne, and Christian Cullen to provide the pyrotechnics behind the scrum.

Mark Allen was given the chance to establish himself as an international-class scrummager. With the All Black midfield pair out of consideration and Scott McLeod and Tabai Matson out of form, Alama Ieremia was joined by Lee Stensness, who earned his place with a string of superb performances in the NPC. The third midfield back was Mark Ranby, who'd shone for the New Zealand Under-19s and acquitted himself well in the NPC even though Manawatu's style wasn't conducive to free-flowing threequarter play. Mark Robinson was Marshall's back-up; his sharp form was one of the few beacons of hope amidst the gloom which descended on North Harbour and he'd given a notably gutsy performance against Auckland when his team was coming apart at the seams.

Andrew Blowers' progress in South Africa cemented his place and Taine Randell was given another opportunity to position himself as Zinzan Brooke's heir apparent. When, late in the day, it was decided to stage the warm-up game on a Sunday and thereby ruling out Michael Jones, Chresten Davis was added to the squad. The panel was keen to promote young propping talent: there were a few contenders but some forceful displays for Waikato pushed Michael Collins to the head of the queue. Anton Oliver understudied Fitzpatrick. The inclusion of Joeli Vidiri and Dylan Mika was a reward for their commitment to New Zealand at the cost of three-year stand-downs from international rugby.

Lomu's season hadn't got any better since his return from South Africa. His lingering knee injury and a suspension for a spear tackle restricted him to two and a bit appearances for Counties Manukau but Hart was anxious to get him back into the fold. "He'd been plagued by injuries and, as we were to find out, his kidney condition was playing havoc with his system. There were also signs that he wasn't getting the right balance between his off-field activities and rugby. I spoke to him and his wife before they went to Kimberley for their second wedding ceremony; I wanted to be sure that he'd be one hundred per cent committed when he joined us in the UK because the England game was the perfect opportunity for him to re-establish himself on the international stage.

"It was spelled out that some players mightn't get a game. For Ranby, Collins, and Robinson, it was primarily a learning experience – about touring, about professionalism, about preparation at the top level. Watching Allen, Brown and Fitzpatrick on and off the field would be an immensely valuable crash-course for a tyro prop like Collins."

PR-wise, the tour would be a learning experience for all concerned. The British press covers the full spectrum – from highbrow broadsheets boasting several specialist rugby writers to sensationalist tabloids staffed by foot-in-the-door sleaze-hounds for whom sport is simply another source of "shock, horror" headlines.

Jane Dent warned the players what to expect: "I told them that it was different over there because of the size, range, and intensity of the media – if there was ever going to be an issue, the tabloids would bring it out even though they weren't the All Blacks. There was the Jonah factor – memories of Mike Catt being trampled underfoot at the World Cup – and the Unsmiling Giants tag which still applied in the UK. By that stage, being friendly and approachable to the media and public was coming naturally to most of the players but there are times when you're tired and fed up and don't feel like smiling – after a thirty-hour flight, for example."

Within a few hours of touching down at Heathrow, the Barbarians management held a press conference followed by a buffet lunch at which the players – less Ian Jones, who was getting married in Fiji, and Michael Jones and Lomu, who were flying in from South Africa – were introduced. It was obvious where the media were coming from: the tourists could call themselves whatever they liked but they were the All Blacks – end of story.

It wasn't the best of times to be touring England. The RFU had made the classic mistake of getting embroiled in simultaneous conflicts on several fronts – with the leading players, the clubs, and the other Home Unions. It was tempting to interpret the turmoil as a final, defiant blast of flatulence from the 57 Old Farts but it was a little more complicated than that.

The RFU's provisional contracts with their leading players had elapsed on September 30 and, whether out of complacency or inefficiency, the administrators had dragged their feet instead of swiftly tying the players into long-term contracts. A number of clubs backed by wealthy individuals had seized the opportunity to sign up a swag of top players. This gave the clubs leverage in their ongoing dispute with the RFU. As is so often the case in sporting power struggles, it was essentially about television.

The entrepreneurs who'd bought their way into clubs and were using their chequebooks to create powerful teams overnight didn't expect to make a return on their investments through gate-takings, although some did plan to develop the clubs' physical assets to turn them into all-purpose sporting and leisure centres. The real pot of gold was money from TV rights and the clubs aimed to secure a much bigger share of the television revenue flowing into the English game. The sums involved were huge, reflecting both the intense competition between the various free-to-air and pay TV operators and the population base. How this pie should be sliced was the core issue in the dispute and the clubs were quite prepared to turn up the heat on the RFU by pulling their contracted players out of representative fixtures. The Barbarians were to be caught in the crossfire of English rugby's civil war.

The boot was on the other foot in England's bitter dispute with Ireland, Scotland, and Wales. The RFU had precipitated this crisis by breaking ranks with the other Home Unions to cut a separate and lucrative deal with Rupert Murdoch's BSkyB. The RFU argued that the Home Unions' joint arrangement with the BBC was unfair since TV revenue should be allocated on the basis of population rather than divided evenly. The Celts reacted by moving to expel England from the Five Nations Championship.

The 57 OFs were trail-blazing into the new era in one respect, contracting the organisation and administration of tours out to private enterprise. Normally all tour arrangements would be made by and through the RFU but the Barbarians management found themselves dealing with a travel company run by the former England prop Mike Burton. Burton is a colourful figure whose entrepreneurial activities and tempestuous relationship with officialdom both during and since his playing days bring to mind Andy Haden. Burton's company had been given budgetary guidelines by the RFU and left to get on with it but the results hardly amounted to a great advertisement for out-sourcing. There were five other teams touring the UK at the time and the Barbarians weren't the only contract Burton's outfit had picked up. They were over-stretched and didn't have the connections or the organisational ability to look after a touring team. The liaison officers didn't help: they tried hard, which was important; they were Burton's mates, which was neither here nor there; after that, it was pretty much all downhill.

Before going up to Leeds for the warm-up game, the Barbarians overnighted in a Hammersmith hotel. It wasn't up to scratch; the rooms smelt of smoke, the facilities for the medical staff were inadequate, and the food revived memories of the lunch from hell in Potchefstroom. Worst of all, they were booked in there for another week when they got back to London.

Mike Banks and Hart sought an urgent meeting with Burton. It began in a business-like fashion; the New Zealanders made it clear that they didn't want to stay in the hotel the following week and requested a list of alternative locations which they could check out before heading north. Burton sympathised but offered the Nuremberg defence – "I was only following orders". He'd complied with the RFU's directives on the appropriate standard of accommodation for what wasn't an international team; it would've been different if they were the All Blacks. Banks and Hart argued that, seeing Twickenham was sold out, the distinction was academic. When it became clear that sweet reason wouldn't get them anywhere, the gloves came off; Burton was told that if that was the way it was going to be, they'd point the team bus towards Heathrow, not Leeds. (Banks had taken the sensible precaution of securing NZRFU support for this stand before going into the meeting.) The ultimatum had the desired effect and they were presented with a list of alternative hotels.

They travelled north. Winter had set in and Saturday's training took place on an icy pitch. Snow fell overnight and they looked out at Christmas card scenes on the bus trip to the McAlpine Stadium in Huddersfield, venue for the match against Northern Counties. The snow was overkill since the game was already a fiasco. A number of clubs had escalated the dispute with the RFU by pulling their players out of the Northern Counties team at the last moment. It's hard to imagine a more dismissive gesture towards a touring team than to use them as pawns in a domestic political power struggle.

There was some discussion as to whether there was any point in proceeding with the game; in any other circumstances, the Barbarians wouldn't have bothered but they needed a run. The game was played in freezing conditions with snow falling, a new and unwelcome experience for many Barbarians, especially Vidiri who'd never seen the stuff before. The referee agreed to unlimited substitutions so everyone except Michael Jones got some time on the field.

While Northern Counties weren't good enough to provide meaningful opposition, the Barbarians handled the conditions well, scoring 14 tries in an 86-0 romp. Towards the end, they stopped taking conversions; a man could have got frostbite standing around while the kicks were taken.

The Barbarians beat a hasty retreat to the south of England and their new digs at the Selsdon Park Hotel in Surrey. Burton was waiting for them, anxious to ensure that everything was to their satisfaction. Not quite: it was a nice location with excellent recreational facilities but a long way out of town. That became less of an issue when the RFU refused to allow them to train at Twickenham. England trained there twice.

"It made me wonder why we let touring teams train at our test venues when this right is so rarely reciprocated," says Hart. "It might seem like a small thing but these are the factors which constitute a thorough preparation, especially when the venue is a unique and slightly overwhelming stadium such as Twickenham."

On the Friday, they were granted visiting rights to walk on the hallowed turf and check out the superb dressing rooms. Hart couldn't help wondering what must have gone through Ed Morrison's mind when he entered the Athletic Park dungeons.

Hart had a second meeting with Ian McGeechan, who'd been appointed coach of the 1997 Lions to tour South Africa, having already coached the 1989 Lions to a series win over Australia and the 1993 Lions to a 1-2 series loss in New Zealand. He'd been in South Africa on a scouting mission during the All Blacks' tour and had requested a meeting to talk about planning and preparation.

"He'd been particularly taken with the 36-man squad concept," says Hart. "When we met again in London, he said that as a result of that meeting in Durban, he and the manager Fran Cotton had drawn up a list of recommendations, one of which was an enlarged squad. McGeechan's an impressive figure and a wonderful coach and it was clear that the Lions wouldn't fail for lack of preparation."

England limbered up by giving Italy a pasting. The pundits seemed to regard it as a watershed performance in which England had thrown off the shackles of the forward-based kicking game and embraced running rugby. Hart was impressed by the mobility and control of the tight five but felt there was less certainty in their loose forward and back play.

Hart: "It said something about the depth of England's commitment to attacking rugby that they left Jeremy Guscott, their greatest attacking weapon, on the sideline because of alleged defensive frailties. The number 8 Chris Sheasby had a good debut against some weak defence but I wasn't sure they had the right players in the right positions in their loose forwards. Phil de Glanville looked to have his hands full with the captaincy but his predecessor Will Carling had a strong game.

"The new halfback, Andy Gomersall, got rave reviews. He was a cocky player and some of his antics weren't designed to endear him to the opposition – or neutral observers for that matter. I wondered if he was a little too confident. Confidence is fine but it has to be measured and, given the quality of the opposition, it looked like his feet had left the ground."

Perhaps it was contagious. The England players interviewed after the game positively oozed confidence and the media followed their lead. Ignoring the absence of six All Black test players and the fact that the RFU wasn't awarding caps, the media were billing it as a showdown between the hemispheres in which England would strike a resounding blow for European rugby.

Before it got to that, the Barbarians management had a more

prosaic issue to deal with. They were concerned about how long the match-day bus trip from Selsdon Park to Twickenham would take. Apart from the distance, it had been abundantly clear during Friday's return trip for the walk in the park that their bus driver didn't know his way around London. Extensive discussions took place between Burton and the RFU; the upshot was an assurance that the journey would take an hour and a quarter, not a minute more. The management then drew up a match-day timetable which had them departing from the hotel at 12.45pm for a three o'clock kick-off.

On Saturday morning, they received a fax from the RFU instructing them to leave the hotel at 12.30pm. A terse reply was fired back, the gist of which was that arrangements had been made on the basis of the RFU's 75-minute guarantee and it was too late to alter them. Notice was served that, as the team required at least an hour at the ground before the game, the kick-off time would be delayed one minute for every minute after 2pm it took them to get to Twickenham. Perhaps it was just as well that the TV executives in charge of beaming live pictures of the game around the world weren't copied in on this correspondence.

Being hard-nosed is one thing; cutting off your nose to spite your face is another. The bus left shortly before 12.45. Accompanied by a police escort, they thundered down closed-off roads like a presidential motorcade; clearly, their threat was being taken seriously. The journey took 55 minutes. The liaison officer was congratulating himself on a logistical triumph until it was pointed out that getting to the ground half an hour early was only marginally less satisfactory than getting there late.

In fact, it worked out well; the players welcomed the opportunity for a leisurely stroll around the ground and the huge dressing room meant there was no danger of anyone getting cabin fever. Spending too long cooped up in a cramped dressing room isn't good for the nerves or the concentration.

The Barbarians fielded a powerful side – only Randell and Vidiri hadn't played test rugby for the All Blacks – but once again the make-up of the reserve bench was a headache. Now that tactical substitutions were officially permitted, Hart wanted to get Carlos Spencer and Osborne on the field. With Robinson covering halfback, Taylor covering the lineout, and Oliver covering hooker, that left room for one more reserve who really should have been a prop given the stipulation that there must be two reserves covering the front row. But Collins was too inexperienced for this company and Hart was keen to use Mika, who'd had a storming game at Huddersfield and promised to make a real impact coming off the bench. That involved a very broad interpretation of the substitution guidelines and meant Fitzpatrick would have to prop if Allen or Brown were injured.

The iron man was characteristically unfazed at the prospect but the coach's heart-rate went into overdrive when Brown went down feeling his calf. Fortunately, Brown lived up to the All Black front five's reputation for durability.

The Barbarians have a tradition of running rugby and the team went out to maintain it. England went out, first and foremost, to win a test match. The game began at a cracking pace. Normally that would have suited the New Zealanders but they were out of season and it was an open question as to who would handle the pace of the game better. The Barbarians' lack of recent matchplay was reflected in inaccuracy and poor finishing; possession was regularly turned over and several threatening attacks petered out when the final pass went astray.

In their pre-match planning, the Barbarians had targeted the excessively bouncy Gomersall and he faltered under the pressure. Going back in cover defence, he made a hash of his clearance, putting the ball out near the corner. Vidiri flung a quick throw-in to Brooke who galloped over. The English commentators made a fuss about Vidiri having a foot in the field of play when he'd thrown the ball in but seeing referees routinely tolerate this practice, it's difficult to understand why they should suddenly apply the letter of the law because a try resulted directly from the throw. A barrage of penalty kicks followed leaving the Barbarians 11-9 in front at the break. It could have been more: Fitzpatrick had tapped and run several kickable penalties, once actually getting over the line only to be pulled back for not taking the tap from the right spot.

England began the second half with a hiss and a roar, scoring two tries and shooting out to a 19-11 lead. The Barbarians' loose forwards weren't making much headway so Hart replaced Randell with Mika, who had an immediate impact, adding some real impetus to the drive. Confidence started to flow. Mehrtens brilliantly opened up the defence for Blowers to motor away down the left and score untouched.

Hart then sent on Spencer for Mehrtens; like Mika, he was quick to make his presence felt. The Barbarians were awarded a penalty within kicking range; Spencer said later that he'd hoped

Fitzpatrick would continue the tap-kick policy but this time the skipper pointed to the posts. Spencer landed it and went on to kick a second penalty and a conversion. It was an impressive display of temperament which demonstrated that, while his technique required fine-tuning, he could certainly handle the pressure of goal-kicking in the big-time. Having made that point, Spencer proceeded to parade his dazzling attacking abilities, bamboozling the English with two electrifying sidesteps and scorching in under the posts.

"Spencer's performance inspired a lot of talk about him now being the front-runner for All Black first-five in 1997," says Hart. "I shared the enthusiasm for his talent but felt obliged to point out that Mehrtens had played outstandingly for sixty minutes while England were putting up a very strong forward effort. His control and composure had kept us in the game and, when all was said and done, it was his ability with the ball in hand which created Blowers' try. In amongst all the good things he did, Spencer had a couple of kicks charged down, which can be very costly in test football."

Victory was sealed late in the game when Robin Brooke and Ian Jones repeated their Pretoria double act to put Vidiri over in the right-hand corner. Once again, the All Black engine-room had shown that, in the modern game, athleticism, skill, and a high work-rate more than compensate for modest physical presence. But, like the South Africans, the Europeans seem reluctant to jettison their obsession with size.

In the dying minutes, England strove mightily to have the last word but the Barbarians responded with a most un-Barbarian doggedness in defence. Osborne was on the field for only a couple of minutes but tackled like a demon – Gomersall must have wondered if it was anything personal. Right at the death, a counter-attack from a tap penalty put de Glanville in the clear. He seemed unstoppable but Marshall, Mr Cover Defence himself, came from nowhere to scythe him down. The shadowing Stensness recovered the ball and banged it into touch and the game was won 34-19.

"I sent Osborne on for Vidiri because I wanted Lomu to finish the game," says Hart. "He'd gone down with an infection a couple of days before the game and was a sick young man – it didn't look like the antibiotics would work in time. We gave him a fitness test on Saturday morning – the spirit was willing but the flesh was struggling. I admired him that day; things didn't go his way, he lacked sharpness, and he didn't put the fear of God into England as he'd done at Newlands – but he hung in there.

"Cullen had brought the crowd to their feet with some scintillating running from the back. There are some outstanding fullbacks in world rugby – Matthew Burke, Andre Joubert, Jean-Luc Sadourney. In 1996 Cullen probably ranked third which is as high as could be expected given the quality of the other guys and the fact that it was his first year of test rugby. He backs his ability to take people on and beat them; he takes risks and therefore he'll make mistakes. With experience, he'll become more selective about when and where he takes people on."

Of the fringe players, Allen had emerged with credit from his confrontation with the redoubtable Jason Leonard. Ieremia might have blown a try in the first half when he took the tackle instead of feeding the flying Vidiri but overall he'd played strongly and advanced his cause. Vidiri and Mika showed that they'd be ready to take the big step when they'd done their time and Stensness re-established himself as a player of test quality, combining characteristic attacking flair and tactical canniness with greater involvement and stiffer defence.

For Randell, however, the game was less a graduation ceremony than a harsh but salutary lesson; "He's an immensely talented young man," says Hart, "but Mika's performance rubbed in the need for him to develop greater upper-body strength and power. The gains in strength and hardness from concentrated weight-training are evident in the body shape of a Michael Jones or an Andrew Blowers. Taine had a lot on his plate in 1996 – captaining Otago, the Maoris, and the All Black midweek side, worrying about his own performance, and completing a double degree in law and commerce. All that left him little time for personal training. I strongly supported what he'd done in his education but now that was behind him and he could focus on what he needed to do to be a serious contender for an All Black test jersey."

21

THE CLASS OF '97

JOHN HART'S second year as All Black coach began on an
inauspicious note with the news that a career-threatening kidney complaint would put Jonah Lomu out of action for an
indefinite period.

"Jonah's had the condition – neophrotic syndrome – for two
or three years and there's been a progressive deterioration," says
John Mayhew. "It causes lethargy, swelling of the ankle joints,
frequent skin problems, and would cause renal failure if
untreated. Mood swings are part of his personality and that
tendency certainly wasn't helped by the condition – he tended to
become withdrawn. There are no examples of a high-profile
athlete having this condition and coming back, so when we
began the treatment, we didn't know what the outcome was likely
to be."

While Lomu's star had waned a little in 1996, Hart believed his
unavailability had major implications for the All Blacks. "It was a
huge loss – Jonah has no peer in pulling in defenders and freeing
space for others. Only once in 1996 did he really do justice to his
awesome prowess and some people were very quick to doubt him.
Now they had some idea of the immense mental and physical
pressures he was under. At least the time out gave him a chance to

take stock and perhaps the expectations of him would be more realistic when he returned."

The panel's analysis of the 1997 programme suggested that it would be a more daunting assignment than 1996's. First up were Fiji, who'd made big strides under the guidance of former All Blacks Brad Johnstone and Gary Cunningham and had announced their resurgence by putting 60 points on Western Samoa. They were followed by Argentina, the sleeping giants of international rugby. The Argentinian rugby establishment are the last of the true-blue amateurs and their unyielding attitude has cost them the services of many of their leading players.

But they, too, seemed to be on the way back. Hart had been impressed by their performance against England at Twickenham in late 1996: "They should have won. They were huge up front with a fantastic scrum and showed some flair out wide. With them coming here off a home series against England and with Alex Wyllie as their technical advisor, we expected a highly competitive series."

The panel's first job was to decide who would attend the pre-season camp to be held at Taupo over the first weekend in February. Forty-six players had attended the previous year's professionalism seminar but that reflected the decision to take an expanded squad to South Africa and the coaches' desire to start building relationships with a wider group. With the UK tour coming late in the year, after the NPC, attendance at the 1997 camp was restricted to players under serious consideration for test selection during the first phase of the international programme – incumbents, established back-ups, and the fastest developers from the 1996 intake.

Seven of the 37 who'd gone to South Africa missed out: Matthew Cooper, Eric Rush, Tabai Matson, Scott McLeod, Phil Coffin, Con Barrell, and Todd Blackadder.

Hart rang them before the announcement to explain the panel's thinking and assure them that the door wasn't closed: "I told them that the Super 12 would be important for them. While Rush was coming towards the end of his career, he'd remain in our plans if he showed he still had the fitness, motivation, and form. We needed to see an improvement in Matson's self-discipline. McLeod had to earn further rewards through performance. He took it very hard but I was impressed to hear him on the radio later, talking about learning the lessons of 1996. He reacted exactly as we'd hoped, making a big impact in his early Super 12 games. The other four had been picked to do specific jobs for the midweek team in South Africa; they hadn't let us down but they needed to make a step up in form to put themselves in line for test selection."

The additions were Lee Stensness, who'd finished 1996 strongly, and Charles Riechelmann, who'd been pencilled in for South Africa until injury intervened.

The previous seminar featured experts in various fields who were brought in to help players and management get to grips with the array of issues thrown up by professionalism. It was felt that steady progress was being made on that front so the 1997 camp could be an in-house affair – more rugby-oriented with an emphasis on re-establishing 1996's unity and team dynamic.

The theme was continuous improvement. "It's a theme that should be taken up by anyone attempting to build a winning team," says Hart. "You must continue to stretch yourself otherwise you'll start to slip. International corporations such as General Electric recognise that they have to increase productivity by five per cent a year just to stand still. The old saying that staying on top is a lot harder than getting there is absolutely true; it's very easy to lose your edge, your hunger, and your focus while the chasers are raising their games to match and surpass you.

"The only way to improve is by effective self-analysis. Our analysis of 1996 told us that we could have lost at Christchurch, should have lost at Brisbane, could have lost in Cape Town, and could easily have drawn at Pretoria. Then the record would have read won five, lost four, drawn one which is a bit different from the glory of nine wins out of ten that we were basking in. We had to go into 1997 taking nothing for granted and aiming to do everything better because our opponents certainly would be."

Hart opened the camp by reviewing the year past and outlining the year ahead. Jane Dent reported on results of the media survey conducted at the end of 1996 and led a discussion on how relations with the public and media could be further improved. They were all about to discover that the consequences of dropping your guard in the PR sense can be swift and embarrassing. TV One began airing *The Footy Show*, copying an Australian format supposedly designed to show that footballers are just like the rest of us, only bigger. In the right hands, the formula involves players indulging in harmless buffoonery between free-wheeling panel discussions of the week's talking-points. Unfortunately, the TV One version went horribly wrong on virtually every count, hitting rock-bottom with a segment in which cricketer Emily Drumm was pawed by two blindfolded All Blacks. Taking its cue from the hostile public reaction, the network first abbreviated the show, then put it out of its misery.

Other topics covered were sponsorship, professionalism, mentoring, the NZRFU's strategic direction and how the All Blacks fitted into it, training methods, sports science, and nutrition, an area in which there was scope for improvement. "Players can be very gullible," says Mayhew. "They get onto fads and think you're being conservative when you ask where's the scientific backing. One player once went on a vegetarian diet and ended up with an iron deficiency."

Zinzan Brooke and Frank Bunce led a discussion on tactics aimed at enhancing the team's tactical sophistication and encouraging innovation. The panel had procured a computer-based video analysis system developed in Transvaal; Gordon Hunter explained how it worked and how it could help the players.

The results of the fitness tests were alarming; they revealed a high incidence of injuries suffered in pre-season training or, worse, dating back to 1996. A third of the players were unable to complete all the tests.

The Super 12 selection process for 1996 had been unsatisfactory and caused the five coaches considerable frustration. At the NZRFU's request, the All Black panel got heavily involved this time around. They drew up a list of the leading players in each position, enabling them to monitor whether the NZRFU was getting the right players onto Super 12 contracts, and worked with the coaches towards the objective of fielding five good teams.

The aim wasn't to create five equal teams – which would have reduced the likelihood of a New Zealand team winning the competition – but to produce five good teams, with two or three who'd be semi-final contenders. The panel were also determined that there'd be no repeat of the situation whereby All Black candidates didn't get on the field because their team had an over-supply of good players in their position.

The trick was to achieve all this and ensure that the Super 12 coaches got the players they wanted. "In the end, we were able to announce the squads without resort to arbitration," says Hart. "Relationships and goodwill were important in that context – without them, you won't get resolutions around a table. There was a dramatic improvement in the overall performances of our Super 12 teams as a result of the thorough review of what had gone wrong the previous year and the steps taken to address those problems. To be fair, in 1996 it was all new and done in a hurry but, apart from the Auckland Blues, the squads showed sweeping changes – a forty per cent turnover in some cases. We don't want to repeat that every year because of the high contractual costs."

The Canterbury Crusaders and the Wellington Hurricanes were the big improvers. Canterbury could easily have finished higher but had no luck at all; Wellington played some vibrant rugby in their charge to the semi-finals. Alama Ieremia's collarbone injury was a body-blow to their chances of getting past the ACT Brumbies but the week in the semi-finals spotlight would have been invaluable experience, especially in terms of managing the media and promotional activity to ensure that the focus remains on the game.

Once again, the Waikato Chiefs under-performed. Their scrum lacked stability and their inside backs were never settled; as a result, they failed to unleash the array of talent in the three-quarters.

Hart: "I firmly believe that we should give preference to New Zealand players but it's pointless going into a demanding international competition without being able to compete. Without Coffin, by-passed in year one and now transferred to Wellington, Waikato were facing the same problem at tighthead which had undermined them in 1996. I suggested they should talk to Alex Wyllie about recruiting one of the leading Argentinians, as ACT did so profitably with Patricio Noriega. In the end, Brad Meurant went for Richard Loe, who wasn't wanted by the Crusaders.

"Some in the Waikato hadn't forgiven him for leaving the province after the support he'd received throughout the Greg Cooper affair. Many inside and outside the region felt Loe had had more than enough chances and wasn't what the game needed in the new era. As it turned out, the leopard hadn't changed his spots; he had a positive influence at training and certainly stiffened the Chiefs' front row but was soon in hot water for a high tackle and stomping against New South Wales and earned a three-week suspension for two punching incidents against the Blues, one on Zinzan Brooke before the game was a minute old."

The young Otago Highlanders also suffered from their selections, especially at lock. At times they looked like boys against men; occasionally they showed flashes of their undoubted potential. The Auckland Blues, the old pros, did it even easier than the year before. After Canterbury gave them their wake-up call, it was just a matter of who'd come second.

In the immortal words of baseball legend Yogi Berra, it was *deja vu* all over again for the panel as they contemplated the trial; the biggest issue was the form and fitness of the Chiefs' All Black backs. Bunce, Walter Little, McLeod, and Glen Osborne all had serious injury problems. As if a knee injury wasn't enough, Osborne stood on a sardine tin when putting out the rubbish and needed major patching up.

Hart again sat down with Bunce to discuss the veteran centre's future. He was being written off in some quarters and the Auckland media machine was beating the drums for Eroni Clarke, who was having another big Super 12. Bunce's foot injury prevented him doing any aerobic training for several weeks and he faced a race against time to be fit for the trial.

"We had a lot of confidence in Bunce," says Hart. "He's mentally very hard. He'd been the cornerstone of Laurie Mains' selection and everything I'd seen vindicated that high opinion. The injury was frustrating him but his enthusiasm was undimmed and he was going to fight all the way to keep his place."

Little's knee problem hadn't gone away. The medical team's view was that he needed a break from the game to give himself any chance of continuing to play at the top level. "Walter's got a grotty knee," says Mayhew. "There's chronic degenerative change on the outside of the knee. He's had several operations which have tidied it up but there's no surgical cure for it."

A month before the trial, coach, doctor and player agreed it was in Little's best interests to take a break and allow the knee to recover. "It wasn't easy for him," says Hart, "but I was impressed with the maturity with which he assessed his future and concluded that, if he carried on, the injury would affect his form and probably cut short his career anyway. He wanted to give himself a chance of getting back but it was a big call for an incumbent All Black."

Injury was also cutting a swathe through the young generation of flankers. Andrew Blowers, who'd looked a player of immense talent in South Africa, missed the early rounds of the Super 12 with a groin injury, then suffered a stress fracture of the lower back which took him out of the frame. Like Little, he'd look to the NPC as his route back into the All Blacks.

Chresten Davis was growing in maturity as a blindside flanker when a wrecked knee suffered in the Hurricanes' epic match against the Blues brought down the curtain on his season. Riechelmann injured his other shoulder on Auckland's pre-season European tour. Fortunately, the healing process was less drawn-out this time and he returned during the Super 12 although his lack of match fitness and the emergence of Leo Lafailaii restricted his appearances.

Josh Kronfeld was also forced to miss games. From Hart's point of view, that wasn't such a bad thing: "Josh puts his body on the line in every game and there's a limit to how much the body can take in a given period. His absences are inevitable and help him to survive."

Justin Marshall and Andrew Mehrtens also had their problems – sternum and hamstring respectively. The original reports on Marshall, after the Queensland match, indicated a broken sternum; Dr Marshall's vehement disagreement with that diagnosis went out live on national television.

"Thankfully, he was right," says Hart. "That would've been a disaster – he'd become a very important component in the All Black machine. Both Jon Preston and Junior Tonu'u had good Super 12s but neither matched his versatility and all-round skills. Tonu'u's the best clearer of the ball we have but an important measure of a top halfback is having the ability to handle pressure and the speed to exploit opportunities from scrums."

Olo Brown's calf tear was another nasty moment for the panel who were now starting to get twitchy. A torn calf muscle is one of the worst injuries a rugby player can suffer and, having searched high and low in 1996 for a ready-made replacement for Brown, they were all too well aware that there wasn't one. His enormous value meant that his rehabilitation had to be managed very carefully and required the Blues' and All Black coaching and medical staffs to follow the same script. The fact that Brown returned ahead of schedule showed the value of co-operation and professionalism in the treatment of injuries.

The panel's search had led them to the conclusion that Craig Dowd was the second-best bet at tighthead and Brown's injury gave him a good run on that side of the front row. It started against Canterbury when the Auckland scrum didn't go well, mainly due to the absence of the world's foremost scrummager, Sean Fitzpatrick. When he returned, Dowd proved himself more than capable at tighthead and the switch opened the way for the young loosehead Paul Thomson to play himself into the trial.

Of the 1996 touring team, Michael Jones, Blowers, Lomu,

Ieremia, Davis, Little, Simon Culhane, Blair Larsen, and Zinzan Brooke were taken out of the trial by injury. Coffin, Cooper, and Matson missed out.

The irrepressible Tana Umaga had been the undoubted find of the Super 12. He'd undergone a complete transformation on and off the field and his power-packed running lit up the tournament although he was turned inside out by Joe Roff when the Hurricanes played the Brumbies. Umaga was hammering on the door but the panel felt that Osborne deserved the opportunity to defend his position. They decided to ease Umaga into the environment by putting him in the reserves and bringing him on during the game, rather than throwing him in against the shadow All Blacks.

With the second-five spot up for grabs, they pitted Stensness against Mark Mayerhofler, with McLeod on the shadow All Blacks' bench. After his arduous tournament, Dowd was rested, which gave Bull Allen a start, and Taine Randell stood in for Zinzan Brooke, who'd been concussed in the Super 12 final. The rest of the shadow All Blacks line-up was predictable with the possible exception of Riechelmann, who was named at blindside flanker. Although Riechelmann hadn't played much rugby, the panel saw him as a real prospect; at the pre-season camp, it was apparent that he'd benefited from doing extensive weight-training during his rehabilitation. What criticism there was of the trial teams centred on Bunce's selection in the senior side ahead of Clarke.

The attrition continued after the teams were announced, giving the panel the opportunity to bring some young talent into the reserves: Xavier Rush, Finau Maka, Darryl Lilley, Norm Maxwell, Mark Robinson, Leon McDonald, and Kees Meeuws, although injury then claimed the latter pair. They'd all had their moments in the Super 12, particularly Maxwell who led the Crusaders' lineout and hurled himself into the fray with a reckless disregard for his slender frame.

The New Zealand A side was a good one. They had flair and solidity in the backline of Tonu'u, Carlos Spencer, Mayerhofler, Clarke, Rush, James Kerr, and Adrian Cashmore, and a big, rugged pack. Thomson joined Anton Oliver and Con Barrell in the front row and at lock Glenn Taylor was partnered by Mark Cooksley, who'd emerged from Frank Oliver's boot camp a different player. The original choice at number 8 was Steve Surridge, a 1991 New Zealand Colt who'd really made his mark with the Crusaders; he pulled out with injury to be replaced by Filo Tiatia. Mark Carter, back in the union fold after his flirtation with league had failed to blossom into a meaningful relationship, was on the openside and Todd Blackadder led the team from blindside.

The trial was a chastening experience for the shadow All Blacks. They were lucky to win and their victory owed more to individual brilliance, notably from Stensness, than teamwork. For the most part, they were out-pointed as individuals and as a team and the likes of Robin Brooke looked in need of a break. The A side had been well-prepared by Wayne Smith and John Phillips and the pack, especially the loose forwards and Oliver, played strongly. Spencer showed his brilliance as well as his occasionally fallible decision-making and Jeremy Stanley, who'd been one of the stand-outs in the speed tests conducted earlier in the week, created havoc when he came on as a replacement.

The NZRFU had given Hart the go-ahead to pick 23 rather than 21-man squads for the home tests. While it involved additional costs for the union in terms of salaries, fares, and accommodation, it gave the panel more flexibility in settling on the bench and meant that, whatever mix of reserves was chosen, the players concerned would have trained constantly with the team.

Because the announcement had to coincide with the release of the New Zealand Maori team who were assembling the next day, the panel had one hour to finalise the team and eight reserves and deliver the bad news to incumbents who'd missed out. The first of those was Preston, who'd had a disappointing match for the shadow All Blacks. Early in the Super 12, he'd overtaken Tonu'u in the rankings but the Aucklander had played outstandingly in the semi-final and final, showing a degree of consistency which his game had sometimes lacked. Preston was bitterly disappointed at his omission from the squad.

The second was Norm Hewitt, who'd had a rousing Super 12 and was still seen as the number two hooker. Assuming, however, that there was no erosion of Fitzpatrick's apparent indestructibility, Hewitt would have gone six weeks without a game by the time the All Blacks got to Ellis Park – not ideal for a big man who needs match-play. The selectors thought it made more sense for him to play for the Maori team against Argentina and Western Samoa, especially since Oliver's trial performance had shown he was ready for the bench. Hewitt was guaranteed a return to the squad when the Maoris completed their programme; in the meantime, he'd be paid as if he was still a squad member, not that he raised the issue of money.

Hewitt didn't like it and said so publicly. One can only imagine what he said privately when Oliver got a reasonable stint on the field against Fiji and played very well. At the post-match press conference, Hart mentioned that he hadn't had a call from Hewitt. But when Hewitt had to come on early in the second half at Johannesburg, the selectors gave themselves a small pat on the back.

The third was Osborne. He was still working his way back from injury and lacking a little speed so the panel decided to give Umaga his chance. "Glen accepted the situation," says Hart. "He was actually expecting to be dropped from the squad. He's been an outstanding squad member, accepting his setbacks without recrimination, working as hard if not harder than anyone, and grabbing opportunities when they've come his way."

The team didn't meet with universal approval. Hewitt's omission was criticised on the grounds that the best possible team hadn't been picked and the decision to persist with Bunce triggered a roar of disapproval from Clarke's supporters.

"It was a matter of us backing our judgement," says Hart. "If we'd dropped Bunce then he was gone, because he wouldn't get any opportunities to play himself back in. We decided we'd use Fiji and Argentina to work him back to full fitness. It's not something we'd normally do but Bunce had qualities that no-one else had. His experience was highly valued by the young outside backs and with a new, inexperienced wing and a second-five who'd been out of the frame for several years we wanted to minimise the disruption."

Randell's selection was questioned, notably by Wayne Shelford who argued that he'd been outplayed by both Tiatia and Blackadder. Hart would probably agree but counters that the selectors were looking beyond that game: "The All Blacks were very disappointed that Shelford saw fit to criticise a young guy's selection at a time when he needed support. To be fair, the interview was used selectively and they omitted Buck's comment that Randell was undoubtedly a player of the future. It put extra pressure on Randell but he got tremendous support from Michael Jones and Zinzan Brooke, who came to training even though his concussion stand-down would force him to miss the test.

"The amount of support the older players in both teams gave the young guys was a feature of the trial and is, in fact, one of New Zealand rugby's greatest attributes. Even if the youngster is a current or potential rival, the knowledge is passed on because players don't want to see other players fail. I remember going into the team-room to find Zinzan Brooke showing Xavier Rush how to improve his passing – they'd been at it for 45 minutes.

"We had a pretty settled team. Apart from Lomu, Ieremia was probably the only player outside the squad named whom we saw as a serious test contender at that stage. He'd been the form midfield back in the Super 12 – his vision and distribution had improved dramatically and, although he didn't have Stensness' kicking skills, he could put the ball behind the opposition backline. He may well have got the second-five berth and would certainly have been a reserve. In the back of our minds, we thought he might be the man against the Springboks when you really need physical hardness because of the greater intensity of the marking."

Some of the players could have happily done without the trial and had played accordingly but Hart sensed the team lift as they prepared for Fiji. The Fijian management took the unusual step of not naming their playing XV until just before kick-off. That would have bothered the media a lot more than the All Blacks; their focus was very much on getting their own game right rather than worrying about the opposition and their assessment of the Fijians didn't get down to individuals.

Jeff Wilson was the star of the night, picking up his second five-try bag at Albany Stadium within a fortnight. Randell had a fine game as did Mehrtens until he suffered the hamstring tear which rather ruined his international season. Five players – Randell, Umaga, Tonu'u, Riechelmann, and Oliver – made their debuts but everything, including the 71-5 scoreline, was overshadowed by the injury to Michael Jones. He suffered a ruptured patella tendon which would require major surgery and keep him out for several months.

Hart: "Most people assumed it was the end and he came under some pressure to make an announcement on his future. That underestimates the man, his love of the game, and his ability to fight back – he intends to play again. The question in everyone's mind was: how would we go without Ice? We couldn't replicate him – no-one else had his combination of qualities – so we had to look for an alternative. Randell's performance encouraged us to switch him to the blindside. There was no doubt about his speed, vision, and skills but he needed to develop his defence."

Although Zinzan Brooke returned for the first test against Argentina, the injury toll was mounting; they were only one game into the test programme and injuries had already taken out almost a third of the team. The coaches spent a lot of time on the whiteboard talking the newcomers through the moves and ensuring that they clearly understood their roles in defence and attack.

A lot of motivation came from wanting to produce a special performance for Jones. At training Hart emphasised that the others would have to take on a greater defensive load. He coined the term "Icepack," a call for the whole forward pack to lift their defensive work-rate to cover for the loss of their best defender.

"The tight forwards made a real commitment to defence," says Hart. "After one game, Fitzpatrick told me that his main concern coming off the field was that he was in line for a ticking-off for missing two tackles. From Wellington on, the tackle counts told the story; there was a much greater spread across the team and at the MCG the count was actually topped by Dowd."

The first test against Argentina brought Hart back into contact – and, before long, conflict – with Wyllie. On the Friday, the All Blacks were booked in for a walk in the park at Athletic Park. This consists of a familiarisation visit to the dressing rooms, a session on the field in tracksuits and running shoes to sample the atmosphere and go through some drills, and goal-kicking practice. On the way to Athletic Park, news came through that the Argentinians had turned up there unannounced and were having a training run. They'd been denied permission to train there the day before because of the condition of the ground. Wyllie's response, 24 hours later, was to redirect their bus to Athletic Park.

Hart didn't want to get into a confrontation with his old colleague cum rival on the eve of the test but, on the other hand, he wasn't going to have his team's routine disrupted. It was decided to proceed to Athletic Park and give the Argentinians time to leave before going out onto the field. That solution foundered on the rock of Wyllie's refusal to curtail his training run. The upshot was the unusual if not bizarre spectacle of the All Blacks strolling around one end of Athletic Park while the Argentinians trained at the other end. Hart stayed in the grandstand.

As psychological ploys go, it was different if hardly subtle. It was also counter-productive: the Argentinians didn't look altogether comfortable going through their drills with the All Blacks looking on and the size of the Argentinian forwards was the best possible reminder to the New Zealanders that they'd have to assert themselves physically. Nor were the implications of such an obvious – and disrespectful – attempt to psych them out lost on the All Blacks. That night, Hart got the three survivors from the Wyllie era – Fitzpatrick, Zinzan Brooke, and Ian Jones – to give the team a few examples of the sort of stuff Wyllie would be pounding into the Argentinians.

Albany Stadium hadn't been sold out for the Fiji test and the Wellington Rugby Union couldn't fill Athletic Park for this match even though the Hurricanes' last two games there had been played before full houses. Perhaps Argentina's shared series with England minus their 20-odd Lions hadn't created too much excitement; perhaps there are too many tests or people had already forked out that chunk of their discretionary spending set aside for rugby on the Hurricanes. Perhaps, too, tests against second or third-rank nations no longer rate with the public.

The shambolic aftermath of the 1996 Bledisloe Cup game had prompted an NZRFU ultimatum to the WRU: fix up Athletic Park or risk losing test matches. The WRU had acted, using funds from benefactors to upgrade the dressing rooms. Before that happened, Fitzpatrick and Hart had agreed that Wellington was too important to New Zealand rugby to lose its test-venue status. If it had come to the crunch, they would have told the NZRFU that the All Blacks were happy to play there, with or without an upgrade, although there was no question that one was needed.

To the frustration of the match officials who wanted to have the toss and inspect sprigs, the Argentinians got to Athletic Park late because Wyllie had decided to have an extended warm-up at a nearby ground. Things went on hold again during the playing of the national anthems; Fiji's wasn't short but Argentina's seemed to go on forever. Spectators will spend a long time on their feet when these two nations meet.

"I get a lot of letters complaining that some All Blacks don't sing the national anthem," says Hart. "I think it's difficult for people who haven't experienced the white-hot atmosphere which prevails in the count-down to a test match to understand what it's like. Each individual has his own way of dealing with it and priming himself. Some gain inspiration from singing, some from listening to the crowd, and for some the inspiration comes from within. For most of our opponents, their national anthem is the emotional high-point when they focus on the fact that they're representing their country. For the All Blacks, the anthem is followed by the haka which involves a lot of pride and emotion."

When the game finally got under way, the All Blacks produced a breathtaking and comprehensive performance, scoring 14 tries to one. The tight five operated at a speed, intensity, and skill-level which the Argentinians, heavily reliant on their upper-body power at maul and scrum, simply couldn't live with. Umaga turned on a block-busting display, repeatedly bringing his home crowd to their feet with his muscular, uninhibited running. He set up the try of the game, exploding onto Randell's switch pass inside the All Black 22 and scattering defenders before handing over to the faithful Kronfeld at the other end of the field. As he'd done in 1996, Cullen began the test programme in overdrive; Randell made a big contribution to the attack and was effective on defence when called upon; and Marshall gave a sneak preview of his brilliant kick for Wilson's try at the MCG. Fitzpatrick scored what in front row terms almost amounted to a runaway try, then generously baled out when Zinzan Brooke's outrageous, perfectly weighted cross-kick pitted him against Robin Brooke in a sprint to the try-line.

Spencer had a dream debut, finishing with a 33-point haul and showing the benefits of listening to the goal-kicking advice he'd been getting. Remembering what the pressure had done to Wilson at Twickenham in 1993, Hart hadn't forced the issue of who'd take the kicks – Wilson and Cullen were other options. But Spencer understood that he had to grasp the goal-kicking nettle if he wanted to compete successfully with Mehrtens; on the Friday night, he told Hart that he was happy to do the job. His first shot at goal – not a "gimme" by any means – came off the boot sweetly and from then on he kicked them from everywhere.

"Carlos showed a lot of emotion and humility in the dressing room afterwards when he was presented with his test tie," says Hart. "I reflected on how much he'd grown from the young man who'd been in South Africa where he'd shown undoubted attacking talent but denied the backline opportunities by doing too much himself – a case of individual flair being exercised at the expense of unit flair. We didn't want to inhibit his capacity to open up defences from broken play, just make him more mindful of the opportunities out wide. At Athletic Park he showed that he'd learned a great deal and presented himself as a formidable contender for the number 10 jersey."

When the panel had first contemplated a schedule of four tests in successive weeks coming off the trial and the Super 12 semi-finals and final and culminating with the Wallabies, they identified the second Argentinian test as an opportunity to rest players. That would have brought the whole issue of picking the best possible team, which had simmered briefly when Hewitt was left out of the squad, to boiling point. However, because the management team felt they'd struck the right balance between work and relaxation and the two tests hadn't been unduly physically demanding, the status quo was maintained.

Test fever had gripped Hamilton. Rugby Park had been sold out for many weeks and the All Blacks were all but buried under an avalanche of public relations and promotional activity; the public's appetite for the All Blacks seemed insatiable. Arriving at Rugby Park for Thursday afternoon's training session was almost like turning up for a game – there were 6000 people there. It was a huge compliment to the All Blacks but the noise made it difficult to hone team communication, which is one of the main objectives of the final training run.

Afterwards the players were due to sign autographs. That commitment had been made before anyone knew how big the crowd would be or how excited they'd get. Security was inadequate and there were extraordinary scenes behind the grandstand; children were stacked ten or twelve deep and the atmosphere of near-hysteria suggested a rock concert rather than a rugby practice. Hart went out to assess the situation and had to scoop up a child who'd fallen over and was in danger of being trampled. Clearly, all hell would break loose if the players went out there. Instead, a group of them armed with autograph sheets circled around to the rear of the crowd to draw the young fans away from the crush behind the grandstand.

With the game being played on the shortest day of the year, it promised to be cold and dewy underfoot. At 2.30pm the sun was shining and – while there's no question night rugby has its place – one had to question yet again the wisdom of staging so many night games when conditions are less conducive to skilful, spectacular rugby. It was certainly cold, as the sight of steam billowing from Allen's shaven head graphically indicated, but ground conditions weren't that bad.

It was a frustrating game. The All Blacks were in a no-win situation in that anything less than a 90-point winning margin would be regarded as failure. After their first test flogging, the Argentinians went into the game determined to do whatever was necessary to keep the score from blowing out. They defended tenaciously but there was no such thing as an off-side line. Add poor goal-kicking and high body positions close to the line and the

All Blacks had little to show for their early dominance apart from a lop-sided penalty count in their favour. It was a situation tailor-made for the sin-bin; although the English referee Brian Campsall came down firmly on Argentina, he could have whistled them off the park – literally. Campsall's view was that if he'd sent an Argentinian off, they might have erupted.

It was a considerably less expansive performance than the week before. With their time and space closed down, the All Black backline stuttered and only the last of the nine tries featured the sweeping movement and support play which had been hallmarks of the Athletic Park extravaganza.

"Even allowing for the Argentinians' negative approach, our first half display was pretty ordinary," says Hart. "Spencer missed a couple of the sort of kicks you just can't afford to miss in a major test. It was a satisfying moment all around when McLeod, who'd worked very hard to regain his place in the squad, replaced Bunce; the fact that his reappearance in the black jersey took place in front of his home crowd was a nice coincidence. Bunce still wasn't where we wanted him to be although he was starting to show a little more speed and there were no worries about his defence. We'd seen enough to keep backing him."

22

MISSION
UNREASONABLE

JOHN HART objected to three aspects of the 1997 Bledisloe Cup and Tri-Nations series playing schedule:
    • the staging of a third Bledisloe Cup game before the Tri-Nations series;
    • the draw which had the All Blacks playing tests in Pretoria and Melbourne a week apart;
    • South Africa's unilateral decision to shift their home test against the All Blacks from Pretoria to Johannesburg after the SANZAR board had ratified the draw.

The decision taken in 1996 to play extra Bledisloe Cup games in 1997 and 1998 was driven purely by financial considerations. In Hart's view, it was putting short-term financial gain ahead of the players' long-term welfare and muddying the waters going into the Tri-Nations series. The Tri-Nations draw became hostage to the Australian Rugby Union's determination to have an All Black test at the Melbourne Cricket Ground; it would be a gate-takings bonanza and a showpiece suitable for presenting rugby union to a new audience. The problem was, July 26 was the only Saturday within the time frame when the MCG was available. The ARU went ahead and made the commitment, then set about securing South African support. The South Africans were only too happy to oblige; building the draw around an All Black-Wallaby game in Melbourne on July 26 meant that both their opponents would have to play in Australasia and South Africa a week apart while the

Springboks would get a two-week break each time they travelled.

"We were given three options on the Tri-Nations draw, two of which we could live with and one we couldn't live with," says Hart. "It appears that Australia and South Africa got together and did a deal which foisted the unacceptable option on us. It's not about the number of tests – that's part and parcel of the new era – but the lack of recovery time between them. Players aren't robots.

"The South Africans decided that the Louis Luyt-controlled Ellis Park in Johannesburg was a more appropriate venue than Pretoria and changed it. When it was pointed out that the draw had been ratified and couldn't be changed without the agreement of all three parties, they took no notice. I agree with the principle that the host country should be able to decide where matches take place but that wasn't the issue – the issue was the way the South Africans want to make or break the rules when it suits them. Not only that, it's done in a way which is almost calculated to offend – the correspondence from SARFU on this issue didn't show much respect for our position."

Hart was disappointed that the NZRFU hadn't taken a more forceful stance on these issues; as he saw it, they'd been bulldozed. NZRFU Chief Executive David Moffett sees it differently: "We agreed to play a third Bledisloe Cup match in 1997 and 1998 – but not beyond that, much to the Australians' dismay – with our $6 million loss very much in mind. You have to get a balance between the financial returns and all the things Hart gets concerned about but there's a clear nexus between the funds the NZRFU can generate and what we can pay the players.

"SANZAR has worked too rigidly within the time-frame originally set down for the Tri-Nations. Six matches in six weeks falls into place but it does mean some teams will be disadvantaged by having to play back-to-back – in 1997 it was New Zealand and Australia. New Zealand had the best draw in 1996 but you can't expect that every year. The ARU quite improperly agreed a date with Victorian Premier Jeff Kennett before telling us. We were presented with a fait accompli: if you've got to schedule six games in six weeks involving three teams home and away and one game is already set in stone, it's very difficult to resolve. We weren't happy about it but it was something we had to live with. Hart has devised a draw which would prevent this situation arising by having a bye-round in the middle of the series. We've taken it up with Australia and South Africa and hopefully this draw will come into force in 1998.

"On the switch to Ellis Park, the South Africans believed it was their sovereign right and just refused to discuss it. What were we going to do – say we wouldn't play? We hammered away for three or four months then said we've got other things to do, let's get on with them. I accept that the coach should always be trying to get the best result. If Hart wasn't an occasional pain in the backside, I'd be worried because he wouldn't be doing what all good coaches do which is to get the best environment for his team. My job is to make him justify what he wants."

There was concern both inside and outside the All Black camp that their build-up had been insufficiently testing. Hart had talked up the aerobic and physical challenges posed by Fiji and Argentina respectively but was privately worried that the team hadn't had enough of a work-out.

Australia seemed to be in good shape. Despite horrendous injury problems, they'd had a highly successful end-of-year tour of Europe and were coming off a bruising two-nil series win over France. The French hadn't clicked as a team but they'd pushed the Wallabies hard in all departments. Although coach Greg Smith and the selectors had continued to tinker with the line-up, they were sticking with their most contentious decision – Tim Horan at first-five rather than David Knox who, along with George Gregan, had been the spark which had ignited the ACT Brumbies' impressive Super 12 campaign.

"I thought the Wallabies were struggling a little with their pattern," says Hart. "They looked as if they were caught between what they had and what they wanted to bring in from the ACT. I had the simplistic view that Horan and Jason Little were an outstanding midfield combination – difficult to mark and putting constant pressure on you – and didn't think Horan showed quite the same skills at first-five. But the Wallaby backline was still an outstanding unit: they had Matthew Burke, who on his 1996 form was arguably the best all-round fullback in world rugby, a magic centre in Little, and emerging stars on the outside in Joe Roff and Ben Tune."

Hart had also been impressed by the way the Springboks had regrouped on their end-of-year tour and discerned a significant step up in skill, continuity, and mobility in their performance against Wales. Andre Markgraaff's fall from grace was a setback but although his replacement, Carel du Plessis, had virtually no coaching track record, he was a renowned rugby thinker. Hart thought his public statements revealed a very clear grasp of the requirements of coaching at the top level in the modern game. The ex-All Blacks who'd encountered du Plessis on the Cavaliers tour and at the Classics tournament in Bermuda held him in high regard.

The du Plessis era began shakily with the Springboks surprisingly going down in their home series against the Lions. "The Lions were written off but any team with that quality of management and coaching staff deserved respect," says Hart. "Their success had a lot to do with planning, organisation, motivation, and unity. They played territory well, kicked their goals, and defended with tremendous commitment led by Scott Gibbs. The Springboks' failure in the first two tests could be placed fairly and squarely on the lack of a goal-kicker but, even so, they could have won both games."

In terms of intensity, the Lions series had provided the Boks with exactly the sort of testing build-up they'd lacked in 1996. With Jannie de Beer kicking the goals, they'd stormed to a decisive win in the third test at Ellis Park which would have given them a lot of confidence going into their clash with the All Blacks at the same venue.

Andrew Mehrtens had been named in the All Black team for the Bledisloe Cup match at Lancaster Park but his hamstring still wasn't right. Carlos Spencer was restored which meant the All Blacks were unchanged for the third match in a row. The Wallabies had real problems: two of their stars, Burke and Little, were ruled out with injury and replaced by Steve Larkham and Daniel Herbert. Lock David Giffin's last-minute withdrawal meant a call-up for Matt Cockbain who'd spent most of his short representative career at loose forward. The All Black coaching staff thought Cockbain's late introduction could affect the Wallaby scrum. The scrum had been the All Blacks' main focus at training and the scrummaging session at Aranui High School was the toughest Hart had ever seen.

Zinzan Brooke, who was about to play his 50th test, came down with a bad dose of 'flu and took little part in training. When the bug hit Josh Kronfeld, the panel opted for a two back/four forward bench in case either of the 'flu victims failed to go the distance. The back reserves were Jon Preston, recalled to the squad as cover for Mehrtens, and Alama Ieremia, who'd replaced Scott McLeod after the panel had received a positive report on his comeback match in Wellington club rugby.

The All Blacks' first-half display was exceptional. There were danger signs for the Australian scrum from the outset; the All

Blacks chugged forward on their own ball enabling Marshall to break dangerously on the blindside. At the next scrum, Gregan delayed the feed because his pack was skidding backwards and conceded a penalty. Zinzan Brooke picked up the inevitable pushover try after the All Blacks had pinned the Wallabies inside their 22 and pounded them mercilessly for several minutes.

The live-wire Kronfeld's ability to get to the ball-carrier's shoulder anywhere on the field earned him two tries. The first was created by Jeff Wilson who rounded Roff as if the Wallaby was wearing fisherman's waders. The second, the try of the game, began with a Wallaby turnover just outside the All Black 22. Spencer flicked the ball through his legs to Frank Bunce; he fed Christian Cullen who hit the line at pace, breaching the defence. Tana Umaga broke Herbert's tackle and rampaged into the Wallaby half. The ball went to ground; Bunce secured it and the forwards, led by Fitzpatrick, hit the ruck like a battering ram. Robin Brooke cleared the ball to Spencer on the left; he waltzed around Marco Caputo and found Kronfeld with another piece of sleight-of-hand.

Setting the pattern for the matches to come, the Wallabies came out firing in the second half with the game beyond their reach. The All Blacks' possession dried up; when they did get the ball, they weren't able to hold onto it for long. Inside the last 15 minutes, a tighthead led to Zinzan Brooke's second try and took the All Blacks out to 30-6. Having scored the tries and run themselves to a standstill, the 'flu victims were replaced. The All Blacks weren't impressed with the old-fashioned Lancaster Park booing served up to Mark Carter.

At the very end of the game came the incident which would dominate post-match discussion and deflect attention from what had been an authoritative All Black performance. Sean Fitzpatrick, loitering on the fringe of a ruck, interfered with Gregan as he went to pick up the ball. He was penalised by Ed Morrison who made a production of giving him a lecture. The television audience heard Morrison utter the fateful words: "Official caution; that's six or seven times I've had to penalise Blacks for professional fouls."

It was an unfortunate comment from a referee who a minute or two earlier had chosen to ignore a similar offence by John Eales on Justin Marshall when the All Blacks were poised on the Wallaby line. Far more unfortunate was the fact that it was invalid, as Morrison himself would later concede. The words would come back to haunt him as they were used by the Australian camp to justify their attacks on his handling of the game.

The comment was manna from heaven for the Australian television commentary team who'd worked themselves into a near-frenzy during the second half, to the point of suggesting that the Wallabies should resort to violence. The professional foul theme was taken up by the media, including Wayne Shelford whose disapproval must have caused a few wry smiles among his contemporaries.

"Smith entered the fray after the game and his comments got a lot more strident on his return to Australia," says Hart. "It was a case of people in glass houses throwing stones because, when we studied the tape, we saw four professional fouls – two from each team. I don't accept them and told Robin Brooke so. I decided not to trade verbal blows with Smith through the media because I don't think slanging matches between coaches are in the best interests of the game. I could have highlighted Troy Coker's 20 minutes in the blood-bin after halftime for a minor hand injury suffered within the first ten minutes; it was a flagrant abuse of the blood-bin and amounted to nothing less than an interchange."

In reality, the only flaw in the All Blacks' performance was their failure to turn an emphatic win into a demolition. Initially, Smith conceded that the professional fouls hadn't made a scrap of difference to the result. However, his subsequent attacks and those of ARU Chief Executive John O'Neill and sections of the Australian media virtually amounted to an attempt to de-legitimise the All Blacks' victory.

At the aftermatch function, Hart was asked to make a presentation to Zinzan Brooke to mark his 50th test: "I was proud to do so. Although we haven't always agreed and grew apart when I was off the scene, I'd had a long association with him – I picked him for his first Auckland game in 1986 and was a selector when he came into the All Blacks in 1987. He'd done it the hard way, suffering from the 'Bring Back Buck' campaign and a lack of faith in his ability on the part of Alex Wyllie and, initially, Laurie Mains. That's reflected by the fact that, even though he and Michael Jones made their All Black debuts in 1987 and Jones missed a lot of tests through injury and not playing on Sundays, he beat Brooke to 50 caps. Zinny fought through it all to become one of the game's key personalities, on and off the field. He has genuine star quality and has brought a new dimension to loose forward play."

Mehrtens was named, subject to a fitness test, in the 26-man squad to travel to South Africa and Australia. He came through a club match unscathed to join the squad. The squad consisted of the 24 players who'd assembled in Christchurch plus Todd Blackadder and Mark Cooksley.

"Cooksley's selection was a recognition that he'd overtaken the back-up locks who'd gone to South Africa a year earlier," says Hart. "His all-round game and scrummaging had improved immeasurably and he'd performed well for the New Zealand Maori team in Western Samoa. Blackadder gave us an extra tight-loose forward capable of covering blindside flanker, number 8, and lock. He's immensely wholehearted and committed to the All Black cause and very popular with players and management. In choosing back-ups, it's important to pick players who'll give everything to the cause rather than allow their frustration to push them into chipping away at the edges."

This time, there was a welcoming committee at Johannesburg airport: Rian Oberholzer, SARFU'S Chief Executive, Johan Prinsloo, Chief Executive of the Transvaal union, and Kobis Ecksteen, who'd prove to be an excellent liaison officer.

Before embarking on Mission Unreasonable, the team took a break from rugby at the Bakubung Resort Hotel in the Pilanesburg National Park, adjacent to Sun City. As at Plettenberg Bay the year before, the squad was divided into teams: Bunce, whose ties of blood to the British royal family had recently come to light, led The Bluebloods; Umaga's team was Bob's Dreaded Mob, a reference to the winger's flamboyant hairstyle modelled on the late, great reggae singer Bob Marley; continuing the younger South Island All Blacks' mysterious infatuation with Wellingtonians of yesteryear, Wilson led Hewson's Heroes, while Dowdy's Freaks speak for themselves.

The team finishing last in the competitions would be the winners' slaves for a day so all four teams had plenty at stake right to the bitter end. The events included team tennis; a sports trivia quiz, the answers to which are still a matter of dispute; team gambling at Sun City; skits; crosswords, a discipline dominated by the Freaks in the form of Ross Cooper, Mehrtens, and Taine Randell and in which the Dreads failed to trouble the scorers; volleyball; and scrabble, in which Lee Stensness, the red-hot favourite, came through under pressure.

The judges were Messrs Hart and Richard Fry and Ms Jane Dent, who had to stand down when an innocent remark was seized upon as proof of bias towards the Freaks. Vehement protests ensued, expertly orchestrated by Fitzpatrick and Zinzan Brooke, and Dent was reduced to observing proceedings from behind the team video camera. The Bluebloods took out the final event, the volleyball, to share first place with the Freaks. The hapless Dreads came in last although their sentence was commuted to four hours on a legal technicality. Allowed to choose on whom they would wait on hand and foot, they sensibly opted for The Bluebloods, the marginally more humane of the joint winners.

The All Blacks were based in Pretoria during the build-up. When the management sought to hold a training run at Ellis Park, they were told that only a light run without boots was permissible. When they tried to get the kickers some stadium time at Loftus Versfeld, they were knocked back. Mike Banks persuaded Prinsloo to allow a proper training run on Ellis Park and after Hart had alluded to the situation at a press conference, word came through that the kickers could use Loftus. But when they got there, they were turned away by an official who claimed that the field was flooded. It was a brilliantly fine day. Hart vented his frustration by booting a traffic cone; it was sturdier than it looked and he had a sore knee for several days.

When it was suggested at a press conference that the All Blacks had a propensity for committing professional fouls, Hart returned serve by saying that he believed the Springboks had deliberately slowed the game down during the 1996 series. This caused quite a stir amongst the attending media, but lost its momentum when, to Hart's surprise, Markgraaff came out in the press the next day admitting that they'd set out to do exactly that.

Although du Plessis had stuck with the team which had beaten the Lions in the final test, he was under pressure over his selections. There was widespread suspicion that the ongoing omission of Hennie le Roux and Kobus Wiese had more to do with the fact that they'd crossed SARFU than rugby considerations. With le Roux overlooked and Japie Mulder and Andre Joubert injured, du Plessis had picked a youthful backline; the newly capped Russell Bennett, Percy Montgomery, and Pieter Rossouw, none of whom had taken part in the Super 12, lined up alongside Danie van Schalkwyk and Andre Snyman, who'd made their debuts against the All Blacks in 1996.

Thursday's session was the All Blacks' first private training run since Hart had been coach: "We wanted to work through a few tactical variations which, as it turned out, we never got the chance to use but it was mostly to give the players some space – they enjoyed being able to sit down and stretch and unwind afterwards rather than having to cope with the demands of the press and public. We picked up some deficiencies in the defensive pattern which we simply wouldn't have been able to talk about if it had been a public session. I came away rethinking my attitude to private sessions."

The Springboks had gone in hard in the third test against the Lions; there'd been some rugged work done in the rucks and the touch judges had had a busy afternoon. Word reached the New Zealand management that they intended to dish out the same medicine to the All Blacks. At his meeting with the Australian referee Peter Marshall, Hart expressed concern about off-the-ball stuff. Marshall told them that he'd watched the tape of the Lancaster Park match and thought the professional foul thing had been blown out of proportion; both sides had been guilty of it. Du Plessis had vowed that he'd tackle Marshall on the All Blacks' professional fouls and scrum tactics but Hart was able to come out of the meeting saying that the All Blacks had no issues with the referee.

On Friday afternoon, Hart got a message from Marshall to say he wouldn't permit the players to wear protective vests. Hart had assumed that the three southern hemisphere countries were on the same wavelength and hadn't bothered to raise the vest issue at their meeting. He spoke to Marshall who accepted his assurance that the All Blacks would cut down the vests and tape them to their bodies.

Three minutes before the All Blacks were due on the field, touch judge Wayne Erickson came into their dressing room. Seeing Ian Jones wearing a cut-down vest taped to his body, he instructed him to take it off. Hart told Erickson that he'd sorted it out with Marshall. Erickson came back with Marshall and the other touch judge, Welshman Clayton Thomas, who'd apparently delivered the same veto in the Springbok dressing room. Marshall told Hart that he must have misunderstood what had been agreed to.

"The thing had gone way beyond a joke," says Hart. "Erickson had no problem with the vests when he refereed us against Fiji. It's a maddening issue because the vests don't do any harm – a padded shoulder does less damage than an unpadded one. They prevent bruising and abrasions and the IRB's medical committee have been recommending them for some time.

"I took them outside and said I wasn't prepared to have the team's preparation disrupted like this. If they insisted on the padding being removed, it would take 25 to 30 minutes because some of the players had adapted their vests to cover medical conditions for which they had certificates. They were taped up in such a way that it would take a while to remove the vests and get re-strapped and they certainly wouldn't be going out until they were ready. Marshall was embarrassed – someone had put him under pressure. He told Thomas to go and tell the Boks they could put their vests back on."

After the game, Hart sought support from du Plessis and Luyt to have the vests officially approved for the Tri-Nations series. Luyt, who doesn't mind thumbing his nose at the IRB, was all for it provided Hart could get the Australians on side.

The crowd of just over 60,000 – Ellis Park can hold 73,000 – must have been a disappointment to those who'd organised the switch from Loftus Versfeld. There was one small group of All Black supporters; in 1996, the All Blacks had got used to having sizeable and very vocal contingents of New Zealanders in the crowds. There was what seemed like a deafening roar when the All Blacks emerged; it was no more than a polite round of applause compared to the wall of sound which greeted the Boks.

Hart: "In my time, the All Blacks had never gone into a game better physically and mentally prepared. We started well: Umaga took the ball up, Spencer kicked deep into Springbok territory, they put it into touch, we won the lineout. Then Bunce took the ball into a ruck and we turned it over. The Boks then proceeded to take us apart. The ferocity of their attack, their ball retention, their control, their ability to put the ball into the corners, their scrum – it was all firing. For the first 30 minutes, they were almost as good as the All Blacks were at Athletic Park in 1996."

The first points came when Fitzpatrick was penalised for being on the wrong side of a ruck. No fewer than four Springbok forwards trampled on him. Although Erickson pointed that out to Marshall, the penalty stood. Given Hart's representations, it wasn't a promising start.

The first try came from another turnover, again engineered by Ruben Kruger who turned Bunce on his back. The Bok forwards piled in and won the ball before the All Black pack got there. De Beer belied his reputation as a kicking machine by breaking, the All Blacks stood off tackles, and Naka Drotske scored in the left-hand corner after some unSpringbok-like improvisation.

Eventually, the All Blacks got some field position. They worked a tap move from a short-arm penalty and Bunce threaded his way through a static defence to score under the bar. To be only three points down after a quarter of an hour on the back foot was as good as the All Blacks could have hoped for and probably better than they deserved. The try lifted them. They produced a huge scrum and Zinzan Brooke and Marshall manufactured a break up the middle. There was an overlap on the left but a couple of imprecise passes slowed the attack and the opportunity was lost. Montgomery, who has real pace, broke from inside his 22 and when the ball came back from a midfield ruck, de Beer stroked over a dropped goal from beyond the 10-metre mark.

The Springboks climbed straight back into the All Blacks. Another turnover allowed Joost van der Westhuizen to probe the blind. Umaga couldn't control the kick and the All Blacks were scrambling. They conceded a scrum under their posts from which the Boks worked a blindside move, catching Spencer and Stensness in two minds. It probably didn't make much difference; the move was perfectly executed and Bennett hit the ball at maximum velocity.

Another de Beer penalty made it 23-7. Even for the Comeback Kings, it was looking dicey. After a few minutes of frantic thrust and counter-thrust in which the Boks looked decidedly more threatening, Wilson got the All Blacks back in the game. He charged down van der Westhuizen's kick on the blindside of a ruck on halfway, recovered the ball and, stepping as surely as a tightrope walker, negotiated the narrowest of paths between the touchline and Kruger's unavailing tackle before clearing out to score. From the kick-off, the All Blacks spread the ball. Wilson bobbed up on the left wing to nudge a beautifully judged kick in behind the Springbok defence and Spencer won the race for the try. Even though he missed the meat-and-drink conversion, the All Blacks had come back from a near-death experience in the blink of an eye.

The second half opened with more helter-skelter. Cullen and Stensness got a little ambitious inside the danger zone and it was panic stations when van der Westhuizen got his hands on the ball. The Springboks knocked on metres from the goal-line but the All Blacks couldn't clear and de Beer kicked another penalty. Once again, it could have been worse.

Ten minutes into the half, Jones picked one off the top of a lineout. Bunce ran onto Spencer's flat pass and broke into space as he crossed halfway. With support runners led by Randell coming from everywhere and Bunce keeping his options open, the Boks hung off and Bunce kept going. Finally, a couple of them tried to wrestle him down but no-one out-muscles Frank Bunce that close to the line. This try was the high-point of one of the truly great individual performances; while the flashes of attacking brilliance live in the memory, his stupendous defence was just as crucial to the cause.

Throughout the week, the All Black medical team had been nervous about the state of Fitzpatrick's knee. A scan showed no significant damage but by halftime it was clear he'd struggle to finish the match. While Spencer was converting Bunce's try from wide out to make it 26-all, Norm Hewitt came on to play the most important thirty minutes of his career.

De Beer dropped another goal to put the Boks back in front but they infringed from the kick-off and Spencer levelled it again. It was penalties from there on, Spencer punching his kicks as straight as laser beams from the "right" side of the field. Ahead 35-32 and with the pack smashing up the middle, it looked like the All Blacks would nail it. But Marshall threw an untidy pass out in front of the South African posts and suddenly the Springboks were running onto a loose ball behind the All Black forwards. Stensness was penalised for shouldering the speedy Montgomery and de Beer kicked his side back onto the attack. And there they stayed. There were mauls on the goal-line, five metre scrums, a kick which hit the upright, and a midfield break – but the All Blacks held on.

Hart: "Bunce was the hero. I said at the team talk that we'd picked him for this game when his experience would be needed. He'd had doubters and critics by the score and it was nice to see him get the accolades from those who'd bayed for his blood. Randell, who'd also taken a lot of flak, was another to shine; he was outstanding on defence and created opportunities on attack. His man-of-the-match award gave us a lot of pleasure. He'd gone through a difficult period when he was shown up in the Barbarians-England game but he'd addressed the problem and made huge progress. Spencer's selection ahead of Mehrtens was based on form and Mehrtens' lack of matchplay as he made his way back from injury. Spencer kicked superbly under intense pressure and, although he blew a certain try by kicking with Wilson unmarked outside him, it's worth remembering that he created the opportunity in the first place. It's part of the learning curve.

"Hewitt gave a great yell as he ran onto the field. He was letting his emotions out – he'd waited an awfully long time for the chance to play a substantial role on a really big stage. He threw in well and took the ball up. Losing Fitzpatrick put the pressure on but Zinzan Brooke's leadership and the support of the senior players, led by Jones, overcame it.

"We might've been a little lucky to come away with a win. We were under pressure at the end and it might've been different if Henry Honiball hadn't chipped ahead after breaking the line. Marshall had his arm up for an off-side penalty against us but took it down when Honiball broke. Watching de Beer's final kick from directly behind, it looked for all the world as if it was going over. At the time, I would've settled for a draw but, on reflection, I feel that a side which scores four tries to two and comes back from 23-7 down deserves to win.

"The dressing room was like a field hospital in a war zone and the mood was downcast, more that of a beaten team. The All Blacks were quite down over their performance. I told them to lighten up – they'd come away from Ellis Park with five points. But looking at the tape, they were right to feel disappointed – it was a flawed performance."

South African rugby was in a strange mood. They'd had a bad trot, losing successive home series, making little impact in the Super 12, and lurching from crisis to crisis off the field. Some of their media people had voiced the unthinkable, expressing the hope that the All Blacks would give the Springboks such a hiding there'd be a cleansing of the stables and a brand-new start. As it was, the Springbok camp found hope in defeat, drawing encouragement from the way they'd played and the quality of the game.

But at the aftermatch function, there was a reminder of the vendettas and animosities which bedevil South African rugby. In his speech, Fitzpatrick congratulated James Small on becoming the most-capped Springbok. There were five speeches by people either connected with the Springboks or SARFU, including Gary Teichmann; not one of them contained a reference to Small. Small went over to thank Fitzpatrick who was talking to Luyt. Luyt had something to say to the most-capped Springbok: "You're bloody lucky."

The All Blacks left Johannesburg on Sunday night, flying to Melbourne via Perth and Sydney. With a delayed take-off, the journey took 26 hours hotel to hotel, ending at one o'clock on Tuesday morning. Three players – Fitzpatrick, Cullen, and Umaga – were in doubt for the MCG; a number of others were bruised and battered. A day on an aircraft isn't the best therapy for sore bodies and the after-effects of Ellis Park were still being felt several days later. Adrian Cashmore and Anton Oliver were summoned to Melbourne as cover.

"At a press conference at Sydney airport, I made the mistake of saying that the scheduling of this game amounted to an ambush cooked up by Australia and South Africa," says Hart. "The comment was seen as a whinge in Australia and perhaps by some in New Zealand as well. I was trying to make a point about the need to revise the structure of the tournament to ensure that teams don't have to make that journey between matches a week apart and all three teams are given an equal chance."

The coaches and medical staff had decided on a regime of training every day but closely monitoring the condition of the players and adjusting the intensity accordingly. The panel re-thought selection and tactics with a view to conserving energy by playing a more structured and accurate game, setting targets from first phase for the forwards to hit in order to get them into the match right from the start.

"I don't like taking a conservative approach but it suited the circumstances," says Hart. "We needed to play in a way which didn't match the Australians' expectations. It all led to a re-think on second-five and a call-up for Ieremia who'd shaped as our number one midfield back earlier in the season."

The Mehrtens-Spencer debate was resumed. At Ellis Park, Spencer's restarts had been disappointing and he'd taken a couple of wrong options. Overall though, he'd had a fine game; he was assured in his calling of set-piece moves and the backline had confidence in him. The unsentimental fact of the matter was that he'd grabbed his opportunity. The issue was settled beyond doubt at the first training run; Spencer had handled the travel well and was on top of his game while Mehrtens failed to allay the suspicion that his hamstring still wasn't 100 per cent right.

Umaga hadn't recovered from the heavy blow to the chest which had forced him off Ellis Park. He was replaced by Glen Osborne who was one of the worst affected by jet lag. The panel thought about making a change in the pack to bring in some fresh legs but the prospect of being without the captain and most experienced player dissuaded them.

Although many of the players didn't sleep overnight, the team trained diligently on Tuesday afternoon. Having to stand aside at training and contemplate the likelihood that he wouldn't take the field was a new experience for Fitzpatrick and not one he enjoyed. Hart talked to Zinzan Brooke about taking over the captaincy. The All Black camp had often heard that Fitzpatrick and Bunce were the two players the Australians feared most. Hart pointed out that that could only mean they didn't have much respect for the rest of the team. The players' attention was also drawn to the fact that the programme for Saturday night contained no reference to a presentation of the Bledisloe Cup, which could be seen as implying that a Wallaby win was a foregone conclusion.

Hart rang Smith to secure his support for the padded vests. Smith volunteered the information that he was under a lot of pressure and people were trying to unseat him; the only way he could survive was to beat the All Blacks. Hart replied that he didn't think he could help him there.

Wednesday's training was a good news/bad news affair. The good news was the way the pack responded to the challenge of covering for Fitzpatrick's absence with some impressive scrummaging. The bad news was that both Zinzan Brooke and Cullen suffered leg muscle strains. The panel seriously considered bringing Blackadder into the reserves to provide some experience and leadership in case they lost both the captain and his lieutenant. By the time training wound down, the players were out on their feet. Zinzan Brooke went to bed at six o'clock and woke up 12 hours later.

Fitzpatrick was hell-bent on playing but no-one in the management team was putting money on it. The plan had been to let him rest the knee through the week and make a decision on Saturday morning. But on Thursday afternoon, Fitzpatrick told Hart that he wouldn't go into the game with any confidence unless he got through training that night.

The All Blacks had a long, slow, private training run at the MCG, soaking up the atmosphere of one of the world's great stadiums. Fitzpatrick took part in most of it; now it was a matter of how the knee reacted to the work-out. The spirit had lifted noticeably; the banter was back, led, as always, by Zinzan Brooke who'd been uncharacteristically subdued earlier in the week. But the sight of players falling asleep on the bus-trip back to the hotel was a reminder that they weren't out of the woods yet.

The huge influx of visitors had created a carnival atmosphere in AFL-besotted Melbourne. There would be a substantial Kiwi presence in the predicted 90,000-plus crowd if attendance at the training runs was anything to go by – Kiwis turned up in their hundreds.

The Wallabies' defeat at Lancaster Park had triggered a flood of caustic media comment which was given a second wind by the extraordinary public tongue-lashing that Smith administered to his team at their first post-Christchurch training run. One could only wonder how the players felt reading headlines along the lines of "Coach tells team: You're soft." Since then, the Wallabies had played a pointless test against a patch-work England team, two-thirds of whom had flown in from South Africa where they'd been on tour with the Lions. England were sacrificial lambs but it took the Wallabies 70 minutes to get them on the spit.

There were eight changes to the team who'd played in Christchurch, three of them injury-related: Burke and Little returned and James Holbeck replaced the injured Pat Howard. They'd bolstered their front row by bringing in Andrew Heath and Michael Foley and added bulk in the form of Garrick Morgan and Daniel Manu. A certain amount of fanfare, not least from Smith, surrounded the introduction of Michael Brial to put some fire in the belly. Brial's loss of control at Suncorp Stadium in 1996 seemed to have earned him enforcer status; former Wallaby turned TV comments man Chris Handy predicted that he'd "knock the wax out of the All Blacks' ears".

Everyone who was anyone in Australian rugby seemed to be having a dig at the All Blacks. Smith had plenty to say about professional fouls, Brown's scrummaging technique – he claimed the All Black tighthead put his hand on the ground to propel himself forward but it was more a case of him trying to prevent the scrum from going down when his opponent couldn't handle the pressure – and Ed Morrison's performance at Lancaster Park. The Wallaby coach said he was looking forward to telling Morrison the facts of life. Then O'Neill got in on the act; he labelled the All Blacks "precious" for not sending the test XV to a civic reception even though the Victorian Premier's office had been advised months beforehand that they wouldn't attend; he attacked Hart for his criticisms of the Tri-Nations draw and made a gratuitous remark about the All Black coach's relationship with the NZRFU; he made an equally gratuitous comment about the NZRFU's sponsorship negotiations.

O'Neill then turned his guns on Morrison, saying that although they couldn't have him replaced, they'd be having some severe words with him. He criticised Morrison's habit of addressing All Blacks by their Christian names, saying it sounded like "old home week". Morrison, of course, had called players on both sides by their Christian names. O'Neill was part of the Australian entourage who met Morrison before the game. Coupled with the fact that he felt free to comment publicly on issues of team performance and selection, his presence indicated that he saw the playing side of the national team as within his domain. It will be interesting to see whether having one's toes regularly trodden on becomes part and parcel of being the Wallaby coach.

Hart bided his time, describing Smith's comments as "disappointing" but saying the All Blacks' focus was firmly on the game. The counter-strike was launched at his final pre-game press conference when he raised a matter which had been bothering him for a couple of weeks: the bawling-out Smith had given his team after Lancaster Park. According to press reports, which Hart had had confirmed, Smith told the Wallabies that they had to take matters into their own hands if the opposition committed professional fouls and other illegalities. If they had to start an all-in brawl to get the message across, so be it – he wouldn't be upset if a Wallaby was sent off as a result.

"It was scarcely believable that a coach could express such views in this day and age," says Hart, "especially when it was clearly aimed at the All Blacks and our next meeting was, to some extent, a missionary expedition into non-rugby territory. A Bledisloe Cup showpiece which degenerated into an all-in brawl in front of 90,000 people would hardly have been what the ARU had in mind when they moved heaven and earth to stage the game in Melbourne."

On Friday morning, Hart and Fitzpatrick met Morrison who'd had his encounter with the Australians the night before. Morrison said he was well aware of the psychological war being waged by the Australian camp and the media and would tell them what he'd told the Aussies: he'd call it how he saw it and he wouldn't be influenced by events off the field. He said he regretted using the term "professional foul" to Fitzpatrick. They went through all the issues which had been aired during the week. Hart asked Morrison if there was anything about the way the All Blacks played the game which concerned him; there wasn't. The New Zealanders left the meeting feeling that the psychological warfare campaign hadn't achieved its objective.

That proved to be wishful thinking. "I was disappointed that Ed reverted to the northern hemisphere approach with us generally on the wrong side of the decisions," says Hart. "I didn't directly criticise him after the game but said I thought the All Blacks were over-refereed and that the yawning imbalance in the penalty count had kept the Wallabies in the game. Watching the tape only strengthened that conviction. I'd like to think the psychological warfare didn't play a part but Smith and O'Neill went in very hard. It raises the issue of whether there should be a code of conduct governing comments about match officials."

There were 90,119 spectators at the MCG. This was sport on an epic scale: the atmosphere was super-charged; the vast stadium throbbed with anticipation. Despite all the talk of the Kiwi invasion, the Wallabies were greeted with a mind-blowing roar and the Australian national anthem must have echoed around Port Phillip Bay.

Wilson showed great skill and athleticism to retrieve Spencer's switch kick-off but the Wallabies killed the ball and got away with it. From the lineout, they drove the maul into All Black territory and were awarded a penalty when it went to ground. Morrison and the touch judge missed a post-whistle stomp on Kronfeld, the first in a series of cheap shots from the home side. Burke pumped over the 47-metre penalty; 3-0 with less than two minutes gone. The Wallabies made the early running but the All Blacks went forward at the first scrum and Brial looked off the pace as he missed Spencer on the blindside. It was clear from the outset that this was a different Ed Morrison: there were no first names; it was numbers and colours only.

Spencer levelled the scores with a long-range penalty, then the All Blacks got down to business. After a series of drives off an attacking lineout, the ball was moved blind. Randell sidestepped Brial and Bunce brushed off Burke to score. A minute later, Brial took the ball up off a ruck. Taking a leaf out of the Springboks' book, Bunce and Brown turned him on his back and Kronfeld ripped the ball free. Marshall went to the open side and, sensing that Burke had come forward looking to make a blindside run, drilled an inch-perfect kick over the Wallaby backline into the right-hand corner. Wilson got there ahead of Roff, Spencer's kick from the sideline sneaked inside the upright, and the All Blacks had suddenly jumped out to 17-3. Those two tries in as many minutes drained the crowd of fervour and largely took them out of the game. In the second half, the ground announcer was reduced to appealing to the crowd to get behind the Wallabies.

After half an hour, Brial the enforcer had departed, replaced by Coker. When Eales was penalised for striking Fitzpatrick, Spencer kicked his third penalty and the All Blacks went to the break ahead 23-3.

"There's no doubt that Eales became rattled under the pressure and Fitzpatrick was relentless in maintaining it," says

Hart. "Eales' captaincy had been criticised by Mark Ella and the air of crisis surrounding his coach can't have helped. He makes a massive contribution but the expectations of him from both his team and the public are just as massive."

The Wallabies played with a lot of determination in the second half. A sequence of penalties in their favour, beginning with a dubious high tackle call on Ieremia, put them on the attack and they battered away for several minutes. Eales wriggled over in the corner only to be penalised for a double movement. It seemed the All Blacks had weathered the storm but Marshall got carried away and tapped and ran from the goal-line, sending the coach's blood pressure to a record high.

Perhaps sensing that they'd let slip their last chance of making a serious contest of it, the Wallabies went off the boil and the All Blacks closed the game out. Mimicking Marshall, Gregan ran a penalty in the shadow of his posts. This time the rush of blood was punished: turnover, black ball. Randell drove over the advantage line and the props carried it on, ploughing to within a metre of the posts. When the ball went left, there were All Blacks lining up to supply the finish. The conversion of Cullen's try made it 30-6 with 18 minutes to go.

The Wallabies scored two tries, narrowing the gap to 12 points, but the All Blacks finished remarkably strongly. A fourth try looked certain after Cullen had carved through but the inside backs took up too much space and Osborne was bundled into touch. When the Wallabies barged at the lineout, Spencer made it seven from seven, 13 out of 14 in the two away games. The All Blacks might still have snatched a bonus point. Right on fulltime, they were hot on attack with a line-up stretching across the field. Being a mere link in the chain wasn't for Zinzan Brooke; he cross-kicked off his left foot but, for once, neither the option nor the execution had much to recommend them. When the ball dribbled into touch, Morrison blew fulltime.

Hart: "The All Blacks should have won more decisively but the inhuman demands on them started to tell. They'd played an all-time epic match in Johannesburg, crossed an ocean and a continent, and won a decisive victory seven days later on what was one of the biggest occasions in the modern game. It had been a great week in All Black history.

"The Wallabies fielded a stronger scrum but weren't able to match the intensity and pace of the All Black pack. We'd targeted them in that area because they had three forwards – Heath, Brial, and Morgan – who'd had very little top football recently. Horan's broken thumb slowed the delivery of the ball to the outsides but our loose forwards defended well and our midfield got in their opposite numbers' faces all night, giving them very little room. Because our scrum was on the front foot, it enabled our backs to be aggressive in defence."

The All Blacks refused to leave the arena until the Bledisloe Cup was produced. One couldn't help but think that, if the roles had been reversed, the trophy would've been out there in a flash for the Wallabies to flourish on their victory lap.

Earlier in the week, Hart had given Australian TV commentator Gordon Bray – for whom he has huge respect – a piece of his mind over his and his co-commentators' call of the Lancaster Park test which had fanned the flames of the professional fouls controversy. At the aftermatch function, Bray's colleague, former Wallaby great Simon Poidevin, told Hart that his intemperate comments were mainly an expression of his frustration with the Wallabies' performance.

Afterwards, Smith claimed the Wallabies were making up ground on the All Blacks. When this was put to the New Zealanders, Fitzpatrick raised his eyebrows. The Australian rugby writers had smelt blood and were circling Smith; perhaps because it made better copy or perhaps to underline their view that the coach was losing his grip, some of them reported that Fitzpatrick had put his head in his hands and shaken with laughter.

Smith was under immense pressure. His post-match press conference was to be the first of several highly charged appearances before the media over the next few days. Having sung Brial's praises all week, he dwelt brutally on the number 8's lapses, virtually blaming him for the defeat; he also rubbished Knox's claims to replace Horan, dismissing him as "a non-tackler". Within 48 hours, he was having to perform a back-flip on that subject.

He would've been better off saying nothing or taking cover behind platitudes but stress and perhaps naivety caused him to dig himself into a deeper hole every time he opened his mouth. The writing was on the wall; his only hope of surviving lay in a Wallaby victory at Carisbrook three weeks hence.

23

SILVERWARE, TAKE TWO

THE aftermath of the Melbourne test wouldn't have been pleasant for Greg Smith. With the ever-higher-profile ARU Chief Executive John O'Neill getting involved, Smith was very publicly rolled over the selection of David Knox in the Wallaby side to play South Africa in Brisbane. To add insult to injury, the ARU vetoed Smith's preferred option of flying in lock John Welborn – who, like Knox, was playing for Natal in the Currie Cup – when Garrick Morgan became a doubtful starter. Owen Finegan eventually took Morgan's place.

Smith was already under heavy fire over his selections and the decisive roles the unwanted duo played in Australia's win over the Springboks cast further doubt on his judgement. But he could take comfort from the pride, passion, and finesse shown by his team and the victory strengthened his claim that the Wallabies had advanced in the international pecking order since he'd taken over from Bob Dwyer. Despite having nine days to prepare for the game and fielding an unchanged side except for the ill Marius Hurter, the South Africans were pale imitations of the super-charged team who'd rattled the All Blacks' fillings at Ellis Park. The result opened up the Tri-Nations series; now all three teams had a chance of winning.

There was one change to the All Black team to meet the Springboks at Eden Park, Glen Osborne giving way to Tana Umaga. It was tough on Osborne whose assertive and error-free performance at Melbourne had included a try-saving tackle on John Eales at a critical point in the game. Alama Ieremia had taken a grip on the number 12 jersey. With him in the team and specialist inside backs on the bench, the third back reserve had to cover the backline from second-five out. As Lee Stensness couldn't do that, there was, unfortunately, no place for him in the 23-man squad; he was replaced by Scott McLeod who'd been in outstanding form for Waikato and in club rugby. Stensness didn't deserve to be dropped but accepted the logic behind the decision when it was explained to him.

The test players deserved a break; they were told to have a week off and enjoy themselves. Josh Kronfeld went surfing, got hit by a board, and collected 15 stitches in his forehead – not everyone's idea of fun. The reserves, on the other hand, needed games. Most of them got a run for the Barbarians against St Stephen's College; it wasn't high-pressure but it was matchplay and it afforded the welcome sight of Andrew Mehrtens moving freely at last. The Bay of Plenty-Auckland game was another such opportunity and the panel was grateful for Bay coach Gordon Tietjens' offer to include Mehrtens in his line-up.

Although the break did the All Blacks a lot of good, it didn't fix Sean Fitzpatrick's knee. Only an operation could do that. In the meantime, he wasn't doing any further damage by playing on it but he found it enormously frustrating not being able to take a full part in training.

"The state of Sean's knee was going to cause a fair amount of disruption to our preparation in Auckland and Dunedin," says Hart. "There are very few players you'd give that leeway but he's top of the list. Some people suggested that there was one rule for Fitzpatrick and another for Mehrtens; it was a false analogy since Mehrtens' injury actually prevented him from playing in several tests."

The South African changes were predictable: Henry Honiball and James Small brought some much-needed experience to the backline while, up front, Hurter and James Dalton, a more accurate thrower-in than Naka Drotske, were fit again. Hart was surprised that they didn't send for Andre Joubert and that they chose to remain in Brisbane until two days before the game. The All Blacks didn't set much store by South Africa's dismal performance in Brisbane; they had vivid memories of the first half at Ellis Park when the Springboks had played what Hart regarded as their best rugby since their return to the international arena in 1992.

Derek Bevan would referee. Hart's less-than-fond farewell to him after the Ellis Park loss in 1996 was obviously water off a duck's back; Bevan was in good spirits and looking forward to the game. He and Hart seemed to be of a like mind on how the game should be played. Thankfully, Bevan had no problems with the vests as long as they were taped to the body. Hart's attempts to broker an agreement between the Tri-Nations participants had foundered at Brisbane at the hands, embarrassingly enough, of New Zealand referee Colin Hawke.

Hart feared the worst when touch judge Brian Campsall showed up a few minutes before kick-off wanting to check the vests. But Bevan hadn't sent him; he was there at the instigation of Springbok coach Carel du Plessis who wanted him to make sure that the All Blacks' vests were taped down. Campsall took Hart's word for it.

Hart: "I wasn't impressed. Perhaps du Plessis was under more pressure than I realised if he was resorting to that sort of gamesmanship. I was even less impressed when Small took his jersey off during the game to reveal that his vest wasn't taped to his body."

The day before the game, the NZRFU advised Hart that Zinzan Brooke had signalled that he was considering bowing out of New Zealand rugby after the end-of-year tour. It was public knowledge that he was one of the few All Blacks who hadn't extended his contract beyond the next World Cup. Brooke and Hart had previously discussed the number 8's future and agreed to review it after the Tri-Nations. Clearly, though, the issue was preying on Brooke's mind.

He and Hart talked it over again. "What it boiled down to was that he didn't want to finish anywhere but at the top," says Hart. "Perhaps Wayne Shelford's sacking was at the back of his mind. I told him that, as long as he was fit, we saw him as part of our plans until the end of the year. People might ask why we'd take him on tour if he was thinking of retiring afterwards. The answer is that the four months Taine Randell spent with Brooke this season have been crucial to his development – why wouldn't we want to continue to make use of that expertise?"

With Brooke pondering his future, there was a possibility that this game would be his last test at Eden Park. There wasn't an announcement to the team but Hart made sure that Fitzpatrick was aware of the situation. The game already had great significance in terms of personal milestones: it would be Frank

Bunce's 50th test and Fitzpatrick's 50th test as captain – Bunce's test career and Fitzpatrick's captaincy overlap exactly. At the aftermatch function, Hart made presentations marking these achievements. Shortly before the game, Hart had made a public presentation to Michael Jones marking his 50 test matches. It was an emotional moment as Jones had been a special player in Hart's coaching career. Both men have had their setbacks; at times, the prospect of Jones reaching 50 tests had seemed as unlikely as that of Hart becoming All Black coach.

The All Blacks had set themselves the objective of minimising mistakes but Josh Kronfeld got offside at the maul following the kick-off. The Springboks gained field position and the throw to the lineout. They drove superbly, using their upper-body strength to keep the maul up. It's difficult to halt a well-executed driving maul without taking it down and the Boks bulldozed to within a few metres of the line before Os du Randt peeled off. Ruben Kruger crashed over and the All Blacks were 7-0 down with barely a minute gone.

From the kick-off, they came within an ace of scoring themselves, Christian Cullen losing the ball as he went to force it. Ieremia exposed the soft centre in the Springboks' defence and again they got within a whisker of a try. Fitzpatrick settled for three points.

The loss of the immensely strong and abrasive Kruger with a broken ankle was a huge blow to the Springboks. What made it worse was that the injury almost certainly deprived them of a try. He'd intercepted Justin Marshall's pass after Zinzan Brooke had tapped down a Bok throw-in on the All Black 22. Although slowed by Jeff Wilson, Kruger was en route to his second try when his ankle gave way. It was a sad end to Kruger's season, especially as he had to remain behind when his teammates flew home. Hart, Fitzpatrick, and John Mayhew visited him in hospital the next morning and did what they could to make his enforced stay as little of an ordeal as possible.

Bunce created the All Blacks' first try when the backs moved lineout ball on halfway. He knocked off Percy Montgomery with a stiff fend, went straight through Russell Bennett, and set up Ieremia with a perfectly timed and weighted inside pass. It was a straightforward conversion but Carlos Spencer's kick hit the woodwork.

After a Spencer penalty, New Zealand conceded 14 points in a few minutes of almost surreal rugby. When the All Blacks worked a blindside scrum move, Joost van der Westhuizen, far and away the Boks' best defender, cut down Cullen. He set the ball but it wasn't claimed by an All Black and Gary Teichmann gave it a hopeful hoof. Instead of going into touch, the ball hopped back into the arms of the Springbok captain who galloped over wearing a slightly stunned expression. A minute or two later, the Boks won a New Zealand throw on the All Black 22. Looking suspiciously like a man who'd run out of ideas, Montgomery aimed an up-and-under towards the right-hand corner. It skewed away to the left, disorienting Cullen who couldn't get to it on the full. The bounce sat up for Montgomery who acknowledged his teammates' congratulations with a wide grin and a fatalistic shrug.

Down 21-11, the All Blacks demonstrated yet again that the combination of speed, skill, and boldness can erase substantial deficits in next to no time. First, some Cullen opportunism enabled them to win ball going forward in midfield. The improvised backline of Kronfeld at first-five, Cullen at second, Wilson at centre, and Umaga on the right wing made the transfers slickly to create an overlap for Spencer.

A couple of minutes later, Marshall punished a poor kick by van der Westhuizen with a telling one of his own which led to an All Black throw-in near the Bok 22. A set-piece move off a short lineout was executed with breathtaking speed and precision, Randell storming onto a sweet Bunce off-load to send Cullen flying to the corner.

The All Blacks were now rampant. A thundering drive down the left seemed certain to produce another try but Bevan failed to play the advantage. The quick tap almost worked but when the Boks were re-penalised, Fitzpatrick opted for the kick. It, too, came back off the upright. That was halftime: after forty minutes of frenetic and at times madcap rugby, it was 23-21 to New Zealand.

The All Blacks quickly extended the lead through two Spencer penalties. Seven minutes into the half, Fitzpatrick tackled Mark Andrews from behind and found himself in harm's way on the wrong side of the ruck. Andre Venter was late to the party and, perhaps in his haste to get a piece of the action before the ball was cleared, planted a boot on Fitzpatrick's face.

He was sent off and Andrews was lucky not to follow. His flick at the recumbent Fitzpatrick after the Venter incident wasn't the act of a man in full control of himself. It was no great surprise that, in the very next sequence of play, he lined up Kronfeld who was pinned in a maul and smashed into his back. The resultant penalty made the count 11-3 in New Zealand's favour. Andrews didn't cover himself in glory that afternoon; a TVNZ tape of the game featuring camera angles not used in the broadcast placed him at the scene of several other unpleasant off-the-ball incidents.

"Venter's sending-off obviously had a bearing on the outcome," says Hart, "although I felt the All Blacks were starting to take control. Andrews is an outstanding player but we felt he was carrying an injury and perhaps that led to his frustration and indiscretions – he's better than that."

The All Blacks turned up the heat. After a long attack featuring wonderful handling and continuity, Kronfeld slipped de Beer's feathery tackle and Olo Brown propelled Marshall over by the posts. Marshall then broke from deep in his own territory and some thrilling running by Spencer and Cullen produced the latter's second try. When the All Blacks shunted the seven-man Bok pack off the ball and Zinzan Brooke adroitly put Randell over, the All Blacks had scored 39 points without reply. With the issue settled and the game winding down, holes opened up everywhere. There were three more tries, two of them to the Springboks.

Hart: "The All Blacks played some brilliant rugby but, once again, with the game won, they took their foot off the throttle. That was a little disappointing but, at the end of the day, I'd settle for putting 50 points and a 20-point margin on our toughest foe.

"After the game, du Plessis said he thought his team had been disciplined. My reaction was to say that, if so, I'd hate to see them when they were ill-disciplined. The All Blacks felt the game had been close to blowing up; I thought they were impressively disciplined in the face of a lot of provocation. I'd continued to hammer on the theme that, no matter how much they might feel like throwing a punch, they had to think about the consequences: conceding an advantageous position, conceding three points, getting a yellow card, even getting a red card and putting their teammates under huge pressure. On his return to South Africa, du Plessis claimed that my criticism of their lack of discipline showed that the All Blacks couldn't handle the Springboks' physical style of play, a comment that was ill-founded. He's a nice guy but he was discovering how relentless the pressure on a coach can be.

"Speaking to the Springboks after the game, it was clear there was a lot of frustration in their camp and concern that the defeat would lead to wholesale changes. In fact, Joubert was finally called up, perhaps in response to public pressure as much as anything, given du Plessis' apparent reluctance. There were clear parallels with Smith and Knox which extended to Joubert's brilliant performance against the Wallabies in Pretoria."

The panel had to do some hard thinking about the line-up to

face Australia a week later. Springbok tests are physically and mentally draining; although there'd been a lot of running and ball movement, the physical contact had been as uncompromising as ever – Kronfeld and Zinzan Brooke in particular had taken a fair battering. They restored Jon Preston to the squad to provide the option of a two-back/four-forward bench but delayed naming the playing XV until they got to Dunedin. The training programme for the week was revised to ease back on the physical stuff.

Hart: "Before we disbanded, we had a long chat about the need to reduce the error rate and exert consistent pressure and the fact that the Wallabies would be on a high after their win at Brisbane. They'd be well aware that victory and a bonus point would put them in with a real chance of winning the series. I asked the team if they wanted to be getting up at three in the morning in a couple of weeks' time hoping for a Springbok win – that could be the situation if they faltered at the last hurdle. I left them with the thought that the achievement of winning in Johannesburg and Melbourne wouldn't mean a thing if the Wallabies took ten points from their last two games."

In the end, the only change was Osborne for Umaga. The selectors saw the two wingers as being pretty much on a par but Umaga wasn't fully over the chest injury he'd suffered at Ellis Park. Mehrtens had been given 15 minutes game-time at Eden Park to get him back into the swing of things – the crowd's warm welcome was in stark contrast to the chilly reception for Mark Carter at Lancaster Park and Junior Tonu'u at Carisbrook – but his lack of rugby and Spencer's excellent form meant that there wasn't an issue at first-five. Not everyone saw it that way; Hart could have wallpapered his office with the letters he'd received – most of them with Canterbury post-marks – criticising him for not putting Mehrtens back in the team.

But when Spencer pulled up at Thursday's training, it looked like a case of he who rises by the hamstring, falls by the hamstring – and vice versa. Mehrtens went into test match mode but on Friday afternoon Spencer was cleared to play. At Tuesday's scrummaging session, Norm Hewitt had blown a calf muscle which brought Anton Oliver back onto the bench.

The panel had intended to name a two-back/four-forward bench to give them maximum cover for Zinzan Brooke and Kronfeld. But with Spencer's injury scare coming so close to the game, Mehrtens had to be in the reserves which forced them back to a three/three split. Since Kronfeld was the main worry, they were anxious to have Carter, the specialist openside flanker, on the bench. With the stipulation that there should be two front-row reserves, that would leave no room for Charles Riechelmann and therefore no cover for the locks. Whatever mix they decided on, they risked being exposed somewhere. Without Eales and with locks who were inexperienced at test level, the Wallabies' lineout was less potent than usual so it was decided to take the risk. If the need arose, Craig Dowd would go to lock.

"I came in for a lot of criticism for failing to use the bench in the second half," says Hart. "I think the critics underestimate the limitations imposed by the six-man bench and the fact that in internationals you can't send substituted players back on. You need seven or preferably eight reserves to cover the whole team and give you the confidence to make tactical substitutions knowing that you won't be exposed in the event of injury. If we'd substituted Kronfeld at halftime – and seeing we were up 36-nil, there wasn't a strong argument for doing so – and one of the loosies had then got injured, we would've had Oliver playing on the side of the scrum.

"Similarly, when Ieremia had to go on for Umaga at Ellis Park, we were criticised for not having Osborne in the reserves but the critics don't always think these things through; the only way we could've covered the back three, the midfield, and the inside backs was by having Preston on the bench instead of Mehrtens and Tonu'u. Six can cover 15 if you stack the bench with utility players but if you want to have the option of bringing on matchwinners like Mehrtens – which is the whole point of tactical substitutions – you're always going to be a little vulnerable somewhere and then it's just a matter of luck. With our bench that day, we were vulnerable if we lost a wing or fullback; not only did that happen but it happened early. Some of the northern hemisphere countries were opposed to the concept of tactical substitutions and they succeeded in restricting their use by limiting the bench to six players. The result is Clayton's tactical substitution."

As usual, Dunedin was showing that it really knows how to host a test match. Test match fever rose steadily even without much input from the Australians who were keeping a low profile. After Melbourne, Smith and his team had copped a hammering from the media and this time around they were happy to be the underdogs.

Hart's award in the Queen's Birthday honours had drawn a swift "please explain" from the Bastards Club, questioning whether he was still a worthy member. He'd been able to allay their fears and with Ross Cooper and Gordon Hunter being inducted into the brotherhood during the week it was now official: the All Black selectors are Bastards.

Hart sometimes asks players to talk to the team before a game. One of those he used in Dunedin was Bull Allen, like Hewitt a model reserve in his attitude to training and commitment to the team. "After the MCG game, Allen told me he'd never seen the test props play better which spoke volumes for the man," says Hart. "Here he spoke about how much the reserves wanted the All Blacks to succeed and finish on a winning note because they felt an integral part of the team."

Fitzpatrick chose to run with the wind in the first half after a local expert advised him that it would drop in the second half and that the sun wouldn't be a factor. The wind actually freshened and the sun did become a factor. Randell has several strings to his academic bow but meteorology obviously isn't among them.

The All Blacks went out and blew the Wallabies off Carisbrook. The Australians couldn't live with the All Blacks' speed and intensity and it was only a matter of time before the dam burst. After a break-out by Ieremia, the Wallabies scrambled desperately to prevent first Wilson then Bunce from scoring but they were only delaying the inevitable; another clinically executed scrum move involving Marshall and Zinzan Brooke opened up a boulevard for Randell to stroll down.

Brooke then leapt to claim an up-and-under and fired a perfect cross-field pass for Cullen to accelerate on to. Running with the effortless freedom of an animal in the wild, Cullen went the length of the field to score, confounding defenders with his pace and ability to switch direction without losing speed. It was a try fit to compare with his miraculous effort against the Scots at the same ground a year earlier. Almost immediately, an aggressive chase by the outside backs rattled Ben Tune and Steve Larkham who co-produced a spectacular bungle. Ieremia scooped up the ball one-handed and passed inside to Kronfeld. The pass was slightly behind the flanker and he grassed it with the line open. Some held the view that such a devastating one-two punch at that point would have broken the Wallabies. As it was, Marshall's try from short range and Spencer's eight goals from eight attempts had put the All Blacks out of reach by halftime.

Once again, the prospect of humiliation galvanised the Wallabies. The coaches were barely back in their seats before Joe Roff was over out wide after they'd snaffled an All Black throw-in and James Holbeck had bustled through some slack defence. Given the scoreline, no-one could get too worked up about the fact that the scoring pass was clearly forward; Roff's try was just a hiccup and normal service would be resumed shortly.

But normal service was never resumed. Looking more lackadaisical by the minute, the All Blacks fell off tackles and turned over what little possession they had. The whistle came to dominate, Frenchman Joel Dumé's piercing blasts the nerve-jangling theme music to a drama whose second act was limping towards an anti-climax. Dume was having major problems at the scrummage where the Wallabies were crowding the mark to prevent the All Blacks getting a good hit at the engagement. Perhaps it was his inability to impose his will at this phase which made Dume so interventionist at the break-downs.

Larkham scored the Wallabies' second try, ghosting through the All Black pack like a child playing among outdoor sculptures. Two more followed to put them ahead in the try count and within 12 points. New Zealand supporters, who'd expected to see the Wallabies put to the sword in the second half, began casting uneasy glances at the clock.

With fifteen minutes to go, Hart substituted Marshall. Television viewers didn't need advanced lip-reading skills to realise that the halfback wasn't too thrilled about it. "He'd taken another knock on the sternum," says Hart, "and didn't have the strength to execute his passes properly. He's determined to the point of stubbornness, one of the most wholehearted and committed players in the team. Under normal circumstances, he'd be one of the last players I'd take off but he was struggling and I didn't see any point in risking an aggravation of the injury. These guys don't want to come off – Justin wanted to see the campaign out and I can understand that. But his reaction wasn't in keeping with the image we'd worked hard to build up and, to his credit, he was well aware of that afterwards and made a public apology.

"Our goal was to start well and produce an eighty-minute performance – we got the first bit right but not the second. In my view, the All Blacks produced their second-best forty minutes of the past two years – to be 36-0 up at halftime against one of the top three sides in the world is as comprehensive as it gets. They took the Wallabies apart up front and out wide. We saw a tremendous exhibition of support play and keeping the ball alive and effective utilisation of the wind. When the Wallabies repeatedly infringed in their danger zone, I couldn't help but wonder if what we were seeing were professional fouls. The final score flattered the Wallabies but the second half was very unsatisfactory for all concerned."

"Harty said the right things at halftime," says Fitzpatrick. "We said the right things. But I think we just felt the job was done – urgency comes from the mental drive which was clearly there at the beginning of the game but not in the second half."

Dume was heavily criticised but Hart sympathised with him: "The constant penalties disrupted the flow and shape of the game and made it hard to get any rhythm but, these days, a lot of refereeing is done with the voice rather than the whistle and when you have very little English, that becomes a problem. French teams have laboured under the handicap of their communication problems with non-French speaking referees for many years."

It was a very flat All Black dressing room; Zinzan Brooke described it as a morgue. The atmosphere wasn't improved by the fact that some of the reserves who were turning out for their NPC teams the next day had to leave straight after the game. They'd made a significant contribution to the overall success and to miss out on the end-of-campaign celebrations was a downer for them and the rest of the squad. Tonu'u's situation was particularly unfortunate; he begged Auckland coach Graham Henry to allow him to stay in Dunedin to celebrate his second cap but he'd made a prior commitment to play for Auckland against Taranaki and Henry, understandably, held him to it. Wearing his provincial captain's hat, Brooke was also quick to remind Tonu'u of his obligation.

The team arrived late at the aftermatch function because they'd attended an event for the winners of a major Coca-Cola promotion involving the All Blacks. As their bus arrived, the Wallabies were walking out. ARU Chairman Dick McGruther told Hart that the All Blacks' tardiness showed a lack of respect for the Wallabies; inside, Mike Banks was upbraided by NZRFU Chairman Rob Fisher and Chief Executive David Moffett. Hart asked Smith if he'd consider bringing his players back into the function; he did so and Fitzpatrick publicly apologised for the All Blacks' lateness. It wasn't intentional but the incident did underline the need to re-think the timing and purpose of aftermatch functions given the heavy demands on players and management in the immediate aftermath of a test match.

Hart admired Smith's role in defusing a potentially damaging situation. The relationship, such as it was, between the two coaches had been generally prickly but that night they had a couple of drinks and a good chat, mainly about the harsh reality that, in the professional era, there was even greater pressure on coaches to achieve results. For Smith, the pressure was becoming unbearable. That afternoon's defeat had probably doomed him and any faint hope he might have had of clinging to his job disappeared a week later when the Wallabies came spectacularly to grief in Pretoria.

Before that game, the media were predicting that the losing coach would get the axe; as it turned out, both men got the chop. The Springboks' resounding victory wasn't enough to save du Plessis who was shown the door after a mere six months in the job. With England's Jack Rowell, who'd also been hounded by detractors, choosing to stand down to concentrate on his business interests, three of the big five rugby nations had shed their national coaches in the space of a month. Professional sport is an unforgiving environment, especially for coaches who tend to be the scapegoats when results don't match expectations. Those who make and break coaches, on the other hand, are rarely called to account.

The All Blacks' second-half performance drew some heavy criticism, particularly on talkback radio. The year before, Hart had returned from South Africa worried that people would only remember the defeat in the final test. That didn't happen but, in 1997, some people seemed to have forgotten everything except the last forty minutes.

"I was criticised for talking about tiredness," says Hart. "DJ Graham said that I should've used the squad system more and rested players. I thought that, overall, we'd managed it pretty well and the first half at Dunedin showed that, if we did miscalculate, it was by forty minutes. Resting players may become unavoidable but there'll be accusations of devaluing the black jersey when it does happen. It also raises a wider question: if internationals are the game's pinnacle and shop-window, shouldn't the overall playing programme be restructured so that there's no need to rest players from test matches?

"David Kirk wrote that the mark of a great team is that they maintain their intensity for eighty minutes and finish off opponents when they have them on the ropes. I think it's possible to go for eighty minutes in a tight, structured game but I'm not sure that it's possible to play sublime attacking rugby for a full game. What we failed to do at Eden Park and Carisbrook was defend with the same skill and intensity with which we attacked but I think we're learning that, with the ball retention that's possible under the new rules, defensive expectations may have to be altered a little.

"The more you achieve, the more is expected of you – that's the way it is. No-one is – or should be – above criticism and fair and constructive criticism is a check on complacency. All I would ask is that the pundits guard against becoming unreasonably critical because that can create unreasonable expectations among their audiences. For all that, I'm sure, in time, 1997 will be recognised as another memorable year for the All Blacks. Given the schedule and the fact that only in Johannesburg did we ever look in danger of defeat, the 1997 team's achievements were at least the equal of, if not better than, the 1996 team's."

Hart had also come under attack for raising the All Blacks' fatigue in the context of their participation in the NPC. At the press conference after the Eden Park test, he'd said, in response to a question, that he didn't think test players should be expected to play NPC matches on the Sunday or Monday after Carisbrook. Wellington were playing Canterbury that Monday and both unions were quick to weigh in with the line that it should be a matter for the players. The NZRFU came down on the provinces' side, saying it was a matter for the NPC coaches and players – in other words, it was nothing to do with the All Black coach or medical team.

Hart felt the NZRFU was being naive. It's all right leaving it to the players as long as they can make a decision without feeling under any pressure but it seldom happens that way. If, in this particular context, Canterbury's All Black opted to play but Wellington's chose not to, it would leave the Wellingtonian wide-open to criticism from his management, his teammates, and the Wellington public. As it happened, events bore out Rob Fisher's argument that there was no need for a mandatory stand-down because the NPC coaches would apply commonsense and look at the wider picture.

Hart: "The argument advanced by Murray Deaker among others that, because the players are professionals, they should stop whining about being tired and front up like everyone else in the work-force, ignores the physical wear and tear of the high-velocity, high-intensity modern game. Bodily-contact sport is different from office work.

"You can talk about the Auckland Warriors or English soccer where they play week-in, week-out but there's not the same pressure in those environments as there is with the All Blacks where defeat is unacceptable. Zinzan Brooke's a key figure in the All Blacks, the Auckland Blues, and the Auckland NPC team which is a huge load to carry. When Zinny, one of our great stars, considers opting out of the game because his mind and body have had enough, we should heed the warning signs."

24
HART PROGNOSIS

IN mid-1997, John Hart was appointed All Black coach through to the 1999 World Cup. It was done with a minimum of fuss; there was no drama, no murky wheeling and dealing, no personality-driven media analysis, no parochialism. It was a far cry from the way the issue had been resolved in the past and from the messy changings of the guard which were to take place in Australia, South Africa, and England later in the year.

Once Hart was satisfied that there was every good reason for him to carry on, the only outstanding issue was whether the All Black management team could be kept together. There was a complication on that score.

The NZRFU had come to see the Super 12 as the testing-ground for future All Black coaches and was therefore keen to get the leading coaches involved with Super 12 teams. The union was also anxious to dispel the malaise surrounding the under-performing Waikato Chiefs. These objectives converged with the result that pressure was brought to bear on Ross Cooper to coach the Chiefs in 1998.

Hart felt that he, Cooper, and Gordon Hunter had formed a successful All Black selection panel. They'd established a good rapport and brought stability and consistency to the selection process. He worried that Cooper's appointment to the Chiefs might be the catalyst for a potentially disruptive re-jig of the panel.

"Given the NZRFU's ruling that Super 12 coaches couldn't be All Black selectors, my worry was that Ross would have to leave the panel and, given the enormous amount of work and planning we've done in the past two years, it wouldn't be easy for someone else to come in and pick up the threads. It's good to have other viewpoints and the panel doesn't operate in an ivory tower – we consult widely and regularly with a range of rugby people around the country."

On the other hand, the panel recognised that it was in the interests of New Zealand rugby that the Chiefs became achievers. A compromise was reached: after the end-of-year tour of Britain, Cooper would take six months' leave of absence from the panel to coach the Chiefs, resuming his selector's role when the Super 12 finished. However, if he elected to continue with the Chiefs in 1999, the make-up of the panel would be reviewed. On that basis, the panel was appointed through to the World Cup, as was the rest of the management team.

In conjunction with the NZRFU, Hart's assistant coaches for the next two years will be appointed after the UK tour. While he stresses the need for continuity and stability in selection, he acknowledges that there may be a case for introducing new voices, new thinking, and new directions on the training field to ensure that the team continues to improve. This is in no way a reflection on the contribution currently being made by Ross and Gordon.

"Delaying the decision is hard on them but they agree with the logic," he says. "There are a number of other well-qualified people. Graham Henry has made it clear that he wants to be the next All Black coach and sees an assistant's role as a stepping stone; Frank Oliver and Wayne Smith probably have similar aspirations. People tend to think it's just a matter of surrounding the All Black coach with the next-best coaches in the country but that's not necessarily the case – successful coaches don't always make successful assistants and vice versa. I'd cite myself as an example; I'd find it difficult to be someone's assistant. Call it what you like – ego, drive, ambition – the attributes that make a head coach aren't necessarily those you want in an assistant.

"You're looking for people who are personally compatible,

who are supportive of your direction and the team culture you're creating, who are team players in someone else's team, who complement your strengths and weaknesses. In the past, I've mentioned Peter Sloane, Robbie Deans, and Graham Mourie as examples of people whose expertise I respect and who would meet these criteria. When you add the high-profile coaches to these names, it adds up to an impressive list of candidates. I'm sure others will emerge when we focus more closely on the issue and think laterally about people who possess specific areas of expertise which complement my strengths."

The All Blacks assemble three days after the NPC finals for a tour whose itinerary was only finalised in August after months of exasperating negotiations with the notorious Four Home Unions Tours Committee. The tortuous progress partly reflected the break-down in trust between England and the three other home unions who see the English as increasingly inclined to go their own way. Unfortunately, the committee viewed the proposed New Zealand-England double-header in this light.

The committee wanted a 13-match tour with one test against each of the four home unions. Hart asked the NZRFU to negotiate a seven-match, three-test tour finishing by the end of November which would give the players the whole of December off. The outcome was a nine-match tour with tests on four successive weekends, the last of them on December 6. Having pushed for as short a tour as possible, Hart found himself having to ask for an extra game at the beginning of the tour to give the test side – some of whom won't have played for four or five weeks depending on the outcome of the NPC – a warm-up game before the first international. Earlier, he'd suggested that, instead of playing Ireland, the tour should start with a Barbarians game in Dublin which would double as the test side's warm-up. However, the Barbarians advised that they wouldn't be able to field an adequate side on the date in question because the leading players were unlikely to be released by their clubs. It was a stark reminder of who calls the shots in British rugby.

According to NZRFU Chief Executive David Moffett, the Four Home Unions Tours Committee is "possibly the most frustrating organisation I've ever had to deal with. They were inflexible towards our desire to play a second test against England which is in return for England coming here in 1999 to help with our World Cup preparation. Secondly, they wanted a 13 or 14-game tour. Thirdly, Wales had secured a test against the Wallabies in 1996 because Ireland forfeited a game; the deal was, Wales would do the same to give Ireland a test against us. They didn't see fit to tell us about this arrangement."

The NZRFU board's decision to accept an itinerary which has the All Blacks playing four tests in four weeks at the end of a gruelling year gave Hart cause for concern: "I understand that the board was staring into a financial hole created by professionalism. The bottom-liners were saying the NZRFU had to get back into profit as soon as possible but, in business, you'd expect to take a number of years to recoup such a strategic investment; in the early stages, it's more important to maximise your product to ensure long-term profitability.

"I don't think we should be arrogant but we should recognise that the All Blacks are in demand, which gives us a strong negotiating position. As it is, the fact that the itinerary was finalised so late gives us little opportunity for the pre-planning that's been fundamental to our success in the past two years. Mike Banks was scheduled to go to the UK in May but had to cancel his trip because the itinerary wasn't finalised. Six weeks before the tour started, he was over there rushing around the place trying to sort out hotels and travel arrangements. This sort of amateurish, last-minute stuff has no place in the professional environment. It's also frustrating that all the midweek games are at night which will disrupt our preparation for the test match on the Saturday. It's another indication of the power of television and the financial pressures facing the game; Tuesday afternoon games don't suit TV and don't bring in the same gate money as night matches. In that context, the touring team's wants and needs count for very little.

"This isn't just about the win-loss record. I don't complain about an unreasonable playing schedule or last-minute arrangements that muck up our planning because I want everything in our favour so we can win every game. We're going to lose games at some stage but if we lose playing well, beaten by a better team on the day, that's okay – that's going to happen in the new era. If we lose playing badly – which will happen if we allow the cards to be stacked against us and we push the players too hard – we put the record and therefore the All Black brand at risk."

During the Tri-Nations series, the panel established the selection guidelines for the 36-man tour squad: they essentially amounted to a fine-tuning of the long-term strategy. Once again, the aim was to ensure that the test players wouldn't have to play midweek games. It was agreed that the midweek team should have a balance of youth and experience while fulfilling the primary objectives of providing quality cover for the test team and winning their games.

"The need to prepare for the World Cup is the sub-text to an awful lot of rugby discussion these days," says Hart. "We see this tour as being partly rather than totally driven by World Cup considerations. We'll be looking to take some young players, particularly in positions where the incumbents' age and/or form may keep them out of the World Cup. It's worth remembering, though, that after this tour, there are still two Super 12s, two Tri-Nations, and several tests against top-notch opposition before we pick the World Cup squad. Without being complacent, that leaves a lot of time for player assessment and development. At the end of 1985, how many people would've said that Michael Jones would play in the 1987 World Cup, let alone be one of the stars?

"There are players we've identified as potential World Cup squad members whom we won't take to the UK because we think it would be better to allow them to develop through the 1998 Super 12, the New Zealand A team, and a possible end-of-season Barbarians tour. Next year the New Zealand A side will play the shadow All Blacks in the trial, England, and perhaps Tonga; I see the A team becoming a very important part of our set-up. It will play a big role in the development of test players and is an answer to the dilemma we face with emerging rugby nations. They desperately want to play us and learn from us but tests which are mis-matches aren't in either country's best interests."

At the conclusion of the Tri-Nations series, the panel drew up a list of 46 players they saw as the leading contenders for the touring team. The list was subsequently expanded to 55 to provide a full complement of stand-bys to cover for injury during the tour. The 55 were put on fitness programmes and tested at the end of September. The injury situation balanced itself out: Michael Jones and Chresten Davis were most unlikely to come into consideration but the indications were that Jonah Lomu and Walter Little could do so.

"Jonah has worked really hard and matured enormously," says Hart. "He's been through hell and come out with a very positive attitude but I was determined that his return should be managed carefully. The absolute priority is to do what's best for him; that might mean taking it slowly and letting him ease his way back into the game."

Overall, the picture was brighter than it had been when the panel had set out on the long process of selecting a squad for

South Africa, primarily because of a marked improvement in the depth in what were then the problem positions. They identified seven genuine contenders at both prop and lock – 18 months earlier, the tight forward cupboard was nearly bare once the test players were taken away. Qualms about depth at test level are now centred on halfback and number 8.

Hart believes that the All Blacks' opponents will have benefited from having had their leading players – 20-plus of them in England's case – in South Africa with the Lions. "England have massive potential. The emergence of Richard Hill on the openside flank has given them a better look but, like Australia, they need to get stability in the inside backs. The new halfback, Austin Healey, has talent and rare speed but they have to decide what they want at first-five. Up front, they remain very big and very well organised. They've certainly set themselves a challenge, taking on Australia, New Zealand, South Africa, and New Zealand again on successive weekends.

"There can't be many rugby people who don't want to see Wales regain its former glory. Wales is a special country in world rugby: they've contributed richly to its tradition and produced some of the all-time great players. Like New Zealand, Wales is a small country where the game is played and followed by all walks of life, rather than being the essentially private school, middle-class game it is in some of the other countries. They've been systematically raped and pillaged by league for the last decade-and-a-half which has made team-building impossible although it must be said that they've compounded their woes with internal bickering, poor administration, and indisciplined selection. Now that the player-flow is going the other way, there's a real promise of better days ahead.

"Coach Kevin Bowring is clearly determined to restore the ball-in-hand style of the golden era and in the last Five Nations they showed glimpses of coming to grips with the new rules. Alan Bateman and Scott Gibbs give them solidity in midfield, Scott Quinnell gives them aggression and a capacity to take it to the opposition, and Rob Howley is an impressive halfback. Their challenge is to develop the skill and mobility up front which you need to play the continuity game.

"When I was explaining to the NZRFU board why I wasn't happy with the itinerary they'd agreed to, a comment was made that Ireland would not be a threat. Tell that to the 1989 All Blacks or the 1991 or 1996 Wallabies, all of whom got hit by an avalanche at Lansdowne Road. On their home patch, the Irish can pose as physical a challenge as anyone. They provided three of the Lions' tight five in the form of Keith Wood, Paul Wallace, and Jeremy Davidson. Add the likes of Nick Popplewell, Paddy Johns, David Corkery, and their exciting young number 8 Eric Miller and you've got a formidable pack by any standards."

And just over the horizon is the biggest prize of all: the World Cup. In Hart's view, managing the playing programme to prevent player burn-out will be one of the keys to mounting a successful campaign. Without an overseas tour involving four tests on successive weekends, the 1998 schedule is low-key by comparison with the last two years. As another phase in the development of a World Cup squad, a Barbarians team, with a similar mix of players as the 1996 team, may visit the UK at the end of 1998 to play two of the home unions.

The 1999 season will be extraordinarily demanding: Super 12, home tests against France and England, the Tri-Nations series, the NPC, the World Cup. All told, the All Blacks could play up to 13 tests, which raises the question of whether it's sensible to have the Tri-Nations series in a World Cup year. With the Tri-Nations finishing in August and the World Cup taking place in October and November, it seems unlikely that the leading All Blacks will take much – if any – part in the NPC.

"In 1999, New Zealand rugby's focus has to be on winning the World Cup," says Hart. "We'll need everyone pulling in the same direction and the key will be to work co-operatively so that things happen by agreement rather than by dictate. After the Tri-Nations, I see us having camps, playing a game or two, and using the NPC to give match-play to fringe players who mightn't have had much rugby since the Super 12."

While some may question the wisdom of the All Blacks playing their major rivals a few months before the World Cup, it does provide the opportunity to score some telling psychological points. Perhaps the most intriguing clash will be with the French. It will be the All Blacks' first meeting since the shared 1995 series with an opponent Hart expects to mount "a truly formidable challenge for the World Cup". "I wasn't surprised France won the 1997 Five Nations because I expected them to adjust to and exploit the new rules quicker than England. The fact that they won with virtually a second-string backline and missing such forwards as Phillipe Benetton, Laurent Cabannes, and Olivier Roumat should have set the alarm bells ringing around the rugby world. With the power base in French rugby shifting from Agen to Toulouse, the way has opened for Pierre Villepreux, a great but long-neglected coaching talent, to get involved with the French team as assistant to Jean-Claude Skrela. Villepreux's influence on their backplay was plain to see."

An important step towards the World Cup was to make sure of the players' availability by contracting them through to 1999 and beyond. The panel gave the NZRFU a list of 60-odd players whom they saw as being in the frame. They'd cast the net wide, all the way out to left field in a few cases. At that stage, Hart hadn't been reappointed so he advised the NZRFU to also canvass the views of the Super 12 coaches, some of whom would be contenders for the All Black coaching postion if it became vacant.

The onus is on the selectors to go into the World Cup with "a team which is on the rise but still has enough test experience to handle the pressure," says Hart. "That doesn't mean they all have to have twenty tests under their belt – Super 12 and touring with the All Blacks, learning the culture, are part of player growth and development. On the other hand, I don't think you can go into a World Cup expecting inexperienced players – especially in tactical positions, as was the case in 1995 – to cope with the pressure.

"Looking at the 1997 All Blacks, it's highly unlikely that they're all going to go through although professionalism changes everything in terms of training and attitude. Even before he suffered his second major knee injury, Michael Jones' assorted injuries had slowed him down and Zinzan Brooke has indicated he won't be there. Sean Fitzpatrick will be 36; you'd think a 36-year-old would struggle in the modern game but, if he's injury-free, I wouldn't bet against him. His attitude to training is such that he may go through because hooker is one position where speed isn't so crucial. You wouldn't say that about centre but for Frank Bunce the issues are fitness, enthusiasm, and freedom from injury rather than age."

Fitness advisor Marty Toomey declares that "chronological age doesn't mean a lot – a 35-year-old can be as fit, fast, and strong as anyone. You set the physical targets for each position and, if the guy can still meet them, his age doesn't worry me. It's physiological age that counts – are they still capable, still hungry? You can't measure hunger. It's only when you watch them week-in, week-out and see the involvement fall off, when you notice they're not going looking for work, that you start to think 'he doesn't want to be there'. Look at what happens to a Phil Coffin when he pulls on the black jersey. Look at the late starters like Joe Stanley and Bunce. If they've still got it, the guys with experience are worth a lot more to you.

"There's also the small matter of rugby-playing ability. If you selected solely on fitness results, half the current All Blacks wouldn't have been heard of – there are guys sitting on the bench in Super 12 who'd leave them for dead. Some All Blacks – Jeff Wilson, Christian Cullen, Josh Kronfeld – are superb athletes but others just have an amazing natural ability to do things with the ball."

In 1996, Andre Markgraaff claimed South Africa was better-placed for the World Cup than New Zealand because the All Black pack would need a substantial infusion of new blood while the Springbok pack would stay together and develop. It would be interesting to know if he'd still make that claim. Hart thinks it's possible that New Zealand's current top three hookers, props, and locks will still be in the frame come 1999. "That's only half the story of course – the other half is whether they're still keen and still the best. In the meantime, we have to develop back-up across the team to cover for injury, loss of form, and the possibility that age will catch up with some players mentally or physically."

In terms of the opposition, Hart expects that hosting the tournament will galvanise Welsh rugby but sees the strongest challenges coming from the usual bunch – Australia, England, France, and South Africa. "We need to bear in mind that both the Wallabies and the Springboks have been racked by instability of one sort or another in the past two years and suffered far more injury disruptions than we did.

"The All Blacks really have had an amazing run when you consider that the same eight forwards played all ten tests in 1996 while in 1997 we had an unchanged pack for seven out of eight tests. There's probably an element of luck in that but it speaks volumes for the players' professionalism and the expertise of our fitness and medical team. I'm sure the combination of making a fresh start under new coaches and the spur of the World Cup will bring more unity of purpose and stability to Australia and South Africa and they'll lift significantly from where they've been for the past couple of years.

"Rod Macqueen has shown himself to be a talented and creative coach with the Brumbies and his comments following his appointment to the Wallaby job indicated a shrewd customer who's determined to make Australian rugby a more cohesive force. At the time of writing, Carel du Plessis' replacement hadn't been chosen but I'd be surprised if Nick Mallett and Hugh Reece-Edwards, who were a very positive influence on the Springboks on their 1996 end-of-year tour, weren't strongly in the frame. Nor would I be surprised if Andre Markgraaff were to re-emerge in some role."

One of the paradoxes of the professional era is that the talent pool at the top has expanded even as the all-round strength of New Zealand rugby has diminished. For years, it suited officialdom to turn a blind eye to the annual exodus to Italy and France because it functioned as a safety valve which prevented a build-up of pressure for professionalism. Now, however, Japan and the UK, particularly England, pose a major threat to New Zealand's player base. An impressive team could be assembled from New Zealanders who've chosen to pursue rugby careers in those countries: Arran Pene, Jamie Joseph, Kevin Schuler, Liam Barry, Ant Strachan, Graeme Bachop, and John Kirwan in Japan; Hemi Taylor and Dale McIntosh in Wales; Simon Mannix, Shane Howarth, and Ross Nesdale in England; and Kurt McQuilkin in Ireland.

There are people in New Zealand working as talent scouts for English clubs, targeting players who aren't offered Super 12 contracts. It's understandable that some of those who miss out prefer to take up substantial offers from overseas rather than staying to put their case in the NPC. While the outflow of second-tier players doesn't generate the headlines which accompany an All Black's departure to Japan or defection to league, it erodes the talent base and weakens the NPC. It's a significant issue for New Zealand rugby as well as an example of market forces at work in the professional game.

"The South African threat to refuse to give players clearance to play overseas is, I believe, unsustainable in the professional era," says Hart. "Apart from anything else, it must be vulnerable to legal action on the grounds of restraint of trade. If the All Black jersey maintains its hold and we're able to offer adequate contracts, that should be enough to persuade our top players to stay. For those just below the elite tier, however, going overseas can be a worthwhile experience in a number of ways but we should encourage them to sign short-term contracts – one or two years – with the NZRFU having first right of refusal so they aren't lost to us.

"The Auckland Rugby Union's move to develop a relationship with an English club may point the way to a solution; players could go to England on NZRFU contracts which could evolve into Super 12 contracts. The Rugby Academy has been a very positive development in this area in terms of putting talented youngsters on contracts and developing their skills on and off the field. The mooted participation of a New Zealand team in a revised Pan-Pacific competition is another progressive initiative."

If players are going overseas because they can't get Super 12 contracts, why not increase the number of contracts on offer by putting another team into the competition? The Pacific Island nations want in, the Australians want to field another team, the South Africans must resent having one less team than New Zealand: why not make everyone happy by expanding it to a Super 16 or even Super 20?

Hart is strongly opposed to the calls for an expanded Super 12 on the grounds of "If it ain't broke, don't fix it". "We should have learned from league that constant tampering with a competition's format is destabilising and creates as many problems as it solves. I don't think we have the player base to justify expansion and there's no point in doing so if it simply lowers the quality and produces poor games because of mis-matches or both sides being mediocre.

"People may point to ACT's success but, to some extent, that's been at the expense of New South Wales and Queensland. As far as the Pacific Islands are concerned, Super 12 is a provincial competition, not a national one, and a number of players from these countries do in fact participate with various teams. The suggestion of a composite Pacific Islands team ignores the significant cultural differences between the various nations. We certainly need to support them but I believe the way to do it is to come up with a structure which provides them with regular international competition rather than expand the Super 12."

Hart believes there's a need for more flexibility on the related issues of overseas-based players and national eligibility. He'd like the Graeme Bachop situation to be revisited to enable the All Black panel to consider New Zealanders playing abroad and he questions the IRB's rule which prevents a player from representing more than one country.

Hart: "It was strongly opposed by New Zealand but pushed by the Argentinians, who've lost a number of their leading players to Italy, with support from South Africa who saw it as a way to stop players crossing over from Western Samoa to the All Blacks. Meanwhile, the old system is still in force in the form of the three-year stand-down which seems illogical as well as self-defeating when it means a drawcard like Joeli Vidiri is lost to the international game for three years for having played one match when he was a very young man.

"I doubt the one-country rule can be sustained. It seems

strange that you can live in a country for several years, you can have citizenship, but you can't represent it at rugby because years ago you played one game for another country. A legal challenge seems inevitable, especially if the player isn't wanted by his country of origin and is wanted by his country of adoption. In that context, I believe there's some merit in the WRC proposal that players would be available to their country of residence if they weren't picked by their country of origin. If a former All Black has been living in Japan for five years and we've chosen not to use him, why not let him play for Japan?"

These issues lead into a subject close to Hart's heart: the need to make rugby a genuinely global game. The quadrennial boasting about how many countries play the game ignores the fact that the vast majority of them simply aren't competitive, as the results of three World Cups have clearly demonstrated. Furthermore, it's arguable that the widening of the north-south divide in recent years means that the established rugby nations are now less integrated than ever before.

"Super 12 and the Tri-Nations series may have driven a wedge between the northern and southern hemispheres," he says. "They were understandable reactions to the threat from Super League and WRC which the north was slow to recognise but the result is a vacuum with no vision or strategic direction. To get the right seasonal structure, we need to be talking to the Australians and South Africans because Super 12 and the Tri-Nations are our premier competitions and that's unlikely to change in the short term. But the challenge facing the IRB is to integrate these competitions with their counterpart competitions in Europe and think laterally about ways to make rugby a genuinely global game. That may involve looking seriously at a global season at the top level."

Hart's desire to see rugby become a truly global game isn't just missionary zeal; there's an element of hard-headed calculation behind it. The size of the economy means that New Zealand rugby has far less capacity to generate revenue, particularly sponsorship, than our major rivals. The vast amounts of money now sloshing around English rugby vividly illustrate the point. Globalisation means exposing the All Blacks to a wider audience which in turn greatly increases New Zealand rugby's access to potential sponsorship revenue.

"There's no doubt that the TV moguls see rugby as one of the few sports with global potential," says Hart. "TV coverage taking rugby to the global village would open up huge sponsorship opportunities. The All Blacks are becoming an international marketing commodity and that would accelerate as the game goes global. At present, the All Blacks are rugby's premium brand, a fact which isn't lost on the Nikes of this world. It's been suggested that the $28 million a year New Zealand rugby gets from News Corporation could be matched by revenue from sponsors."

Meanwhile, back on the home front and, on the face of it, a far cry from talking telephone numbers with corporate big-shots, New Zealand rugby has a mission which is critical to its long-term well-being: to ensure that the amateur game survives and flourishes in the professional era.

"The amateur game – school, club, and provincial – is critical to New Zealand culture and New Zealand rugby and a fundamental reason for our success," says Hart. "We learn the game very young which is why our players appear more natural and comfortable than those from some other countries. We must grow the amateur game and integrate it with the professional game."

In his view that means:

• nurturing club rugby and giving it a degree of recognition and responsibility which it doesn't have at present. To attract sponsorship and media support that may require, in some areas, regionalising club competitions, leading to a national club knockout format.

• giving all prospective Super 12 players the opportunity to reach that level and pursue a professional career while ensuring that the structure still caters to amateur players, coaches, and officials and encourages them to maintain their involvement in the game. Rugby's infrastructure at all levels remains totally reliant on the network of volunteers who do what they do for love of the game.

• creating an even NPC competition to avoid the situation which exists in English soccer where the financial clout of a handful of clubs ensures their dominance and condemns the majority of clubs to being permanent also-rans.

The NZRFU is already doing a great deal. The union pumps $6-7 million a year into grass-roots development and, at the time of writing, was preparing to undertake a major review of club rugby. The NZRFU's transfer system has gone some way towards addressing the issue of the disparity of resources and talent among the provinces although it's still difficult to see how most provinces can compete with Auckland and Canterbury with their squads of fully professional players.

If anyone doubts that the dark side of professionalism poses a very real threat to the amateur game, they only need to look at what's happening in England. Entrepreneurs who buy into clubs are solely interested in the top team; they don't believe in developing young talent within the club and won't waste – as they see it – money on that. The money is needed to pay the top team's salaries and buy more stars when the need or opportunity arises. The entrepreneurs certainly aren't interested in continuing the club's historic role of fostering the game within its catchment area. With that attitude at the top, it won't be long before the grass-roots begin to wither.

"Rugby retains its hold on New Zealand because it's an integral part of our culture," says Hart. "It's a game that can be played by anyone and everyone at the level that suits them. We must do all we can to preserve that. We need to ensure that a sufficient proportion of the revenue coming into our game is put towards grass-roots development in terms of administration, coaching, facilities and grounds."

Which brings us back to the glittering prize. "We must give the World Cup our best shot," he says. "Winning it is a catalyst for sponsorship and bringing money into the game. The more I'm involved, the more I see the need to support the amateur game and winning the World Cup would bring in the revenue to sustain our game at all levels."

STATISTICS

JOHN HART COACHING RECORD
(to October 30, 1997)
Compiled by Geoff Miller

AUCKLAND

Year	Played	Won	Lost	Drawn	For	Ag
1982	14	12	2	-	371	149
1983	17	13	3	1	326	176
1984	21	20	1	-	828	160
1985	17	16	1	-	499	135
1986	21	17	4	-	698	221
Totals	**90**	**78**	**11**	**1**	**2722**	**841**

NEW ZEALAND COLTS

1989	4	4	-	-	164	57
1990	3	3	-	-	107	37
1991	4	4	-	-	191	38
Totals	**11**	**11**	**-**	**-**	**462**	**132**

NEW ZEALAND TRIALS

1996	1	1	-	-	72	18
1997	1	1	-	-	29	22
Totals	**2**	**2**	**-**	**-**	**101**	**40**

NEW ZEALAND BARBARIANS

1994	1	1	-	-	59	35
1996	2	2	-	-	120	19
Totals	**3**	**3**	**-**	**-**	**179**	**54**

NORTHERN ZONE

1988	**2**	**2**	**-**	**-**	**96**	**27**

NEW ZEALAND XV

1991	**3**	**3**	**-**	**-**	**153**	**48**

CORONATION SHIELD DISTRICTS XV

1994	**1**	**1**	**-**	**-**	**51**	**23**

PAGE TOTALS	Played	Won	Lost	Drawn	For	Ag
112	**100**	**11**	**1**	**3764**	**1165**	

NEW ZEALAND

1987

Japan B	94-0
Japan	74-0
Asian Barbarians	96-3
Japan	106-4
President's XV	38-9

Played 5; won 5; points for 408; points against 16

1991 (WORLD CUP – co-coach with Alex Wyllie)

ENGLAND	18-12
UNITED STATES	46-6
ITALY	31-21
CANADA	29-13
AUSTRALIA	6-16
SCOTLAND	13-6

Played 6; won 5; lost 1; points for 143; points against 74

1996

WESTERN SAMOA	51-10
SCOTLAND	62-31
SCOTLAND	36-12
AUSTRALIA	43-6
SOUTH AFRICA	15-11
AUSTRALIA	32-25
Boland Invitation	32-21
SOUTH AFRICA	29-18
Eastern Province	31-23
SOUTH AFRICA	23-19
Western Transvaal	31-0
SOUTH AFRICA	33-26
Griqualand West	18-18
SOUTH AFRICA	22-32

Played 14; won 12; lost 1; drew 1; points for 458; points against 252

1997

FIJI	71-5
ARGENTINA	93-8
ARGENTINA	62-10
AUSTRALIA	30-13
SOUTH AFRICA	35-32
AUSTRALIA	33-18
SOUTH AFRICA	55-35
AUSTRALIA	36-24

Played 8; won 8; points for 415; points against 145

GRAND	Played	Won	Lost	Drawn	For	Ag
TOTAL	145	130	13	2	5188	1652